D1327198

Jikoni

Jikoni

RAVINDER BHOGAL

Proudly Inauthentic Recipes from
an Immigrant Kitchen

BLOOMSBURY PUBLISHING
LONDON · OXFORD · NEW YORK · NEW DELHI · SYDNEY

Introduction 7

15 *Naashta* Breakfast and Brunch

63 *Kazuri* Small and Beautiful Snacks and Nibbles

103 *M'boga na Saladi* Vegetables and Salads

153 *Samaki* Fish and Shellfish

193 *Kuku na Nyama* Poultry and Meat

243 *Tamu Tamu* Sweet Things and Desserts

Ingredients 286

Index 292

With Thanks 302

Jikoni
means 'kitchen' in Kiswahili,

the spirited language spoken in Kenya, the country where I was born. I grew up in Nairobi, in a whitewashed house built by my *bhaji* (grandfather). Like many Indians before him, he left his native Punjab in the 1940s in search of work. Most of them worked as labourers building the railways – lines of neat-as-needlework stitches across wild terrain – to link Kenya with Uganda. Many later settled in Uganda, only to be expelled in the 1970s under the bloody regime of Idi Amin. *Bhaji* spent much of his time constructing properties in Kenya, but he also spent a great deal of it

falling in love with the red-earthed, blossoming landscape

of this tropical East African clime, so much so that he decided to lay down roots.

Our family was neither small nor quiet – there were six just in my nuclear clan, but the tradition of living with extended relations meant that there was anywhere between fifteen and twenty-five people in our house at any one time – a source of both cosiness and chaos. Mealtimes for a tribe that never seemed to stop breeding had to be handled with military precision, and every woman and girl was recruited to the cause, willingly or otherwise.

I was a reluctant assistant to my mother, who had a stern approach to all domestic duties. Taking pity on me, my grandfather would let me hop onto his strong broad shoulders, and take me off for a weekly treat. We would drive into town in his rickety Volkswagen and head straight for Sno Cream, a kitsch ice-cream parlour where gelatos like dreamy sherbet-hued clouds came in cut-glass dishes. It was over our love of the naughty-but-nice stuff that we bonded, and I think this was where my association of food with pleasure began. One day, in the season of the long rains,

when the garden bloomed madly and insects seemed to congregate

in every corner of it, *bhaji* bought me a little aluminium stove that could actually be lit with crumpled-up newspaper. I took to making towers of chapattis that were singed and bitter, but he would praise and encourage me, eating them with relish. This made me realise that feeding someone made love expand, and so I decided to embrace my kitchen duties.

After that I spent most of my time making a nuisance of myself, squeezed into a small *jikoni* full of women confidently throwing a series of fragrant seeds and pods into pots, gossiping in a unique patois made up of several inherited tongues including Swahili, Punjabi, Gujarati, Urdu, Hindi and English.

This was also my initiation into the secret language of cooks

— where recipes were never recorded in ink on paper, but sung down the generations like feminine gospels, until every daughter knew them off by heart. It was here that I felt truly alive, my every sense awake to the subtleties of the kitchen: the cheery whistle of a pressure cooker; the cloud of steam rising from an ochre broth gilded with turmeric, its sweet, sour, hot, salty and deeply, deeply spicy flavours all expertly balanced. My nose was acutely attuned to the potency of each spice my mother crushed in her crude stone pestle and mortar. Everything was safe. Everything was familiar.

When I was seven, we made an abrupt voyage to England. Our usual trips to visit family in London had always been a merry-go-round of Fortnum & Mason, Hamleys and shiny biscuit tins, but after several weeks of living in a frigidly cold flat above a shambolic shop that was very much in need of a woman's touch, it became clear that this trip was different, and we were not going back.

Homesickness was an ordeal I found difficult to shake off. I felt displaced and alienated, bullied at school for my foreign accent and NHS specs. I existed in a strange sort of suspended animation, carrying the burden of living between two worlds. I had been accustomed to creepers, colossal jamun trees and rugged, open terrain – my new landscape was barren, the horizon heavy with haggard buildings set against a terrifying Milky Way of artificial lights. I longed for the familiar, and for the foods that signified the familiar for me.

I developed a sensual nostalgia for the smell of wet, red Kenyan earth,

for the scent of guavas warming on the trees in the garden.

I can't remember exactly how long it took me to settle – and even when I did, the dream of returning endured. Nostalgia makes the things you hastily leave behind feel more precious than ever: the favourite dolls, the language, the neat and beloved grandmother, the culture. But for me it was the distinctive taste and smell of home I missed the most. Eventually, the hole in my stomach and soul led me into our modest English kitchen with my mother, where we learnt to merge our old and new worlds. We occupied a hinterland where we fused new ingredients with our old traditions, unwittingly creating a new cuisine.

Our recipes displayed a rebellious spirit –

lawless concoctions that drew their influences from one nation and then another. We took the traditions of our ancestors and their regional home cooking and overlaid them with the reality of our new home and whatever its various food markets, delis, canteens and multicultural supermarkets had to offer on any given day. This is what I suppose could be loosely termed 'immigrant cuisine',

proudly inauthentic recipes that span geography, ethnicity and history.

It was in the kitchen that I found my sanctuary and made peace with my new nation. As I grew up and graduated to cooking alone, unaided by my mother, I realised that a kitchen might provide a little bout of perfection, disappearance and luxury, amid the stresses of constantly trying to fit in. I relished every opportunity to cook and, more importantly, to feed, quickly identifying that the happy stability of mealtimes – from breakfast to the very last titbit before bedtime – was just the tonic for an uprooted family. Even now, a day punctuated by great meals still really matters to me.

You could say that it was cooking that liberated me. In fact having a kitchen of one's own could be considered, in the Virginia Woolf mode, a matter of personal freedom. Growing up in a patriarchal Punjabi family as daughter number four was at times stifling. I chafed at the constraints of what was permissible (embroidery, crochet, cooking for family, the oompah of the creaking harmonium at prayer ceremonies) and what was verboten (discos, climbing trees, boys, and dreaming of cooking for anyone other than your future husband and children).

Cooking is a highly skilled and often selfless endeavour, especially when it is women who are doing the feeding. As I watched my grand-mother, mother, aunts and sisters join the cult of domesticity, I felt restless, and inwardly rebelled at the drudgery of it all. At the same time, I found solace in cookery books and cookery shows – powerful female role models like Madhur Jaffrey and Nigella Lawson gave me the faith that cookery could be a career prospect, rather than just a feminine duty.

Many years later, after graduating and working as a journalist, opportunity finally knocked and, unexpectedly, the career I had been daydreaming about all my life became a reality. I began writing about food, cooking at pop ups and doing private catering – until, finally, after a decade, I plucked up the courage to join the cohort of brilliant women at the helm of their own food establishments and opened Jikoni in 2016. Even now, in the restaurant kitchen, the maternal figures who shared their culinary wisdom with me stand alongside me, in spirit, at the pass. I feel immensely grateful to them for giving me the best education they knew. Instead of a brood of children, however, it is my guests I feed with the same love and affection they taught me when I was little.

It's sustaining, it's precious, and it's what keeps me coming back to my *jikoni*.

Naashta

Breakfast and Brunch

When I moved to this country aged seven, I didn't feel at home for quite some time. Most nights I curled up next to my bone-tired mother, puffs of warm air blowing from her drooped mouth, relaxed and unsmiling in sleep. The bedroom, with its few pieces of makeshift furniture, looked out onto a main road, and the glare of car lights, foggy through the sheets we'd put up for curtains, seemed never to stop zipping across the horizon.

I tried everything – rote prayers, counting sheep, counting backwards from three hundred, reading in the dark – but I remained alert, twitching and bereft of sleep.

Sometimes I would pad to the kitchen in slippered feet,

stand for a few moments in the pale light of the fridge, peel and eat a clementine from the fruit bowl, and then shuffle back to bed, to finally fall asleep just as the rising sun bathed the room in light.

Being suddenly uprooted from a familiar landscape and thrust into an unfamiliar one left me rattled and anxious. I was freaking out – I transferred the worry in my parents' hushed voices onto my small, sloping shoulders. My stretching and yawning through school the next day was evidence of a sleepless body, a restless mind, a worrier.

It took me a few years to figure out how to unravel myself out of this tense fold, but I did. I finally discovered that a meditation on meals was a welcome distraction from the weary tedium of insomnia. I drifted off planning meals – particularly breakfast – and woke up woozy, but with a sharp appetite.

There is a certain optimism about breakfast.

If you find yourself, mug of hot tea in hand, with a stack of generously buttered toast in front of you, you know that things could be much worse.

While weekday breakfasts can be pressurised, weekend brunches should be savoured. I still yearn for my mother's Sunday-morning parathas – fried flatbreads that are India's equivalent of a fry-up. Of course there are no eggs, bacon or sausages, but there is still the seductive sizzle of something hissing in a pan, burnished and golden. These gave me the taste for something other than just bacon (though I can never resist a crisp rasher or two) for breakfast. So – if you find yourself unable to sleep at night, plan breakfast or brunch for yourself or someone you love in the morning.

It makes things better, always.

125g small tapioca pearls
150ml coconut milk
250g condensed milk
4 passion fruit
Chopped pistachios or flaked
  almonds, to serve

For the coconut caramel bananas
100g soft brown sugar
100ml coconut milk
4 small bananas, peeled
  and cut into slices

Overnight Tapioca Porridge with Passion Fruit and Coconut Caramel Bananas

For some, tapioca is a rediscovery of the past – of that squishy British milk pudding, which was at worst a lumpy unsavoury paste, at best sublime and creamy. But in Asia, tapioca pearls are mainly cooked with some form of milk, from coconut to condensed, to make rich and refreshing desserts that are often served with fruit.

Tapioca is less about flavour and more about its texture, which is both brilliant and absurd, with more than a passing resemblance to frogspawn. This delicate porridge reminds me of the taste and smell of my grandmother's fruit bowl in Kenya, which was never without a few ripe bananas and some wrinkly, geriatric passion fruit. The sharpness of the passion fruit balances the sweetness of the caramelised bananas wonderfully.

- Thoroughly rinse the tapioca pearls under cold running water in a large sieve until the water runs clear, then tip into a large heatproof bowl.
- In a small saucepan, bring the coconut milk to a simmer, then pour over the tapioca, along with the condensed milk. Once cool, cover and leave in the refrigerator overnight to swell up and chill.
- In the morning, stir in the pulp from the passion fruit and loosen the tapioca with some cold coconut milk if it is a little too thick.
- For the coconut caramel bananas, combine the sugar and coconut milk in a saucepan and heat until the sugar has dissolved and the milk has come to the boil. Reduce the heat to a low simmer, place the bananas in the milk and cook for about 5 minutes, turning gently, until they are lightly caramelised.
- Divide the tapioca between six small bowls or glass dishes. Spoon the bananas on top and sprinkle with some chopped pistachios or flaked almonds for a pleasing crunch.

2 ripe bananas
500g yoghurt
200ml whole milk
Seeds from 4 green cardamom
    pods, crushed
Ice – optional

Banana and Cardamom Lassi

Lassi is a tangy sweet-and-sour drink that takes its roots from my ancestral state of Punjab. At its purest it is made from yoghurt and water either sweetened with sugar or made savoury with salt and a little cumin. Of all the fruit lassis, mango is probably the most popular, but really you can use whatever fruits you find languishing in your fruit bowl. I always seem to have too many ripe bananas, which are so sweet that I never need to add any honey or sugar to sweeten my lassi, just some invigorating cardamom for a little punch. The bananas add a sort of custardy heft and body – a long swig of this at breakfast will really set you up for the day.

- This couldn't be simpler. Simply place all the ingredients in a blender. Whizz enthusiastically and then pour into tall glasses to serve. Pour the lassi over ice if you are after something extra-refreshing.

500g jumbo rolled oats
100g almonds
100g hazelnuts
50g cashew nuts
100g jaggery, grated
100g clear honey
2 tbsp groundnut oil
½ tsp ground cinnamon
2 heaped tsp fennel seeds,
   toasted and lightly crushed
100g dates, chopped
100g dried apricots, chopped
100g dried baby figs, cut in half
Milk or yoghurt, to serve

Jaggery and Fennel Seed Granola

I have fine-tuned this recipe over the years, and the end result is a nutty, fruity bowl of breakfast bliss. Roasting the granola tickles a wonderfully deep toasty flavour out of the nuts and oats, and the fennel seeds and jaggery are great for kick-starting your digestive system.

- Preheat the oven to 180°C/Fan 160°C/Gas Mark 4 and line a large baking tray with baking parchment.
- Mix together the oats, nuts and jaggery in a heatproof bowl.
- In a saucepan, gently heat the honey and oil, then stir in the cinnamon and fennel seeds.
- Pour the warm syrup over the oats and nuts and toss to coat. Spread out over the baking tray and bake for 15 minutes until crisp and golden brown.
- Leave to cool on the tray, then break up any big clumps and mix in the dried fruit. The granola will keep in an airtight container for a month.
- Serve with milk or yoghurt.

Parathas, Please

In mainstream Indian restaurants, the paratha has often been a culinary nobody, overshadowed by the fluffier naans glistening with butter or the flaccid handkerchief of a roti. At first glance parathas may seem unremarkable, but when they're done right, these buttery, flaky flatbreads are far more than just a vehicle to carry meat and vegetable curries into your mouth. I can never resist the tender, crisp chew of any paratha, but my favourites are the stuffed varieties, filled with anything from meat or potatoes to unripe green papaya and grated daikon. They are a meal in themselves.

Unsurprisingly, it was my mother who taught me how to make parathas — a graduation permitted only once I had mastered a beginner's chapatti. Before I was even allowed to try rolling one, there were years of studying the master at work.

I would stand on a red plastic stool so l could reach the worktop, and watch her knead the dough,

1 flat cast-iron pan

then deftly roll it out and slap it on a *tawa*,[1] a relic bought or inherited well before I was born. She never followed a recipe, but just went on instinct — eyeballing the dry ingredients as she brought them together with just enough water to make a firm but springy dough. She'd roll the fist of dough around the steel *paraath*[2] until it picked up every last fleck of sticky flour and the metal was shiny and almost spotless again.

2 shallow dish for kneading dough

Stuffing parathas requires dexterity. You need to lay just the right amount of filling onto a flattened disc of dough and then pinch the sides of the *atta*[3] over the stuffing so it is tightly encased and sealed, and will not spill out when flattened into a larger, thinner circle with a rolling pin. While shaping parathas may seem daunting, the dough itself is pretty much foolproof — you can whizz it up in a food processor in a couple of minutes and, unlike yeasted dough, it needs no time to rise. The rest is simply down to practice.

3 dough

600g kimchi (see page 114
    or use ready-made),
    plus extra to serve
375g chapatti flour, plus extra
    for dusting
1 tsp sea salt

4 tbsp oil or ghee, plus extra
    for shaping and frying
About 200ml lukewarm water
Fried eggs, thinly sliced spring
    onions, coriander cress
    or coriander leaves and
    sesame seeds, to serve

Kimchi Parathas

Kimchi, Korean fermented cabbage, seems to have found its way into everything from burgers to tacos these days, so I thought I would attempt a little Korean-Indian mash-up by stuffing it into parathas. Adding a fried egg makes this perfect for a lazy Sunday breakfast. What's more, you can use the drained liquid from the kimchi to make a spicy Kimchi Bloody Mary too – just add 25ml to your tomato juice and leave out the Worcestershire sauce and Tabasco.

- Place the kimchi in a muslin-lined sieve set over a bowl and refrigerate for a couple of hours or overnight to drain. Discard the liquid (or keep if you want to make Kimchi Bloody Marys), then chop the kimchi finely and set aside.
- To make the paratha dough, combine the flour and salt in a large bowl, then add the oil or ghee and mix with your hands. Slowly begin to add the warm water, a little at a time, kneading well until you have a soft, springy, malleable dough. If it is too wet add a little more flour, and if it is too dry, just add a little water – the dough should not be sticky. Cover it with a clean, damp tea towel and leave to rest for half an hour.
- Divide the dough into approximately 8 balls. Dust them with a little extra flour and keep covered with the damp tea towel to prevent them drying out. With lightly oiled hands, take one ball at a time and roll it between your palms to make a ball. Using a rolling pin, roll out to form a disc about 8cm in diameter. Place a generous tablespoon of the kimchi in the centre, then bring the edges up around it and seal at the top (this is a similar process to making a dumpling). Flatten the paratha slightly with the palm of your hand, then turn it so it is seam side down and roll again into a 15cm round, dusting with extra flour if it starts to stick. Repeat with the remaining dough and filling.
- Heat a non-stick frying pan or *tawa* over medium–high heat. When the pan is hot, add about ½ teaspoon of oil or ghee and place a paratha in the centre of the pan. Cook for about 2 minutes on each side, or until it is lightly blistered and seared. Place the cooked paratha on a plate lined with kitchen paper and keep warm while you cook the rest in the same way.
- Serve with extra kimchi, fried eggs, spring onions, coriander and sesame seeds.

Date and Pistachio Parathas
with Orange Blossom and Saffron Shrikhand

While parathas generally tend to be savoury, there are also sweet versions filled with jaggery that are normally eaten to break a fast. This one, stuffed with a date paste, is crisp and gooey at the same time, which makes it irresistible. Shrikhand is a creamy dessert made simply by straining yoghurt and sweetening it. Traditionally it is flavoured with nuts and a hit of cardamom, but I have used orange blossom water and saffron as I love these perfumed Middle Eastern flavours with dates.

NAASHTA

300g plain flour, plus extra
   for dusting
75g chapatti flour
4 tbsp ghee, plus extra for
   shaping and frying
About 250ml lukewarm water

For the shrikhand
500g yoghurt
Generous pinch of saffron
   threads
1 tbsp warm milk
2 tsp orange blossom water
35g icing sugar
1 tbsp shelled pistachios,
   finely chopped

For the filling
175g pitted Medjool dates
60ml warm water
50g shelled pistachios

- First make the shrikhand. Place the yoghurt in a muslin-lined sieve set over a bowl and refrigerate overnight to drain – you should end up with a dense cream. Add the saffron to the warm milk and let it steep for half an hour. Put the strained yoghurt into a bowl and stir in the saffron-infused milk, orange blossom water and sugar. Turn out into a serving bowl, sprinkle with chopped pistachios and chill until you are ready to serve.
- To make the paratha dough, combine both flours in a large bowl, then add the ghee and mix with your hands. Slowly begin to add the warm water, a little at a time, kneading well until you have a soft, springy, malleable dough. If it is too wet add a little more flour, and if it is too dry, just add a little water – the dough should not be sticky. Cover it with a clean, damp tea towel and leave to rest for half an hour.
- Meanwhile, for the filling, soak the dates in the warm water for 20 minutes or until soft. Whizz the pistachios in a blender or small food processor until finely ground, then add the drained dates and blend again until you have a smooth, spreadable paste.
- Divide the dough into approximately 6 balls. Dust lightly with flour and keep covered with the damp tea towel to prevent them drying out. Take one ball at a time, dust it with a little more flour and roll it between your palms to form a smooth ball. Using a rolling pin, roll out into a disc about 10cm in diameter. Spread half the disc with the date filling, leaving a 3mm border round the edges. Fold the paratha in half to make a semi-circle, and then in half again so you have a quarter. Dust with a little more flour, then carefully roll with your rolling pin until it is about 3mm thick. Repeat with the remaining dough and filling.
- Heat a non-stick frying pan over medium–high heat. When the pan is hot, add about $\frac{1}{2}$ teaspoon of ghee and place a paratha in the centre of the pan. Cook for about 2 minutes on each side, or until lightly blistered and seared. Place the cooked paratha on a plate lined with kitchen paper and keep warm while you cook the rest of the parathas in the same way.
- Serve the parathas with the shrikhand alongside for dunking.

Cornbread with Creamed Corn, Eggs and Green Chilli Relish

I love picking corn at the end of the summer when it is at its sweetest. There are many pick-your-own farms dotted across Britain where you can do this – I have great memories of a bounty of different fruit and vegetables at Hewitt's Farm in south-east London when I lived nearby, but it was the September corn that always got me. I would peel away the husk and the silk and sink my teeth into it right there in the field.

Sweet, starchy and rich, creamed corn is one of my favourite comfort foods. This version includes spices and a hit of chilli, ginger and garlic to prevent it from being too saccharine. This recipe is really three recipes in one: the creamed corn can be eaten on toast, or is rather lovely on a jacket potato; equally, the cornbread makes for a great snack on its own pan-fried with a little butter; and the jalapeno relish is the perfect condiment to spice up anything, but especially eggs. If you can't get fresh corn, just use frozen or tinned.

Sea salt
Butter, for spreading
Fried or poached eggs, to serve

For the cornbread
225g plain flour
200g fine polenta
150g mature cheddar, grated
1 heaped tsp dried oregano
3 tsp baking powder
½ tsp bicarbonate of soda
Finely grated zest of 1 lemon
200g sweetcorn kernels
300ml buttermilk
25ml whole milk
2 eggs, beaten
60g butter, melted

For the creamed corn
Glug of rapeseed oil
2 tsp brown mustard seeds
Pinch of asafoetida
15 curry leaves
1 cinnamon stick
1 tsp cumin seeds
Thumb of ginger, finely grated
3 garlic cloves, finely chopped
1 red chilli, finely chopped
100g chopped tinned tomatoes
2 tbsp tamarind concentrate
1 tbsp soft brown sugar
450g sweetcorn kernels
90ml single cream
Handful of chopped coriander

For the relish
2 green jalapeno chillies
Juice of 1 lime
50ml olive oil
1 spring onion, sliced
1 small garlic clove, chopped
Handful of chopped coriander

NAASHTA

- Preheat the oven to 180°C/Fan 160°C/Gas Mark 4. Grease a 900g loaf tin and line it with baking parchment.
- For the cornbread, combine the flour, polenta, cheese, oregano, baking powder, bicarbonate of soda, lemon zest, corn and 2 teaspoons of salt in a large bowl. In a separate bowl, whisk together the buttermilk, milk, eggs and melted butter, then stir into the dry ingredients until combined. Spoon into the loaf tin, level the top and bake for 45 minutes, or until the cornbread is golden brown and feels firm when lightly pressed with a finger. Let it cool in the tin for 10 minutes, then turn out and cool on a wire rack.
- For the creamed corn, heat the rapeseed oil in a saucepan over medium—high heat. Sprinkle in the mustard seeds and as soon as they pop, throw in the asafoetida and curry leaves, quickly followed by the cinnamon and cumin. Once all the spices are fragrant, lower the heat and add the ginger, garlic and chilli. Let the ginger and garlic soften and colour a little, then pour in the tomatoes and tamarind, sprinkle in the sugar and cook for 5 minutes. Add the corn, season with salt and bring to a simmer, then cook for 15 minutes. Stir in the cream and take off the heat. Mash coarsely with a hand blender, leaving some kernels whole for texture. Finish with the coriander.
- For the relish, simply blend together all the ingredients in a food processor or blender until smooth.
- To serve, thickly slice the cornbread, butter each side and fry in a frying pan over medium heat until golden brown on both sides. Spoon over the warm creamed corn, top with a fried or poached egg and drizzle over the chilli relish. Any leftover cornbread can be kept in an airtight container for 3 days or frozen, to be enjoyed on another day.

Pina Colada Pancakes

Who doesn't love griddled slabs of carbohydrate that just beg to be drenched in maple syrup? Pancakes are incredibly versatile and this kitsch, cocktail-inspired interpretation is a crowd pleaser – an opportunity to booze at breakfast without raising too many eyebrows. You'll need to begin the recipe a day ahead, to give the coconut ice cream time to freeze.

→

3 large eggs
240ml coconut milk
2 tsp vanilla extract
300g self-raising flour
1 tsp baking powder
Pinch of salt
30g desiccated coconut
Coconut oil, for frying
Roughly chopped pistachios,
  to serve

For the ice cream
50g fresh or defrosted frozen
  grated coconut
300ml double cream
300ml whole milk
100g jaggery, grated
6 egg yolks
20ml dark rum

For the caramelised pineapple
1 pineapple
300g brown sugar
100ml maple syrup
100g butter
1 tbsp dark rum

- For the ice cream, heat a heavy-based saucepan over medium heat, spread the coconut over it and toast until it turns golden brown, tossing or stirring it frequently so it doesn't burn. Add the cream, milk and jaggery, turn the heat down to low and bring to a simmer. Let it simmer for 1 minute, then remove from the heat, cover and leave for 30 minutes to infuse.
- Meanwhile, whisk the egg yolks in a mixing bowl for a few minutes until pale and frothy, then slowly pour in the coconut-infused cream, whisking constantly. Keep whisking until you have a silky custard. Return to the pan and cook over low heat, stirring continuously with a wooden spoon, until it coats the back of the spoon. Strain through a fine sieve, pressing on the coconut with the spoon to extract all the liquid and flavour. Discard the solids, stir in the rum and leave to cool completely. Freeze in an ice-cream machine according to the manufacturer's instructions. Store the ice cream in a lidded container in the freezer until required.
- To make the pancakes, mix together the eggs, coconut milk and vanilla in a large bowl. In another bowl, combine the flour, baking powder and salt. Stir the dry ingredients into the wet ingredients in three stages, making sure each addition is well combined before adding the next one. Finally, add the desiccated coconut and beat again.
- Heat a large frying pan over medium heat, add a little coconut oil and swirl to cover the surface of the pan. Then you can either pour ladlefuls of the pancake mixture directly into the pan – or for neater, more uniform pancakes, put the mixture into a piping bag and pipe into 15cm pastry rings. Cook until the edges of the pancakes look dry and the bottoms are nicely browned, then flip and cook on the other side for a few minutes. Keep the cooked pancakes warm while you cook the rest.
- For the caramelised pineapple, thickly slice the pineapple into rounds, then trim the edges and remove the core with a round pastry cutter. Roll the pineapple rings in the brown sugar and lay them in a non-stick frying pan over medium heat. Keep a close eye on the pan as the sugar melts and caramelises, turning the pineapple to coat. Stir in the maple syrup, butter and cheeky tablespoon of rum for a silky, boozy caramel.
- To serve, stack 2 pancakes on each plate, top with a slice of caramelised pineapple and spoon over some caramel. Finish with a scoop of the coconut ice cream and a scattering of chopped pistachios.

Tamarind and Maple Bacon
with Fenugreek Waffles and Fennel and Apple Slaw

Bacon is rarely terrible, but the sublime fatty pleasures of this home-cured one are especially pleasing. The spices, tamarind and pineapple juice in the cure bring out the intensely porcine quality of the pork belly. The processes involved are fairly simple but need time — an overnight cure and 6 hours in the oven — so you'll need to get started two days in advance.

The bacon is good with a variety of things, from eggs and pancakes to the unusual waffles and refreshing slaw in this recipe. You can even serve it as part of a Sunday lunch, or make the best sandwich you'll ever eat: a BKC, bacon, kimchi and pickled cucumbers on sourdough.

1.3kg pork belly
1 onion, thinly sliced
Thumb of ginger, finely grated
4 garlic cloves, finely chopped
1 star anise
1 cinnamon stick
1 black cardamom pod
5 cloves
300ml pineapple juice
60ml maple syrup
50ml tamarind concentrate
Sunflower oil
Sea salt and black pepper

For the cure
3 star anise
2 cinnamon sticks
3 black cardamom pods
8 cloves
250g sea salt
250g demerara sugar

For the waffles
1 tsp cumin seeds
Handful of fresh fenugreek, leaves
    picked and finely chopped
225g plain flour
170g fine polenta
2 tsp baking powder
2 tsp sea salt
1 tsp bicarbonate of soda
1 tsp chilli powder
600ml buttermilk
90g butter, melted
2 eggs

For the slaw
60g soured cream
2 tbsp cider vinegar
1½ tbsp extra virgin olive oil
1 garlic clove, finely chopped
1 tsp fennel seeds, toasted
    and roughly crushed
Finely grated zest and juice
    of 1 lemon
2 fennel bulbs, shaved on
    a mandoline
2 Granny Smith apples,
    thinly sliced
1 red onion, thinly sliced
Handful of chopped parsley
Handful of roughly torn mint

- Using a very sharp knife, ideally a Stanley knife, score the skin of the pork belly right down to the meat (but without actually cutting into the meat), making the cuts as close together as possible.
- For the cure, toast the spices in a dry frying pan over medium heat until fragrant, being careful not to burn them. Put in a spice grinder and blitz until coarsely ground. Mix the spices with the salt and sugar, then pat the cure over all the surfaces of the meat. Put on a tray or plate, cover and refrigerate overnight.
- Next day, preheat the oven to 150°C/Fan 130°C/Gas Mark 2.
- In a frying pan, heat 1 tablespoon of oil over low heat and fry the onion until it turns golden brown. Add the ginger and garlic along with all the spices and cook, stirring frequently, until fragrant; then stir in the pineapple juice, maple syrup and tamarind. Season with salt and pepper, let it come to a gentle bubble and simmer over low heat for 15 minutes.
- Rinse the pork belly thoroughly and then dry it with kitchen paper. Place it, skin side up, in a heavy roasting tin that holds it snugly. Pour over the hot tamarind mixture and bake for 6 hours or until the meat is very tender.
- Once it is out of the oven and cool enough to handle, pull out the rib bones from the meat and transfer it to a clean tray or plate. Put another tray over the meat, place some weights on top (a few tins of tomatoes work well) to press it down, and chill for at least 4 hours. Stored in a sealed container, the bacon will keep in the fridge for up to 3 days.
- Place the roasting tin, with all its cooking juices, over low–medium heat and simmer for 15–20 minutes until you have a sticky glaze. Allow to cool, then transfer to a small sealed container and keep in the fridge until needed.
- For the waffles, heat a little oil in a frying pan over medium heat. Add the cumin seeds and fenugreek and fry until the fenugreek is soft. Remove from the heat and, when cool enough to handle, squeeze out any excess liquid.
- To make the batter, combine the dry ingredients thoroughly in a bowl, then make a well in the centre. In another bowl, whisk the wet ingredients together, then pour into the well in the dry ingredients and mix until smooth. Stir in the cumin and fenugreek and let it stand for 15 minutes.
- In the meantime, make your slaw. Whisk together the soured cream, vinegar, oil, garlic, fennel seeds, lemon zest and juice in a bowl. Add the fennel, apple, onion, parsley and mint and toss to coat all the ingredients in the dressing, seasoning to taste with salt and pepper.
- Heat a waffle iron and cook the waffle batter in batches, according to the manufacturer's instructions, until golden and crisp. (If you don't have a waffle iron, you can make pancakes with the batter instead.)
- To serve the bacon, cut into thick slices. Heat a heavy-based frying pan or griddle and sear on both sides until the fat crisps up. Paint over the glaze and turn the bacon a couple of times in the pan to caramelise. Serve hot.

The Agony and the Egg-stacy

A few years ago I came to possess, of all things, a restaurant. Like any newborn, a restaurant becomes your sole focus and obsession, leaving you with no time for anything else – even eating, ironically. It was in those tense opening months that I came to really appreciate one indispensible ingredient that gives us all the ability to conjure supper from next to nothing: the humble egg.

I love the dependability of eggs – how reliable and versatile they are.

No other ingredient in the kitchen has their fragile, shape-shifting magic. Yolks can be emulsified to make rippling, silky sauces, while the whites can be whipped into airy clouds to make meringue or to add an ethereal lightness to cakes. At the peak of my student poverty, eggs were an eternal standby for making *akuri*[1] or spaghetti carbonara, but as economical as they are, good eggs are one of life's luxuries. Organic eggs, with lavish custardy yolks as orange as ripe apricots, make it clear why the Italian for egg yolk is *rosso d'uovo*, 'the red of the egg'. To come home and find half a dozen eggs in your kitchen is a gift, and the basis for a satisfying breakfast, lunch or dinner.

In my childhood home in Nairobi we always had a supply of fresh eggs. My uncle kept a clutch of chickens – an assertive rooster and a gaggle of hens that waddled after him, plumping up his ego. I was forbidden to go past the backyard to where the hens were housed. I didn't really care for the hens, but I'd heard from the *totos*[2] beyond the wrought-iron gate which served as a border between my world and theirs, that a cat had a litter of precious kittens among the hay there. One hot afternoon, when the balmy weather had caused my mother to nod off, embroidery hoop still in hand, and my *aayah*[3] was distracted, I took my chance and commandeered the pluckiest of the *totos* to accompany me to the coop. We ran the few yards from the gate to the hen house and snuck in like hopeful foxes. As I busied myself with distracting the possessive cat so I could pocket a pet, I heard an almighty shriek from the barn – my companion had a gash across his cheek where an irate hen had flown at him and pecked his face for trying to steal her eggs. We ran as fast as our legs would carry us, terrified and empty-handed. For quite some time afterwards, my mother wondered why I shirked the boiled eggs I used to love so much at breakfast.

[1] Indian scrambled eggs

[2] children

[3] nanny

100g white spelt flour
1 tsp baking powder
½ tsp cumin seeds
½ tsp ajwain seeds – optional
1 egg
150ml whole milk
100g sweetcorn, drained
2 spring onions, thinly sliced
Handful of chopped coriander
Rapeseed oil, for frying
Sea salt and black pepper
Poached eggs and coriander
    leaves, to serve

For the guacamole
1 garlic clove, peeled
1 red chilli, deseeded if you
    don't like too much heat
100g cherry tomatoes,
    quartered
2 large avocados, peeled and
    stones removed
1 small red onion, very finely
    chopped
Juice of 1–2 limes, to taste
Handful of coriander leaves,
    chopped

½ tsp cumin seeds, toasted
    and lightly crushed
Sea salt and black pepper

For the chorizo crumbs
100g stale sourdough bread,
    broken into chunks
60g ready-to-eat chorizo
    sausage, roughly chopped
1 fat garlic clove, roughly chopped

Sweetcorn Pancakes with Guacamole and Chorizo Crumbs

These spelt and sweetcorn pancakes are designed for the savoury-breakfast person who is looking for a natural bedfellow for eggs. They are great eaten for brunch if you want something more exciting than avo-toast and are also terrific if you emerge from your bed in the afternoon after a heavy night out. The chorizo crumbs add flavour as well as texture, and any leftovers are great scattered over all sorts of dishes, from pasta to grilled scallops or squid.

- Begin by making the chorizo crumbs. In a food processor, blitz the sourdough to fine crumbs, then transfer to a bowl. Next, blitz together the chorizo and garlic until finely minced. Heat 2 tablespoons of oil in a frying pan and fry the chorizo and garlic for about 5 minutes until crisp and sizzling. Fold in the breadcrumbs and continue to fry until they are crisp too. Set aside to cool.
- To make the guacamole, bash the garlic and chilli to a paste using a pestle and mortar. Add the tomatoes and avocado and gently pound until the avocado is roughly crushed and well mixed with the chilli and garlic. Stir in the remaining ingredients and chill in the fridge until needed.
- For the pancakes, sift the flour and baking powder into a mixing bowl and season well with salt and pepper. Add the cumin and ajwain seeds, if using. In a jug, whisk together the egg and milk, then pour into the dry ingredients and mix until you have a smooth batter. Stir in the sweetcorn, spring onions and coriander.
- Heat a little oil in a frying pan over medium–high heat. Ladle a quarter of the batter into the pan and fry for 1–2 minutes on each side, or until the pancake is golden brown on both sides. Set aside on a warm plate and cover loosely with foil to keep warm. Repeat with the remaining batter.
- To serve, place 2 pancakes on each plate, top with the guacamole and a poached egg and scatter over some chorizo crumbs and coriander leaves.

Rapeseed oil, for frying
250g manouri cheese
    (or halloumi or anari),
    thickly sliced
Plain flour, for dredging
Honey, for drizzling

For the latkes
1kg sweet potatoes, peeled
    and coarsely grated
1 small red onion, finely grated
1 long red chilli, finely chopped
1 tsp ground cinnamon
Handful of chopped parsley
1 tbsp plain flour
1 tbsp cornflour
1 egg, lightly beaten

Sweet Potato Latkes with Fried Manouri Cheese and Honey

Manouri is an exceptional Greek cheese that is made from sheep's and goat's milk. It has a rich, buttery flavour, and its firm texture means it can be fried or grilled like halloumi, but it is much creamier. To make the latkes, I would suggest ditching your box grater and using a food processor with a grater attachment to reduce your effort to almost zero. You could of course make these with waxy potatoes like Desiree, but the sweet potato ones are an excellent foil for the savoury cheese and make great hangover food. They're also a good alternative to the muffins in eggs Benedict.

- For the latkes, soak the grated sweet potato in cold water for 10 minutes. Drain thoroughly, using your hands to squeeze out any excess liquid – this is essential if you want crisp latkes.
- In a bowl, mix together the sweet potato, onion, chilli, cinnamon, parsley, both flours and the beaten egg.
- Preheat the oven to 140°C/Fan 120°C/Gas Mark 1.
- Heat a 1cm depth of oil in a large frying pan over medium heat. Using wet hands, take about 2 tablespoons of the latke mixture and shape into flat fritters, then carefully place in the hot oil and fry for 3 minutes on each side until crisp and cooked through. Drain on kitchen paper, then keep warm in the oven while you cook the rest.
- For the fried cheese, clean out the pan you used for the latkes, then pour in a little oil and place over medium heat. Dredge the cheese slices in flour, shaking off any excess. Working in batches, fry on the first side for 3 minutes without moving so it forms a crust, then flip over and fry on the other side until golden brown. Serve with the latkes and a drizzle of your favourite honey.

150g rolled oats
100g chickpea (gram) flour
125g butter
1 banana shallot, thinly sliced
500g mixed mushrooms
   (such as field, shimeji, oyster,
   chestnut, shiitake, porcini),
   cleaned and sliced

1 tbsp dried oregano
3 fat garlic cloves, thinly sliced
Finely grated zest and juice
   of 1 lemon
Handful of finely chopped tarragon
Handful of finely chopped parsley
Sea salt and black pepper
Soured cream, to serve

Oat and Chickpea Flour Cheelas with Fried Mushrooms and Soured Cream

A cheela is an Indian crepe that can be made with almost any flour. These chickpea and oatmeal ones make great wrappers for a variety of fillings, but I particularly love them with hearty mushrooms. The trick to frying mushrooms is to use plenty of butter and a really hot pan, so they go crisp and golden and nutty – if the heat is not high enough, they will steam and go watery. Add finely diced pancetta if you are feeling extra-indulgent.

- Pulse the oats in a food processor or blender until you have a fine flour. Tip into a bowl and mix with the chickpea flour and ½ teaspoon of salt, then slowly whisk in about 250ml of water, a little at a time – add just enough water to give a double-cream consistency. Set the batter aside while you fry the mushrooms.
- Heat a frying pan and melt the butter over high heat. When it is foaming, fry the shallot until golden, then add the mushrooms, oregano and garlic and fry until the mushrooms are dark golden brown and nutty. Season with salt and pepper. Scatter over the lemon zest and squeeze in the juice. Finish with the tarragon and parsley, then keep warm while you cook the cheelas.
- Heat a *tawa* or non-stick frying pan over medium heat and brush with a little oil. Pour a ladleful of the batter into the centre of the pan and, using the back of the ladle, spread out the batter in concentric circles, spiralling out from the centre, to make a thin crepe. Cook for a few minutes until it comes away easily from the pan. Drizzle with a little oil, then flip and cook the other side until it is golden. Drain on kitchen paper and keep warm while you cook the rest of the cheelas.
- To serve, top the cheelas with fried mushrooms and soured cream.

250g sashimi-quality salmon,
  sliced
1 avocado, sliced
5 radishes, thinly sliced
2 spring onions, thinly sliced
Handful of coriander cress
1 tbsp black sesame seeds
  – optional

For the dressing
40ml rapeseed oil
1 tbsp light soy sauce
1 tbsp rice vinegar
½ tbsp mirin
1 tbsp finely chopped
  pickled ginger

For the rice
100g sushi rice
½ tsp sea salt
½ tsp matcha green tea powder

Green Tea Rice Bowls with Salmon and Ginger and Soy Dressing

If you want a healthy breakfast that is more interesting than just eggs or a bowl of muesli, this Japanese-inspired fish and rice bowl will be a revelation. It is both light and nourishing, which means you'll be left feeling full but never heavy, awakened by the strong but nuanced flavours and ready to take on the day.

- To make the dressing, shake all the ingredients together in a screwtop jar and set aside.
- For the rice, place all the ingredients in a saucepan with 200ml of water and leave to soak for 1 hour. Place the pan over medium heat and bring to the boil, then turn down the heat to very low, cover with a tight-fitting lid and cook for 10–15 minutes or until the rice is soft. Take off the heat and leave, still covered, for a further 10 minutes, then fluff up with a fork.
- To serve, spoon the rice into 2 bowls and top with the salmon, avocado, radishes and spring onions, then pour over the dressing and sprinkle with the coriander cress and some sesame seeds, if you like.

250g basmati rice, rinsed
125g white urid dhal
1 tsp fenugreek seeds
Ghee, for frying
Sea salt
Grated fresh coconut and fried
    eggs, to serve, if desired

For the filling
40g ghee
2 tsp brown mustard seeds
Pinch of asafoetida
20 curry leaves
1 red onion, finely sliced
40g cashews
2 tsp cumin seeds
1 tsp ground turmeric

2 green chillies, finely chopped
Thumb of ginger, finely grated
1kg Desiree potatoes, cut into
    1cm cubes and boiled until
    tender, then drained
Juice of 1 lime
500g smoked mackerel,
    shredded and bones removed
Handful of chopped coriander

Smoked Mackerel and Potato Dosas

Dosas are thin fermented pancakes from South India. I love their slightly sour blini-like tang against the smoky fish in the potato curry. You'll need to plan ahead to make these, as the lentils and rice have to be soaked overnight, and then ground and left to ferment for at least 8 hours. Once that's done, they are light work, with no kneading or rolling required. Spreading the batter thinly enough in the pan does take some practice. To help the batter spread more easily, cool down your pan between dosas by wiping it with a clean, damp cloth.

- For the dosa batter, place the rice and lentils in a bowl, add enough cold water to cover by 5cm, and leave to soak overnight.
- The next morning, drain the rice and lentils, then blend in a food processor with 100ml of water until smooth. Place in a bowl and gradually whisk in more water until the batter thickly coats the back of your spoon. Stir in the fenugreek seeds and season with salt, then cover and leave to ferment at room temperature for at least 8 hours, or overnight.
- To make the filling, heat the ghee in a frying pan and add the mustard seeds. As soon as they begin to pop, follow with the asafoetida and curry leaves and fry very briefly. Now add the onion, cashews and cumin seeds. Fry over medium heat until the onions are golden brown, then add the turmeric, chillies and ginger and keep frying until aromatic. Add the potatoes, stir to coat in all the spices and season well with salt. Squeeze over the lime juice, then scatter in the mackerel and coriander. Set aside.
- When you are ready to cook the dosas, heat a non-stick frying pan over medium heat and brush with ghee. Pour a ladleful of the batter into the centre of the pan and, using the back of the ladle, spread out the batter in concentric circles, spiralling out from the centre, to form a thin pancake. Drizzle with a little more ghee and cook for 2 minutes, then flip and cook for another minute or until golden. Keep warm while you cook the rest.
- To serve the dosas, you can either spread the filling on one half of a dosa and then fold it over, or you can fill and roll it up. My personal favourite for brunch is to leave it open, with a few spoonfuls of mackerel and potato, a grating of fresh coconut and a fried egg on top.

1 tbsp extra virgin olive oil
500g baby spinach
6 slices pancetta, chopped
50g unsalted butter, plus extra
　for greasing
2 leeks, chopped
½ tsp chilli flakes

A few sprigs of thyme, leaves
　picked and chopped
1 brioche loaf
300g creme fraiche
2 eggs
2 egg yolks
2 tsp Dijon mustard

200ml double cream
Finely grated zest and juice
　of 1 lemon
A good grating of nutmeg
150g mature cheddar
　or gruyere, grated
Sea salt and black pepper

Spinach, Pancetta and Cheese Bread and Butter Pudding

Bread and butter pudding is a minimalist sort of dish, with little more to it than stale bread, butter, eggs and milk. As much as I like it sweet, with a flourish of sugar and sultanas, a savoury version is much more appealing to me. I love to use brioche for this, but challah or white country bread with the crusts taken off works well too.

· Heat the olive oil in a frying pan over medium heat and add the baby spinach. Cook, stirring, for a minute or so, just until it has wilted, then remove from the heat. When it is cool enough to handle, use your hands to squeeze out any excess liquid, then roughly chop. In the same pan, fry the pancetta until it is golden and crisp, then remove and set aside.

· Wipe out the pan with kitchen paper and put it back over low–medium heat. Add the butter and, once it is foaming, add the leeks and fry until they are soft and melting, but do not let them brown. Add the chilli flakes and thyme and fry for a further minute before taking off the heat.

· Preheat the oven to 180°C/Fan 160°C/Gas Mark 4. Line a baking tray with baking parchment and butter a 900g loaf tin.

· Cut the brioche into rough 2cm cubes, spread out on the baking tray and bake for about 5–8 minutes, shaking occasionally, until golden and toasted. Remove from the oven and turn the temperature down to 150°C/Fan 130°C/Gas Mark 2. Whisk the creme fraiche, eggs, yolks and mustard in a bowl until smooth, then whisk in the cream, lemon zest and juice. Grate in the nutmeg and season with salt and pepper.

· Scatter a third of the cheese in the base of the loaf tin, followed by half each of the leek mixture, spinach, pancetta and brioche cubes. Repeat these layers, then pour over the egg mixture, pressing with a fork to submerge the brioche. Leave to stand for half an hour.

· Top with the remaining cheese and bake for 1 hour, until golden and a skewer inserted in the centre comes out clean. Leave to cool in the tin, then serve.

8 thick slices white bread
125g butter, softened
50g mature cheddar, grated
50g mozzarella, grated

For the curried cauliflower
2 tbsp rapeseed oil
1 onion, finely chopped
1 tsp cumin seeds
1 tsp fennel seeds
1 tsp coriander seeds
Thumb of ginger, finely grated
1 green chilli, finely chopped
200g chopped tinned tomatoes

1 tsp sugar
1 tsp ground turmeric
1 cauliflower, cut into
   small florets
250g fresh or frozen peas
A good squeeze of lime juice
Handful of chopped coriander
Sea salt

Curried Cauliflower and Cheese Toasted Sandwiches

No one can smoosh filling into a toasted sandwich the way my mother can. This one was originally born out of the need to use up leftover cauliflower curry, and for me it is now the reason to make cauliflower curry. I use cheddar for tang and mozzarella for its seductive melt and ooze. I love how the turmeric stains the bread with its Midas touch, and for extra golden-brown crispness, be generous with the butter. If you have a sandwich toaster or panini press, use it, but otherwise fry these sandwiches in a non-stick frying pan, ideally with a weight such as a cast-iron pan on top. This stretches the bread, increasing the surface area to give you more crunch!

· For the curried cauliflower, heat the oil in a frying pan and fry the onion until soft. Lightly crush the cumin, fennel and coriander seeds, then sprinkle over the onion and continue to cook until the onion has caramelised. Throw in the ginger and chilli and fry until softened. Add the tomatoes, sugar and turmeric. Let it simmer and reduce for 5 minutes, then add the cauliflower, stirring to coat it in the sauce. Cover and cook for about 15 minutes, until the cauliflower is tender. Add the peas and cook for another 5 minutes. Season with salt and a good squeeze of lime juice. Finish with a scattering of coriander. (At this point the curry is more than ready to eat with some fresh chapattis, but I like to make toasted sandwiches with it.)

· Heat a sandwich toaster or non-stick frying pan. Butter both sides of the bread. Place 4 of the slices on a sheet of baking parchment, then cover each one with a mixture of both cheeses and 3 tablespoons of the curried cauliflower. Top with the remaining slices of bread. Cook in the sandwich toaster or frying pan until the cheese has melted and the corners are slightly charred – if you're using a frying pan, you'll need to carefully turn over the sandwiches halfway though.

· Serve immediately. Any leftovers are also irresistible eaten cold.

Pea and Mint Stuffed Fishcakes
with Curry Hollandaise

There's something about kedgeree that always leaves me cold. It doesn't help that I'm not a fan of smoked haddock, but perhaps it's the lingering taste of a colonised India I find hardest to swallow, or else simply the muteness of spices trying and failing to speak.

I have tinkered around with the traditional recipe, however, and created a punchy little fishcake (minus the dreaded smoked haddock). Who doesn't love the economy of a fishcake, plumped out with mashed potatoes? They are especially frugal when you have ends or trimmings of fish that can be stored away in the freezer until there are enough.

The pea stuffing here has a little kick of heat, and the curry-powder-infused hollandaise provides the quintessential flavours of kedgeree. Serve with a poached egg for brunch, or a side salad for a pleasing supper. If you want to go crazy and double-carb, knock yourself out with a side of shoestring fries.

400g Maris Piper potatoes, peeled and cut into chunks
250g salmon fillet, skinned and pin-boned
250g cod fillet, skinned and pin-boned
About 500ml whole milk
2 bay leaves
½ tsp black peppercorns
Finely grated zest of 1 lemon
Handful of chopped coriander
1 onion, finely chopped

2 garlic cloves, finely chopped
1 green chilli, finely chopped
Thumb of ginger, finely grated
1 tsp cumin seeds, lightly crushed
1 tsp coriander seeds, lightly crushed
1 tsp ajwain seeds
1 egg
200g polenta
4 tbsp rapeseed or groundnut oil
Sea salt and black pepper

For the hollandaise
1 heaped tsp curry powder
200g butter
3 egg yolks
1 tbsp lemon juice

For the stuffing
150g frozen peas, defrosted
Handful of chopped mint
5 spring onions, thinly sliced
A few drops of lemon juice
1 tbsp extra virgin olive oil

- For the hollandaise, put the curry powder and butter in a saucepan over low heat and let it slowly melt, then remove from the heat, cover and leave to infuse for at least an hour, or overnight.
- To make the stuffing, pulse all the ingredients in a food processor until you have a coarse rubble.
- For the fishcakes, boil the potatoes in plenty of salted water until tender. In the meantime, lay the fish in a saucepan and pour over enough milk to cover. Add the bay leaves and peppercorns and bring to the boil, then reduce the heat and simmer for 5 minutes. Remove from the heat and leave to stand for 10 minutes to let the fish gently finish cooking, then transfer to a plate and let it cool a little. Discard the cooking liquor.
- Drain the cooked potatoes and mash or put through a potato ricer, then flake in the fish and add the lemon zest, coriander, onion, garlic, chilli, ginger and spices. Mix well and season to taste with salt and pepper.
- Shape the pea stuffing into 8 patties, then divide the fishcake mixture into 8 and mould around the pea patties. Beat the egg in a shallow bowl and put the polenta in another shallow bowl. Dip each fishcake into the beaten egg, then roll in the polenta so it is well coated. Chill in the refrigerator for 30 minutes.
- Meanwhile, finish the hollandaise. If the butter has set, gently melt it again, then strain. Whizz the egg yolks and lemon juice in a blender for a few seconds and then, with the motor still running, slowly add the butter in a thin steady stream until you have a silky hollandaise. Season well with salt and pepper.
- Heat the oil in a non-stick frying pan over medium heat and, working in batches, fry the fishcakes for 5 minutes on each side, until golden brown. Drain on kitchen paper, then serve with generous spoonfuls of the curry hollandaise.

450g white spelt flour,
plus extra for dusting
1 × 7g packet fast-action
dried yeast
250ml whole milk
1 egg, beaten
30g butter, melted
Olive oil

Sea salt and black pepper
Chopped parsley and sumac,
to serve

For the filling
1 onion, finely chopped
2 garlic cloves, finely chopped
½ tsp chilli flakes

Finely grated zest and juice
of 1 lemon
900g spinach
1 bunch of dill, finely chopped
250g ricotta
250g feta cheese, crumbled
Good grating of fresh nutmeg
1 egg, beaten
4 eggs

Turkish Spinach, Cheese and Egg in a Hole

This is a riff on a Turkish pide or the Georgian cheese bread called 'khachapuri', and it's ideal for lazy Sunday brunches. Its filling of cheese, spinach and a runny egg make it salty, cheesy and spectacular.

- Put the flour, yeast and 1 teaspoon of salt into a large bowl and mix together with a fork. Make a well in the centre and pour in the milk, egg and melted butter. Now bring everything together with your hands to make a soft dough. Turn out the dough onto a floured surface and knead until it is smooth and elastic. Wash, dry and lightly oil the mixing bowl, then return the dough to it, cover with cling film and leave to rise in a warm place for 2 hours, or until doubled in size.
- In the meantime, make the filling. Heat 1 tablespoon of oil in a large frying pan and fry the onion until soft and golden. Add the garlic, chilli flakes and lemon zest and fry for another 2 minutes, then take off the heat and squeeze in the lemon juice. Blanch the spinach in a pan of boiling water for about 10 seconds, then tip into a colander and refresh in ice-cold water. Drain well, using your hands to squeeze out any excess liquid, then roughly chop. Add the spinach and dill to the onion mixture in the frying pan. Stir in the ricotta and feta, grate in the nutmeg and season with salt and pepper. Finally, add the beaten egg and mix well, then set aside.
- Preheat the oven to 240°C/Fan 220°C/Gas Mark 9 and line a baking tray with baking parchment.
- Divide the dough into 4 equal pieces. On a lightly floured surface, flatten each one with your hands, then use a rolling pin to roll out into an elongated oval shape approximately 24cm x 16cm. Spread a quarter of the filling over each one, then fold in the two long sides and twist the ends to create a canoe-like shape. Make a little indentation in the centre, using the back of a spoon, and crack an egg into it. Repeat with the remaining dough, filling and eggs. Place the breads on the baking tray and bake for 5–8 minutes or until the eggs are set to your liking. Scatter with parsley and sumac and serve at once.

300g clear honey
1 vanilla bean, split and seeds
  scraped
1 star anise
Finely grated zest and juice
  of 1 orange
4 pears, peeled, cored and
  cut into wedges
4 Bramley apples, peeled, cored
  and cut into wedges
200g blackberries
Yoghurt or custard, to serve

For the topping
100g rolled oats
50g flaked almonds, toasted
30g demerara sugar
½ tsp ground cinnamon
Big pinch of salt
80g butter, melted and slightly
  cooled

Apple, Pear and Blackberry Breakfast Crumble

No matter how many berries and chia seeds and nuts you add to it, there is always something muted and austere about a bowl of porridge. That's unless you turn the ingredients into a delicious fruit crumble. Yes, you can have dessert for breakfast. Really.

This can be prepared in the morning, or the night before, for ease. If you are preparing it the night before, keep the fruit and crumble topping separate to prevent sogginess.

- Put the honey, vanilla seeds, star anise, orange zest and juice into a saucepan, then bring to a simmer over medium heat. Let the liquid reduce for 5–6 minutes until it thickens and goes syrupy, then add the pears and apples and cook for about 10 minutes, or until they are caramelised. Spoon into a baking dish and scatter over the blackberries.
- Preheat the oven to 180°C/Fan 160°C/Gas Mark 4.
- To make the topping, mix together the oats, almonds, sugar, cinnamon and salt in a bowl. Pour in the butter and mix well, making sure all the ingredients are coated with butter. Spread the crumble topping over the fruit, then bake for 15–20 minutes until the topping is golden brown and the fruit is bubbling.
- Serve with yoghurt at 8am or dollops of custard at dinner time. Leftovers (if there are any) are perfectly fine eaten cold or gently reheated.

100g plain flour
75g cornflour
Pinch of salt
115g chilled unsalted butter,
  cubed
70g icing sugar
¼ tsp ground cardamom

Seeds from 4 green cardamom
  pods, crushed
1–2 tbsp whole milk
Raspberry jam, for filling
Dried rose petals, to decorate –
  optional

Jam-filled Indian Shortbreads

I love a good biscuit with a mid-morning cup of tea. These Indian-influenced biscuits are normally studded with pistachios or almonds – but, inspired by Jammy Dodgers, I wanted to fill their bellies with jam. There is no better time to eat them than when they're still slightly warm from the oven: their crust will have crisped up in the air, forming a tight seal around the warm dough within. Most importantly, they should have cooled enough for you to actually taste the flavours – and for the jam not to burn your tongue! I never remember just how many I have eaten, because the experience for the true biscuiteer is trance-like, hypnotic. Their heady cardamom fragrance and melting velvetiness are soothing to the palate in a way no other food can be.

- Line two baking trays with baking parchment.
- In a bowl, combine the flour, cornflour and salt. Use your fingertips to rub the butter into the flour until it resembles breadcrumbs. Add the icing sugar and cardamom (ground and crushed), then mix with your hands until the dough starts to come together. Add just enough of the milk to form a firm dough, but avoid working it too much.
- Take heaped teaspoons of the dough and roll into balls between your palms, then flatten into a disc, pressing your thumb into the top to make an indentation for the jam to sit in. Place the biscuits a few centimetres apart on the baking trays. Fill each dent with a little jam, then chill the biscuits in the fridge for around 20 minutes, until they're nice and cold and firm.
- Meanwhile, preheat the oven to 180°C/Fan 160°C/Gas Mark 4.
- Bake the biscuits for 20 minutes, or until golden. Remove from the oven and decorate with a few dried rose petals, if you like. Transfer to a wire rack and leave to cool slightly, then serve warm with a cup of tea.

¾ tsp dried yeast
75ml warm water
300g plain flour, plus extra for
    dusting
30g caster sugar, plus extra
    for dusting
1 tsp sea salt
2 eggs
Finely grated zest of 1 lime
130g butter, softened
Rapeseed oil (or any neutral-
    flavoured oil), for deep-frying

For the filling
3 egg yolks
50g caster sugar
25g plain flour
25g cornflour
350ml whole milk
150g Alphonso mango pulp
    (around 3 mangoes)
Squeeze of lime juice

For the sherbet
45g icing sugar
35g citric acid
½ tbsp bicarbonate of soda
5g dried kaffir lime leaves

Mango Doughnuts with Lime Leaf Sherbet

*I make these doughnuts every time Alphonso mango season comes around
but you can make them any time you have a good ripe mango or two to hand.
The lime leaf sherbet is unrestrained and fun, the mango filling sweet and
rich, and the doughnut over-inflated and puffy. Anyone who cares about
doughnuts should make these immediately! You should be able to get the citric
acid from health food shops or online – and you'll need to make the dough the
day before, so it can rest overnight. The filling can also be made in advance
and kept in the fridge.*

· Sprinkle the yeast into the warm water and stir until the yeast has
    dissolved, then set aside for 10 minutes or until frothy. Put the flour,
    sugar, salt, eggs and lime zest into the bowl of an electric mixer fitted
    with the dough hook. Pour in the yeast mixture and knead on low speed
    for 10 minutes until you have a smooth and elastic dough. Add the butter,
    a quarter at a time, mixing well between additions.
· Transfer the dough to a lightly floured bowl, cover with cling film or
    a clean, damp tea towel and set aside in a warm place for 2 hours,
    or until doubled in size. Punch the dough down, cover again and
    refrigerate overnight.

- For the filling, whisk together the egg yolks and sugar in a heatproof bowl until the sugar has dissolved, then sift in both flours and mix to a smooth paste. Pour the milk into a small saucepan and bring to a simmer, then slowly add to the egg mixture, a little at a time, whisking as you go, until you have a smooth custard. Pour the custard back into the pan and bring to the boil, whisking constantly. Keep whisking until it thickens, then take off the heat. Leave to cool, then stir in the mango pulp and lime juice. Refrigerate until needed.
- Next day, lightly butter a baking tray. Divide the dough into 15 golfball-sized (45g) pieces and roll each one into a ball, then place on the baking tray, leaving space between them for proving. Cover with a clean, damp tea towel and set aside in a warm place for an hour, or until doubled in size.
- For the sherbet, sift the icing sugar, citric acid and bicarbonate of soda into a clean and perfectly dry bowl. Put the dried lime leaves into a blender and whizz to a powder, then add to the bowl and mix well.
- Fill a large, heavy-based saucepan a third full with the deep-frying oil. Heat the oil to 180°C – if you don't have a thermometer you will know the oil is ready when a cube of bread turns golden brown in 20 seconds. Fry the doughnuts in batches until golden and cooked through, turning so they become golden all over. Drain on kitchen paper and set aside to cool.
- Meanwhile, take a piping bag fitted with a small metal nozzle and fold down the top to make a cuff. Use a spatula to transfer the filling into it – pop the piping bag, nozzle down, in a tall glass or jug to hold it steady while you do this. Fold the cuff up again, then twist the bag at the top.
- Pierce each doughnut with a skewer and push around the crumb on the inside to make room for the filling. Carefully insert the nozzle of the piping bag into the centre and pipe in as much mango creme patissiere as you can, until it oozes out at you. Sprinkle sparingly with the sherbet – it is mouth-puckeringly sharp.

Kazuri

Small and Beautiful Snacks and Nibbles

My father was a compulsive eater. He knew what he liked, and he ate it to excess. While he'd prod, and complain about, the growing tubbiness around his middle, he took a simple, reliable pleasure in eating and drinking. He ate even when he didn't need to. It's true that his work was physical and made hunger bloom in his belly, but most of his eating was emotional. My father could be distant, self-absorbed and stern, but he rarely showed signs of stress – he simply let his daily graze distract him from his worries...

with each nibble he would become more soporific.

Sure, he loved the feasts my mother proudly laid out on the dining table, but they didn't inspire the same fervour in him as the snacks he scarfed between meals. As soon as he got in from work, he'd rush to the bathroom to scrub the day from his hands, change into his flannel pyjamas, pour himself a free measure of whisky and embark on his rummage around the kitchen cupboards. He rarely cooked, and certainly showed no interest in any kind of household chores, but even as he unwound, listening to his favourite *ghazals*[1] on the record player or watching the BBC evening news, he'd make several trips from the living room to the larder. A slice of bread painted edge-to-edge with butter would not interfere with dinner. A gigantic scoop of Bombay mix did not seem to ruin his appetite – it simply primed and encouraged it.

Even when the house was still and the lights were all out, he'd scuttle to the kitchen, looking for

a last titbit before bedtime – an edible lullaby.

In between stirring spices spitting in the pan, puffing up chapattis on a naked gas flame and being bad tempered with her squabbling children, my mother prepared

a snack tray of small and beautiful morsels for my father.

The tray was silver and shaped like a betel leaf, with three separate compartments for varying delights, which were different each day. Perhaps a simple fry of cashew nuts, doused in eye-watering chilli powder and black salt, or tiny crisp samosas filled with minced meat and peas, or a crunchy tangle of sev[2] — my father made light work of each of these.

Even on the frequent occasions when they quarrelled and were barely on speaking terms, the tray was readied like an offering regardless. It was like the glue that held their marriage together.

In the 1990s, the doctors told my father that his passion for snacking had set him up for a heart attack in the near future, so he underwent a successful triple bypass operation and was advised to lay off munching between meals. He abstained for a while, but then, as his stitches healed, leaving only a faint scar down his torso, he cajoled my mother into dusting off the snack tray and heating her wok of oil. He returned to crunching and masticating noisily — the sound intolerable to the rest of us was music to my mother's ears. And so this chapter of delectable morsels is dedicated to my dearest dad, who I am sure would have approved of all the frying and crunching that's going on here!

SMALL AND BEAUTIFUL SNACKS AND NIBBLES

1 Urdu love poems or odes set to music
2 Indian snack of crisp-fried noodles made from chickpea flour

1 × 375g sheet of ready-rolled
   puff pastry
1 egg, beaten
1 tbsp fennel seeds

For the filling
1 tbsp sunflower oil
1 onion, finely chopped
1 tsp cumin seeds
½ tsp ground cinnamon
½ tsp ground cloves
Thumb of ginger, finely grated
3 garlic cloves, finely chopped
1 green chilli, thinly sliced

350g peeled raw prawns,
   deveined and roughly chopped
½ tsp ground turmeric
100g fresh or frozen peas
4 tbsp coconut milk
½ tsp caster sugar
Handful of roughly chopped
   coriander
Juice of 1 lime
Sea salt

Pondicherry Prawn Puffs

When it comes to Indian cookery, France doesn't normally spring to mind, but the cultural remnants of France's colonial empire have left their mark on Pondicherry's architecture, language, design and food. Imagine a rich French sauce tinged with turmeric, mottled with spices and finished with coconut milk instead of cream — that is typical of the food of this southern Indian enclave. Flecked with prawns, the thick sauce is then wrapped in puff pastry for a more pronounced Gallic accent. These make a perfect alternative to the better-known samosas.

- For the filling, pour the oil into a large frying pan and fry the onion and cumin seeds over low heat until sticky and caramelised. Add the cinnamon and cloves and fry until aromatic, then add the ginger, garlic and chilli and fry for 3 minutes. Now add the prawns and turmeric, season with salt and cook until the prawns are almost done, about 5 minutes, then stir in the peas, coconut milk and sugar and simmer for another 3 minutes. Remove from the heat, stir in the coriander and lime juice and leave to cool.
- Lay out the pastry sheet on a lightly floured surface and use a 9cm round pastry cutter to cut out 12 rounds. Place 1 tablespoon of the cooled prawn filling on one half of each pastry circle. Brush the edges with beaten egg, then fold in half to make a semi-circle and seal by pressing with your fingers to crimp the edges. If you are making these ahead of time, cover and refrigerate for up to 24 hours.
- When you're ready to cook the prawn puffs, preheat the oven to 220°C/ Fan 200°C/Gas Mark 7 and line two baking trays with baking parchment.
- Brush the pastries with beaten egg and sprinkle with fennel seeds, then place on the baking trays. Bake for 15–20 minutes, or until they are irresistibly golden brown. Serve immediately.

500g raw peanuts
350ml rapeseed oil
20 kaffir lime leaves, stems
  removed

Finely grated zest of 1 lime
2 tbsp shichimi togarashi
½ tsp sea salt
3 tbsp maple syrup

Lime Leaf and Togarashi Peanuts

Nothing satisfies the need for crunch like a handful of peanuts. Flavoured with fragrant lime leaf and the potently peppery shichimi togarashi Japanese spice blend, these ones are a cut above any you'd buy ready-made. They are especially welcome with an ice-cold beer.

- Preheat the oven to 180°C/Fan 160°C/Gas Mark 4.
- Spread out the peanuts on a baking sheet and bake for 8–10 minutes or until they are golden and toasted.
- Heat the oil in a small, heavy-based saucepan with a lid. When the oil is hot, carefully drop in the lime leaves (they will spit!) and immediately put the lid on the pan. Once they have stopped spitting, remove with a slotted spoon and drain on kitchen paper, blotting them with the paper to absorb as much of the oil as possible.
- Using a pestle and mortar, crush the lime leaves, lime zest, togarashi and salt together.
- Drizzle the maple syrup all over the nuts, then scatter with the spice mix, making sure the nuts are well coated. Leave to dry, then serve at once or store in an airtight container for up to 3 weeks.

200g cornflakes
125g puffed rice (mamra)
150g roasted daria (split gram)
50g cashew nuts
50g almonds
50g peanuts

For the spice tempering
3 tbsp rapeseed oil
1 heaped tsp brown mustard
  seeds
¼ tsp asafoetida
25 curry leaves
2 dried red chillies
1 cinnamon stick, broken up
5 cloves

1 heaped tsp cumin seeds
½ tsp ground turmeric
2 tbsp raisins
2 green chillies, roughly chopped
1 tbsp caster sugar
1 tsp chilli powder
½ tsp citric acid
Sea salt

Baked Cornflake Chevdho

My father-in-law has fierce cravings for crunchy things. Sadly for him, most foods that crunch are deep-fried, and they are forbidden to him on account of a dodgy ticker. Chevdho is his favourite — it's a sort of Indian deep-fried trail mix or savoury granola that is salty, spicy, tangy and highly addictive. He finds it miserable not to be able to munch it by the handful, so I make him this healthier baked version, packed full of nuts, puffed rice, spices and extra-crunchy cornflakes. It keeps well for up to a month in an airtight container, but somehow it never seems to last that long.

- Preheat the oven to 180°C/Fan 160°C/Gas Mark 4.
- In a large bowl, mix together the cornflakes, puffed rice, daria and all the nuts. Transfer to a large baking tray and roast in the oven for about 10 minutes until dark and toasty, giving it a shake every so often and keeping a close eye on it, as it can quickly burn.
- For the spice tempering, heat the oil in a large saucepan over medium heat and add the mustard seeds. As soon as they pop and splutter, follow with the asafoetida, curry leaves, dried chillies, cinnamon, cloves and cumin seeds and cook for 30 seconds or until fragrant. Finally, add the turmeric, raisins and green chillies, then turn off the heat.
- Add the cornflake mixture to the pan, tossing to make sure everything is well coated. Season with sugar, chilli powder, citric acid and salt to taste. Allow to cool, then serve at once or store in an airtight container for up to a month.

1 cauliflower, cut into
    small florets
Small handful of Thai basil leaves
6 spring onions, thinly sliced
2 red chillies, thinly sliced
4 garlic cloves, thinly sliced
Groundnut oil, for deep-frying
Lime wedges, to serve

For the dipping sauce
100ml Chinkiang black vinegar
80ml light soy sauce
1 red chilli, finely chopped
Small thumb of ginger,
    finely grated
2 tsp toasted sesame oil
1 tsp caster sugar
1 tbsp sesame seeds, toasted

For the batter
2 tsp Sichuan peppercorns
2 tsp black peppercorns
2 tsp sea salt
200g plain flour
4 tbsp cornflour
About 300ml ice-cold
    sparkling water

Cauliflower Popcorn with Black Vinegar Dipping Sauce

Deep-frying is like the icing sugar of cookery — it just makes everything taste so much better! This crisp, battered manifestation of the humble cauli is based on one of the dishes I can never resist when I go to a Chinese restaurant: salt and pepper squid. The batter is laced with mouth-tingling Sichuan peppercorns, which are dry-roasted to tease out their fragrance and flavour, along with some more assertive black peppercorns for a bit of heat. Importantly, the popcorn should really be scarfed as soon as it hits the plate.

· To make the dipping sauce, simply whisk together all the ingredients.
· For the batter, heat a dry frying pan over medium heat and toast the peppercorns until they are aromatic. Tip into a pestle and mortar, along with the salt, and crush to a coarse powder. Empty out into a mixing bowl, add both flours and mix well. Now whisk in the sparkling water, adding just enough to make a batter with a double-cream consistency, and being careful not to overbeat.
· Fill a large, heavy-based saucepan a third full with the deep-frying oil. Heat the oil to 180°C — if you don't have a thermometer, you will know the oil is ready when a cube of bread turns golden brown in 20 seconds. Dip the pieces of cauliflower into the batter, one at a time, letting the excess drip off, and deep-fry until golden. Remove with a slotted spoon and drain on kitchen paper. Dip the basil leaves in batter and fry in the same way.
· When you have finished frying the cauliflower and basil leaves, carefully pour out most of the oil from the pan, leaving just a few tablespoons. Place over medium–high heat and flash-fry the spring onions, chillies and garlic for a minute or so, until the garlic is just beginning to colour. Drain on kitchen paper, scatter over the cauliflower and toss. Serve immediately, with lime wedges for squeezing and the dipping sauce alongside.

500g pork skin
Groundnut oil, for deep-frying

For the fennel seed and chilli salt
1 tbsp sea salt
1 tsp fennel seeds, toasted
1 tsp chilli flakes
½ dried chipotle chilli, chopped
Finely grated zest of 1 lime

Pork Scratchings with Fennel Seed and Chilli Salt

If you were to look up the word 'irresistible' in my dream food dictionary, it's likely there would be a picture of pork scratchings next to it. My late father was extremely fond of pork scratchings — even the intensely salty ones sold in packets in pubs. With their fennel seed and chilli salt, these are far superior.

· Cut away any fat from the underside of the pork skin, then cut the skin into 4cm pieces. Bring a large saucepan of salted water to the boil and add the pork skin. Lower the heat and simmer for half an hour. Drain on kitchen paper, using the paper to dab away any moisture and dry it thoroughly.
· Preheat the oven to 150°C/Fan 130°C/Gas Mark 2 and line a baking sheet with baking parchment. Lay the pork skin on the baking sheet and bake for 1 hour or until completely dried out.
· In the meantime, make the spicy salt by grinding all the ingredients together using a pestle and mortar.
· Fill a large, heavy-based saucepan a third full with the deep-frying oil. Heat the oil to 180°C — if you don't have a thermometer, you will know the oil is ready when a cube of bread turns golden brown in 20 seconds. Add the pork skin in batches and cook for 1–2 minutes, or until puffed and crisp, allowing the oil to return to temperature between batches.
· Drain on kitchen paper, then season generously with the spicy salt and serve immediately.

3 garlic cloves, roughly chopped
Thumb of ginger, roughly chopped
2 green chillies, roughly chopped
700g shelled fresh peas
1 small red onion, finely chopped
Large handful of finely chopped
   coriander
Large handful of finely
   chopped mint

2 tsp cumin seeds, toasted and
   lightly crushed
2 tsp coriander seeds, toasted
   and lightly crushed
1 tsp ground cinnamon
2 tbsp chickpea (gram) flour
Sea salt
Groundnut oil, for deep-frying
Pickled chillies, to serve

For the saffron yoghurt
½ tsp saffron threads
1 tbsp warm water
500g Greek yoghurt
1 garlic clove, finely grated

Pea Koftas with Saffron Yoghurt

*The word kofta comes from the Persian 'koofteh', and generally refers to
a meatball made with meltingly tender pounded beef or lamb. Meat-free
versions, made from various gourds, hung yoghurt and paneer, are very
popular in India, where a significant percentage of the population is
vegetarian. This is my mother's recipe and was one of the first things I helped
her to make: as a five-year-old, I was sat on a wooden stool in the garden
and given the task of shelling sacks of peas. The result was a red plastic bucket
brimming with shelled peas, like gleaming malachite marbles. As master
podder, it was my privilege to check the first kofta for seasoning, while it was still
hissing with oil from the fryer. I remember the sweet vegetal flavour of the peas
contrasting with the heat of chilli and spices – and I still find them irresistible.
To take these from snack to dinner, simmer them in a curry sauce or eat with
linguine spiked with fried lemon zest, garlic and chilli.*

- To make the saffron yoghurt, crush the saffron and steep in the warm
  water for 5 minutes. Beat the yoghurt until smooth, then whisk in the
  saffron with its soaking liquid and the garlic. Season with salt to taste,
  then set aside in a small bowl.
- In a food processor, blitz the garlic, ginger and chilli to a fine paste, then
  transfer to a mixing bowl. Put the peas into the food processor and blitz
  until they are coarsely chopped. Tip into the mixing bowl, then stir in the
  onion, herbs, spices and chickpea flour. When everything is well mixed,
  refrigerate for half an hour to firm up. Season with salt to taste, then shape
  into gobstopper-sized balls and place on a tray, ready for frying.
- Fill a large, heavy-based saucepan a third full with the deep-frying oil.
  Heat the oil to 180°C – if you don't have a thermometer, you will know
  the oil is ready when a cube of bread turns golden brown in 20 seconds.
  Add the koftas in batches, being careful not to overcrowd the pan, and
  cook for 3 minutes, or until crisp and golden, allowing the oil to return
  to temperature between batches. Remove with a slotted spoon and drain
  on kitchen paper.
- Serve the koftas while hot, with saffron yoghurt and pickled chillies.

Prawn Toast Scotch Eggs with Banana Ketchup

These are the bonny love children of a Scotch egg and a prawn toast – both perennially popular in their own right, and outrageously good when they come together. You can use just panko breadcrumbs to coat the eggs if you can't get hold of uncooked prawn crackers, but I especially like the spicy Thai variety that puff up when fried to give an off-the-Richter-scale crunch.

The idea for the ketchup may seem bananas – but please indulge me, and I promise you'll end up with the kind of condiment that will have you scraping the jar! The bananas, especially if slightly overripe, lend a sweet toffee flavour, while the spices bring an addictive heat. The main spice mix here is Madras curry powder. Curry powders can sometimes be a bit of a travesty: musty yellow dust, often with too much chilli and turmeric, but good ones these days can be delicious and time-saving too. There is nothing really authentic about Madras curry powder and, despite its name, it's actually a British invention. However, once you develop a taste for it (maybe in curry sauce for chips, or the thick brown sauce that smothers a breaded fillet of pork in Japanese katsu curry), it is impossible to dislike. It may have zero finesse, but it lends its own unique savoury note to this ketchup, which is equally good in a burger or hot dog – in fact, it tastes good slathered on pretty much anything.

For perfectly soft-boiled quail's eggs, start with a saucepan of cold water (enough to cover the eggs) and once it comes to the boil, slip in the eggs, simmer for 2 minutes and 15 seconds precisely, then quickly fish out the eggs with a slotted spoon and plunge into ice-cold water before shelling.

300g raw prawn crackers
300g panko breadcrumbs
Plain flour, for dredging
3 eggs, beaten
300g raw tiger prawns, peeled
 and deveined
2 fat garlic cloves, finely chopped
Thumb of ginger, finely grated
1 tsp chilli flakes
1 tsp caster sugar
1 tsp sesame oil

1 tsp light soy sauce
5 spring onions, thinly sliced
12 soft-boiled quail's eggs,
 shelled (see page 74)
Groundnut oil, for deep-frying
Sesame seeds, to garnish

For the ketchup
1 tbsp groundnut oil
1 red onion, finely chopped
1 tsp finely grated ginger

3 garlic cloves, crushed
1 red chilli, finely chopped
1 tsp ground cinnamon
1 tsp ground allspice
2 heaped tsp Madras
 curry powder
6 ripe bananas, mashed to a puree
3 tbsp dark brown sugar
200ml cider vinegar
4 tbsp light soy sauce
Sea salt

- To make the ketchup, heat the oil in a large saucepan and fry the onion over low heat until dark and caramelised. Add the ginger, garlic and chilli and fry until soft and fragrant, then follow with the cinnamon, allspice and curry powder and fry for a few minutes until their scents fill your nose. Now stir in the bananas, sugar, vinegar and soy sauce and let it simmer gently for 20 minutes, stirring occasionally. Pour in 125ml of water and cook for a further 5 minutes. Season with salt to taste, then blend to a smooth paste with a hand-held blender, or leave it slightly chunky – the choice is yours. Set aside to cool.
- Blitz the prawn crackers to a breadcrumb consistency in a blender or food processor. Tip into a shallow bowl and mix with the breadcrumbs. Put the flour into another bowl, and the beaten egg into a third.
- Pat the prawns dry with kitchen paper, then pop them into the blender or food processor. Add the garlic, ginger, chilli flakes, sugar, sesame oil and soy sauce and whizz to a coarse, sticky paste – do not over-blend. Stir in the spring onions, then divide the prawn mixture into 12 equal portions and place on a plate.
- Now enclose each soft-boiled quail's egg in a portion of the prawn mixture: with wet hands, roll the prawn mixture into a ball, then flatten it into a circle large enough to wrap around the egg. Press the edges together to seal, being careful not to squash the delicate egg inside.
- Once all the eggs have been wrapped, roll them in the flour, then in the beaten egg and finally in the breadcrumb mixture. Place on a plate and freeze for 5 minutes to firm them up slightly.
- Prcheat the oven to 200°C/Fan 180°C/Gas Mark 6 and line a baking tray with baking parchment.
- Fill a large, heavy-based saucepan a third full with the deep-frying oil. Heat the oil to 180°C – if you don't have a thermometer, you will know the oil is ready when a cube of bread turns golden brown in 20 seconds. Place the Scotch eggs in the oil in batches, being careful not to overcrowd the pan, and fry for 2 minutes until crisp and golden. Use a slotted spoon to transfer them to the baking tray. Allow the oil to return to temperature before repeating with the other batches.
- When all the Scotch eggs have been fried, cook them in the oven for a further 2 minutes. Slice through the middle to check they're done – the prawn mixture should be pink and cooked through, and the egg yolk should still be runny. Serve with the banana ketchup and a sprinkling of sesame seeds.

SMALL AND BEAUTIFUL SNACKS AND NIBBLES

The Samosa Sisterhood

I suppose I will never again experience the nub of security I felt on the communal cookery days when a band of aunties convened at our house to help my mother roll and fill some five hundred samosas. The Samosa Sisterhood gathered whenever my mother needed help to cater for a party – a soiree without a samosa was like a picnic without a sandwich.

In my memory, these aunties are like flickering fragments of female spirit, a sort of pageant of womanhood.

They would tousle my hair playfully, and pull at my cheeks adoringly. I loved them all. I remember the staccato of their dusty sandals clip-clopping across the pistachio-green terrazzo floor, their smell of dough and fried onions, the warmth of their cotton *salwars*,[1] their *kurthas*[2] salty with perspiration.

1 Indian trousers
2 Indian tunic

One aunty had a face as round as an 'O', large kind eyes lined with cow-like eyelashes, and a strong upper body with muscly arms, no doubt built from decades of kneading dough. She wore gold bangles that jangled as she chased the dough around a large metal bowl with the heel of her hand, thwacking it contentedly once it was as smooth and springy as a baby's bottom. Another had gleaming silver hair pulled back into a neat chignon at the nape of her neck. She wore ebony-rimmed glasses that magnified her eyes to cartoonish proportions. Her yellow-gold *matarmala*[3] suited her aristocratic demeanour as she reclined, aloof, on a chair, swatting away flies with quick swipes of her small, henna-ed, work-shy hands.

3 necklace made from gold beads shaped likes peas

This was my childhood. Even though I lived among the chaos of an extended family – parents and grandparents, siblings, uncles and aunts, cousins, house staff, visiting guests, cats, dogs, chickens and a talkative parrot – I had no one I could really play with. I was pierced by loneliness. My siblings were all much older, and far too cool for a five-year-old hanger-on, and my mother was always too fraught managing a household where guests constantly dropped in, with no notice or invitation. So I escaped into books, sometimes reading them over and over. I became obsessed with Enid Blyton's garden fairies, and would spend hours looking for them with a magnifying glass, leaving my grandmother's prized flowerpots upturned.

On samosa-making days, my mother woke with the first birdsong of the dawn to prepare a sustaining lunch of rice and dhal, and to lay plastic sheeting across the table where the women would work. By 11 o'clock they would be milling around our large dining-room table, sharing dirty jokes and masala chai with cardamom-flavoured *naan khatais*.[4] Our African grey parrot, not to be left out of the conversation, would squawk along noisily. I sometimes lay under the table on the cool stone floor, relaxed by their calm and cheering grown-up chatter.

4 chickpea flour and semolina cookies

By the end of the day, my stomach would be growling with greedy keenness to sample their wares. I've eaten too many samosas in my life, but none have lived up to these. Influenced by our Gujarati neighbours, they were smaller than the usual bulky Punjabi ones, and crisper too. They were made with close attention to detail and, despite the jumble of hands making them, were uniformly perfect – the three points of their prism sharp and pointed like a starched shirt.

These delicacies were made with something that felt like love, neatly stuffed and with the pastry carefully folded over, like an envelope containing a missive full of tenderness.

They were best eaten straight out of the fryer. Hot peas and potatoes would explode into your mouth with that first bite, the spike of chilli heat setting your tongue on fire. At teatime, their work would be complete and the women would gaze euphorically at a landscape of pale triangular pastries neatly laid out on newspaper. 'Let's eat!' my mother would shout over the joyful scene – and, just like that, a hundred or so samosas, reserved for the cooks' privilege of tasting, would disappear.

SMALL AND BEAUTIFUL SNACKS AND NIBBLES

Clove-smoked Venison Samosas with Beetroot Chutney

Immigrant recipes are open-ended and ready for adaptation to new lands. Traditionally the meat used for filling samosas is lamb, but I also love using British game when it is in season. Venison is delicious and lean, and it can really stand up to the hefty Mughal-influenced spices in this recipe. I've gone one step further and taken inspiration from the classic pairing of venison and earthy beetroot by making a robust beetroot chutney to accompany these meaty parcels.

Kewra water is an Indian floral essence extracted from pandanus, or screwpine. Although by no means a key ingredient here, it does add a heady sweetness and fragrance that nods to the opulence of the Mughal kitchen.

1 tbsp rapeseed oil
1 small red onion, finely chopped
1 heaped tsp cumin seeds
25g cashew nuts
2 tbsp ghee
Large thumb of ginger,
  finely grated
3 garlic cloves, finely chopped
1–2 green chillies, finely
  chopped
1 tsp fennel seeds, toasted
  and lightly crushed
1 heaped tsp cumin seeds
Seeds from 5 green cardamom
  pods, ground

½ tsp ground mace
¼ tsp ground cloves
1 tsp ground cinnamon
350g venison mince
5 cloves
A few drops of kewra water
  (screwpine essence) – optional
Handful of finely chopped mint
24 strips of samosa pastry or
  8 sheets of filo pastry
3 tbsp plain flour, mixed with
  about 2 tbsp water to make
  a paste
Rapeseed oil, for deep-frying
Sea salt and black pepper

For the chutney
2 tbsp rapeseed oil
1 tbsp split chickpeas
  or channa dhal
1 tsp white urid dhal
Pinch of asafoetida
12 curry leaves
2 dried red chillies, torn in half
1 green chilli, finely chopped
250g beetroot, peeled
  and grated
2 tbsp tamarind concentrate

- To make the chutney, heat 1 tablespoon of the oil in a frying pan over high heat, then add the split chickpeas and urid dhal and turn down the heat. When they begin to darken, sprinkle in the asafoetida, following swiftly with the curry leaves and the dried and fresh chillies. Fry for 30 seconds, then tip into a small bowl and set aside to cool. In the same pan, heat another tablespoon of oil and fry the beetroot over medium heat until it is soft and cooked.
- Put the cooked spices into a blender and whizz to a paste, then add the beetroot, tamarind and salt to taste and blend again. Spoon the chutney into a serving bowl and set aside until you are ready to use.
- Heat the oil in a frying pan. Fry the onion with the cumin seeds over low heat until dark and caramelised. Next add the cashews and fry until they are golden brown. Transfer to a blender and whizz the mixture to a paste.
- To make the samosa filling, heat 1 tablespoon of the ghee in a frying pan over medium heat. Add the ginger, garlic and green chillies and fry until soft and fragrant. Add all the spices and fry for a minute before adding the venison mince. Fry until the meat is cooked, then fold in the cashew paste and cook for another minute. Take off the heat.
- In a small, heavy-based saucepan, heat 1 tablespoon of ghee until it is starting to smoke, then add the cloves. Let them go dark but not burnt. Immediately fish out the cloves with a spoon and pour the ghee over the venison mix. Stir in the kewra water, if using, and the mint, then leave to cool completely.
- If you are using filo pastry, cut each sheet into equal thirds lengthways. Lay a strip of pastry on your benchtop, with one of the short ends nearest to you. Place 1 rounded tablespoon of the filling at the end of the strip furthest away from you, leaving a 1cm border. Now take the right-hand corner of the pastry and fold it diagonally to the left, enclosing the filling and forming a triangle. Fold the filled triangle down towards you, and keep folding until you reach the end of the strip, sealing the last fold with the flour paste. Repeat the process, making 24 samosas in total.
- Fill a large, heavy-based saucepan a third full with the deep-frying oil. Heat the oil to 180°C – if you don't have a thermometer, you will know the oil is ready when a cube of bread turns golden brown in 20 seconds. Fry the samosas in batches and cook for about 4 minutes, or until golden brown and crisp, allowing the oil to return to temperature between batches. Remove with a slotted spoon and drain on kitchen paper.
- Serve the samosas hot, with the beetroot chutney.

500g chickpea (gram) flour
1 tsp garlic powder
1 tsp sea salt
Handful of fresh fenugreek, leaves
   picked and finely chopped

2 tsp cumin seeds, toasted and
   lightly crushed
Groundnut oil, for deep-frying

Franca's Chickpea Chips

This recipe is inspired by the great aunt of a chef who worked with me at Jikoni. Aunt Franca comes from Genoa, where golden fritters made with chickpea flour and called 'panisette' are an immensely popular snack. They look exactly like chunky potato chips (and are just as easy to eat) but contain no potato. Chickpea (gram) flour – or 'farina di ceci', as it is known in Italy – is used all over India to make a multitude of snacks, and panisette reminded me so much of these that I decided to take Aunt Franca's basic recipe and oomph it up with some Indian spices. The result is a chip with a delicate crust on the outside and a creamy interior. Beware, these rank highly on the addictiveness scale!

- In a large, heavy-based saucepan, whisk together the chickpea flour and 1.5 litres of water – keep whisking until it is completely smooth and lump-free. Put the pan over medium heat and bring to the boil, then turn down to a simmer and stir continuously for 15 minutes, or until the mixture starts coming away from the sides of the pan. Stir in the garlic powder, salt, fenugreek and cumin, then pour into two large (about 35cm x 25cm) baking trays, smoothing it out so it is around 1cm thick. Set aside to cool and firm up, then cut evenly into chunky chips.
- Fill a large, heavy-based saucepan a third full with the deep-frying oil. Heat the oil to 180°C – if you don't have a thermometer, you will know the oil is ready when a cube of bread turns golden brown in 20 seconds. Fry the chips in batches for 5–7 minutes, or until golden brown and crisp, allowing the oil to return to temperature between batches. Drain on kitchen paper and serve hot.

3 tbsp plain flour
125g panko breadcrumbs
2 eggs
Groundnut oil, for deep-frying

For the filling
75g unsalted butter
100g plain flour
400ml hot milk
100g shankleesh, crumbled

50g soft goat's cheese, crumbled
1 large cooked beetroot, grated
Good grating of nutmeg
Sea salt and black pepper

Beetroot and Shankleesh Croquetas

Croquetas are basically deep-fried balls of bechamel, and are undisputedly my favourite snack in tapas bars. These ones have a dreamy, creamy, luscious centre full of sweet, earthy beetroot and sharp cheese. If you can't get shankleesh, just use another 100g of goat's cheese, or replace it with the same amount of salty feta.

- For the filling, melt the butter in a saucepan over medium heat, then add the flour and cook, stirring constantly, for 3 minutes. Gradually pour in the milk, still stirring constantly, and let it bubble for a minute or so until you have a thick white sauce. Remove from the heat and fold through both cheeses and the beetroot. Season with the nutmeg and salt and pepper to taste. Allow to cool to room temperature, then cover with cling film and chill until firm.
- Line a baking sheet with baking parchment. Using wet hands, shape the firmed mixture into 3cm balls, place on the baking sheet and freeze for 1 hour.
- Put the flour in a shallow bowl and the panko breadcrumbs in another one. Beat the eggs in a third bowl. Carefully roll each ball in flour, then in beaten egg and finally in the panko breadcrumbs.
- Fill a large, heavy-based saucepan a third full with the deep-frying oil. Heat the oil to 180°C – if you don't have a thermometer, you will know the oil is ready when a cube of bread turns golden brown in 20 seconds. Fry the croquetas in batches for 2 minutes, or until golden brown and crisp, allowing the oil to return to temperature between batches. Drain on kitchen paper, then serve immediately.

300g floury potatoes,
  such as King Edward
100g bulgur wheat
30g plain flour
1 tsp coriander seeds, toasted
  and ground
1 tsp cumin seeds, toasted
  and lightly crushed
½ tsp ground allspice
1 tsp ground cinnamon
Groundnut oil, for deep-frying
Sea salt and black pepper
Pickled chillies, to serve

For the filling
2 tbsp olive oil
1 onion, finely chopped
2 garlic cloves, finely chopped
1 heaped tsp cumin seeds
150g cooked beetroot,
  finely diced
1 tbsp walnuts, toasted and
  finely chopped
75g drained tinned chickpeas,
  blitzed in a blender
1 tsp ground allspice
Juice of ½ lemon

Handful of finely chopped mint
Handful of finely chopped parsley

For the sauce
100g tahini
1 garlic clove, crushed
Juice of 1 lemon
6 tbsp warm water
1 tbsp olive oil
Pinch of cayenne pepper

Beetroot and Walnut Kibbeh with Tahini Sauce

This is a vegetarian take on kibbeh — the classic Levantine patties, usually stuffed with minced lamb or beef. Here beetroot lends its earthy flavour to the filling. Eat these hot, either just as they are, or with tahini sauce and fiery pickled chillies. Like falafel, they are good wrapped in folds of lavaash or pitta.

- To make the sauce, whisk together all the ingredients until smooth, then season with salt to taste. Set aside.
- For the kibbeh, boil the unpeeled potatoes in a saucepan of salted water until tender. Drain and peel, then return to the pan and let them steam-dry over low heat for 10 minutes.
- Meanwhile, soak the bulgur in cold water for 5 minutes, then squeeze dry. Pass the potatoes through a ricer or mash them, then mix in the bulgur, flour and spices. Season with salt and black pepper. Set aside.
- For the filling, heat the olive oil in a saucepan over low heat. Add the onion and garlic and cook until soft and golden. Increase the heat to medium, add the beetroot and cook for a few minutes. Spread out the beetroot mix and let it cool, then combine with the walnuts, chickpeas, allspice, lemon juice, herbs and salt and pepper to taste.
- Take a pingpong-ball-sized piece of the kibbeh, place it on a sheet of baking parchment and flatten it to a 4mm-thick disc. Place a heaped tablespoon of the filling in the centre and shape the dough around it to form a seamless oval. Repeat with the remaining kibbeh and filling.
- Fill a large, heavy-based saucepan a third full with the deep-frying oil. Heat the oil to 180°C — if you don't have a thermometer, you will know the oil is ready when a cube of bread turns golden brown in 20 seconds. Add the kibbeh in batches, being careful not to overcrowd the pan, and cook for 4 minutes, or until crisp and golden, allowing the oil to return to temperature between batches. Remove with a slotted spoon and drain on kitchen paper. Serve the kibbeh with tahini sauce and pickled chillies.

250g plain flour, plus extra
  for dusting
1 × 7g packet fast-action
  dried yeast
1 tsp sea salt
About 150ml lukewarm water
Sesame seeds, for sprinkling

For the filling
1 small red onion, finely chopped
Drizzle of olive oil
2 garlic cloves, finely sliced
500g Swiss chard, stalks finely
  chopped, leaves torn
Handful of finely chopped parsley
3 tbsp finely chopped dill

15g pine nuts, toasted
175g feta cheese, crumbled
1 preserved lemon, rind only,
  finely chopped
Good grating of nutmeg
2 tsp sumac
Sea salt and black pepper,
  to taste

Chard, Feta, Pine Nut and Preserved Lemon Fatayer

These fat, yeasty Middle Eastern pastries are not dissimilar to turnovers, but instead of apples they are stuffed with chard, feta, pine nuts and preserved lemon. They make a perfect portable snack and are equally good hot or cold, and so are ideal for picnics.

· Combine the flour, yeast and salt in a large bowl. Gradually pour in the water, adding just enough to form a dough. Knead well on a lightly floured surface until you have a smooth, springy dough. Place in a lightly oiled bowl, cover with a clean, damp tea towel and set aside in a warm place to rise for 1½ hours, or until it has doubled in size.

· In the meantime, prepare the filling. Fry the onion in the oil until it is soft but not brown, then add the garlic and the stalks of the chard. Fry until tender and before adding the chard leaves. Take off the heat and stir in all the remaining ingredients. Leave to cool completely, then drain off any excess liquid.

· Preheat the oven to 200°C/Fan 180°C/Gas Mark 6 and line two large baking sheets with baking parchment.

· Divide the dough into 20 equal pieces and cover with the damp tea towel to stop them drying out. Taking one piece at a time, roll the dough into a ball and flatten with your hands. On a lightly floured surface, use a rolling pin to roll it out to a circle about 4mm thick. Place a heaped tablespoon of the filling in the centre, then fold the dough inwards from three points on the edge of the circle to form a triangular parcel, pinching the edges together firmly to seal the parcel. Transfer to one of the baking sheets and brush with a little oil. Repeat with the remaining dough and filling. Scatter with sesame seeds and bake for 20–25 minutes until golden and hot all the way through.

· Serve hot, or allow to cool and then store in an airtight container in the fridge for up to 3 days.

1 × 375g sheet of all-butter
  puff pastry
1 egg, beaten
Nigella seeds, for sprinkling

For the baharat
1 tsp cumin seeds, toasted
  and finely ground
1 tsp ground cinnamon
1 tsp ground allspice
1 tsp coriander seeds, toasted
  and finely ground
½ tsp freshly ground black pepper
Good grating of nutmeg

For the filling
500g fatty lamb mince
1 onion, very finely chopped
40g pine nuts
35g hot Turkish pepper paste
  (biber salcasi)
30g currants, soaked in hot
  water for 30 minutes
Handful of finely chopped parsley
Handful of finely chopped mint
Sea salt and black pepper

Lamb and Baharat Sausage Rolls

*Few things compare to the sensory pleasure of a warm sausage roll. This one
uses minced lamb instead of pork, and is pepped up with baharat — a spice mix
that is as indispensible across the Middle East as garam masala is in India.
If you can't find Turkish pepper paste, use harissa for a similar effect.*

- First make the baharat by mixing all the spices together.
- For the filling, combine the lamb, onion, pine nuts, pepper paste, drained
  currants, parsley, mint, baharat and season with salt and pepper to taste.
  Mix well.
- On a lightly floured surface, roll out the puff pastry sheet until you have
  a 45cm x 30cm rectangle. Cut in half lengthways and work with one piece
  at a time, keeping the other one chilled in the fridge. Spoon the lamb
  mix along one of the long sides of the pastry, then roll the pastry over to
  enclose it and seal. Trim and repeat with the remaining piece of pastry.
  Brush with the beaten egg and scatter with nigella seeds, then refrigerate
  for 15 minutes to firm up.
- Preheat the oven to 200°C/Fan 180°C/Gas Mark 6 and line a large baking
  sheet with baking parchment. Cut the sausage rolls into 5cm lengths and
  arrange on the baking sheet. Bake for 20 minutes, until golden brown,
  then serve hot.

The
Pickle Maker

1 pickle maker The entrance to the bungalow where the *achaar-waali*[1] lived was always difficult to get to, on account of the two feral white geese she kept for security, in lieu of guard dogs. There had been a mongrel once, but he had proved puny and insignificant — nothing more than a soppy bundle of caramel-coloured fur. So now she had the twin shadows Sita and Gita — vicious and territorial, pecking everything in their wake.

2 aunty The *achaar-waali*, who we called *maasi*[2] out of respect, was a widow and lived alone. Her bungalow was in creaking disrepair; the dusty, uncared-for veranda was empty apart from a washing line bent under the weight 3 scarves normally worn with an Indian *shalwar kameez* of several drying *dupattas*[3] and a white goat tethered to a tree. She had no funds to fix it up or move, as her only income came from making pickles and chutney. Nearing eighty, she still had pale, youthful, liquid eyes and 4 jasmine an abundance of grey *chameli*[4]-scented hair, which she kept tied in an unfussy knot at the nape of her neck. As a child she had received no formal education, but when her husband died, she taught herself enough basic arithmetic to set up a little business that earned her just enough profit to keep her out of a pickle.

She lived frugally but independently. As the demand for her wares grew in the city, she became astute, tenacious and emancipated, decades ahead of many of the younger women, like my mother, who were her customers.

5 pickle Occasionally, on Sunday afternoons, when my mother noticed her *achaar*[5] stock dwindling, she'd send me along with an older cousin to *maasi*'s house to pick up new supplies. We'd walk down the dirt track to her house, empty glass jars clinking in our satchels. Age had left her in the fuzzy space between sound and silence, and sometimes we'd stand at the gate in the open sunlight for what felt like hours, hurling small stones at her bungalow walls to get her attention, too terrified of the spitting geese to let ourselves in. Once the geese were safely penned in, we'd follow her into a little shed where she'd set up her factory. I loved nosing around in that space, which reeked of vinegar and spices. 'What's that?'

I'd say repeatedly, picking up bits of cooking paraphernalia – she never once got impatient with me. She'd display the fruits of her craft for her customers, laying out open jars of *gor keri*[6] or sticky *chhunda*[7] like bait, to see if they would respond – and they almost certainly did.

In most Indian households, no meal is complete without a smidgen of *achaar*. Traditionally they are a side-show to curries and dhals, but when you had *maasi*'s pickles they overshadowed every other player on the plate.

> She made eye-wateringly hot ones, and mouth-puckeringly sharp ones, but the one I loved the most was her sweet lime pickle, which trod the tightrope between sweet and sour with immaculate balance.

Almost fifteen years after leaving Nairobi as a child, I went back to my old neighbourhood. Most of the houses, including hers, were vacant. Rot, tarnish and decay had set it. The street seemed like an ailing old friend, houses hanging off its shrunken shoulders like a suit that no longer fitted. That evening, I found myself craving the reassurance of home-cooked food – dhal, rice and *achaar* – so I went to the supermarket and bought a commercial brand of lime pickle, knowing that it would be far inferior.

Unsurprisingly, it tasted nothing like the ones *maasi* had made in her little pickling shed. Yes, there were limes and vinegar, sugar and spices, but it tasted flat and unfamiliar. I thought of her then, of her pickling ceremony: laying out limes and chunks of mango to dry on an old *duppata* in the sunniest part of the yard, using a giant pestle and mortar to grind huge quantities of whole spices. I remember her lifting and turning the glass jars, the light from them glinting in those pale, knowing eyes. The joy, satisfaction and magic of whole limes treated with little more than salt and spices, transformed into a mature pickle after a few weeks in the sun. In those jars, she had kept more than just *achaar*, she had preserved the memories of our neighbourhood and a taste of home.

50g butter, melted
60ml hot water
185g plain flour, plus extra
    for dusting
1 heaped tsp ajwain seeds
1 heaped tsp cumin seeds
¼ tsp coarsely crushed
    black pepper
½ tsp sea salt
25g softened butter

2 tbsp cornflour
Rapeseed oil, for deep-frying

For the achaar
2 Bramley cooking apples,
    cut unto 5mm dice
1 tsp sea salt
1 tsp ground turmeric
2 tbsp rapeseed oil

2 tbsp paanch phoran,
    coarsely ground
3 cloves
1 tsp chilli flakes
1 tbsp finely grated ginger
1 tbsp finely chopped garlic
3 tbsp grated jaggery or soft
    brown sugar
3 tbsp white wine vinegar

Ajwain Seed Mathis with Apple Achaar

A 'mathi' is a sort of deep-fried North Indian cracker that is shamefully addictive. Normally eaten in India as a snack at tea time, with a little mango chutney, I find they work just as well as part of a cheeseboard. As they cook, they billow and brown into lots of golden flakes, a bit like puff pastry, but are much sturdier, making them the perfect vehicle for cheese and chutneys.

- For the achaar, put the apples into a muslin-lined sieve set over a bowl. Sprinkle with the salt and turmeric and leave for 2 hours, or overnight.
- Heat the rapeseed oil in a frying pan over medium heat and add the spices. Once they are crackling, add the ginger and garlic and fry until fragrant, then sprinkle in the sugar and vinegar. Bring to the boil, then simmer for 6 minutes, or until the vinegar has reduced to a rich sauce. Throw in the apples and toss well, then take off the heat, spoon into sterilised jars and leave to cool. It will keep in the fridge for up to a week.
- To make the dough for the mathis, mix the melted butter with the hot water. In a large bowl, combine the plain flour, spices and salt, then add the butter-water mix and knead until you have a smooth pliable dough – you could do this in the food processor, if you like. Cover with a clean, damp tea towel and leave to rest for half an hour.
- Divide the dough into 4 equal pieces and, on a lightly floured surface, roll out each one into a round about 2mm thick. Brush generously with the softened butter and sprinkle lightly with cornflour. Roll into a tight sausage, then cut diagonally into 8mm-thick pellets. Roll each one out into an oval cracker about 7cm long and 2mm thick. Repeat with the rest.
- Fill a large, heavy-based saucepan a third full with the deep-frying oil. Heat the oil to 180°C – if you don't have a thermometer, you will know the oil is ready when a cube of bread turns golden brown in 20 seconds. Add the mathis in batches, being careful not to overcrowd the pan, and cook for 3–4 minutes, or until crisp and golden, allowing the oil to return to temperature between batches. Remove with a slotted spoon and leave to drain on kitchen paper.
- Once the mathis are cool, serve with the apple achaar.

200g padron peppers
Rapeseed oil, for frying

For the paneer
2 litres whole milk
4 tbsp lemon juice

For the stuffing
1 small onion, very finely chopped
1 green chilli, very finely chopped
3 tbsp finely crushed cashews
1½ tsp cumin seeds, toasted and
    roughly ground
1½ tsp chaat masala, plus extra
    for sprinkling

1 tsp dried mango powder
    (amchur)
Large handful of finely chopped
    coriander
Juice of 1 lime
Sea salt and black pepper, to taste

Paneer-stuffed Padron Peppers

Blistered padron peppers scattered with sea salt are one of the best Spanish tapas to nibble on with a glass of something cold and bubbly. I ate my first one about a decade ago at the original Brindisa tapas bar in London Bridge, and it was so hot it made me curse! A Spanish diner at a neighbouring table calmly commented: 'Padron peppers – sometimes they are hot, sometimes they are not.' In all the years since, I have eaten plenty of them, and they have been fragrant and mild, never as hot as that first one.

While I love padron peppers simply fried and sprinkled with flaky salt, I also think they lend themselves really well to being stuffed with a cool, creamy cheese and fried. Paneer is an Indian cottage cheese that is ridiculously simple to make at home, but 250g ricotta can be substituted here, if you don't fancy making your own.

· Begin by making the paneer. Pour the milk into a saucepan and bring to the boil, then take off the heat and slowly pour in the lemon juice, stirring all the time. It should begin to curdle immediately. Leave to stand for 20 minutes.
· Pour the curds into a muslin-lined sieve set over a bowl, letting the whey drain through. Discard the whey. Rinse the curds well under cold running water, then gather the muslin in your hands and squeeze out any excess liquid from the paneer.
· For the stuffing, place the paneer in a bowl, crumbling it between your fingers, then add all the other ingredients and mix well.
· Carefully make a vertical slit in each pepper. Stuff gently with the paneer mix and press together the slit to close. Take a large frying pan and pour in enough oil to cover the base. Place over high heat and, when the oil is hot, fry the peppers until they are blistered and wilting. Drain on kitchen paper – sprinkle over a little extra chaat masala and serve while hot.

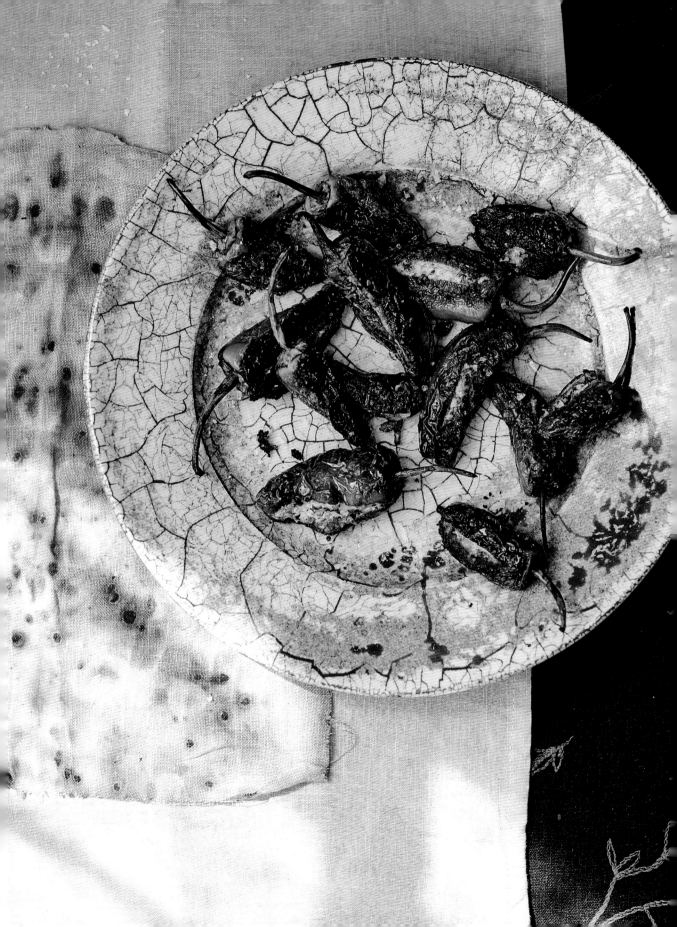

Salt Cod Fofos with Romesco Sauce

Across the Mediterranean, Africa and the Caribbean, planks of salt cod, as stiff as boards, are a kitchen staple. There are a multitude of recipes and ways of preparing it, but I favour those involving garlic and potatoes.

These more-ish little fritters, or 'fofos', have their roots in Portugal, but are also very popular in Goa, where they are mainly made with prawns. I have added ajwain seeds to the batter, which impart a beautiful aniseed flavour that pairs very well with fish. I find a garlicky romesco sauce the ideal accompaniment, along with an ice-cold glass of champagne — because, frankly, there is no bad time to drink champagne.

500g salt cod
1 litre whole milk
6 garlic cloves
2 bay leaves
75ml extra virgin olive oil
200g floury potatoes, peeled
   and diced
Small handful of finely
   chopped coriander
Finely grated zest of 2 lemons
Thumb of ginger, finely grated

1 tsp ajwain seeds
Groundnut oil, for deep-frying
Lemon wedges, to serve

For the sauce
75g blanched almonds
75g stale ciabatta (or any other
   crusty white loaf)
2 medium-ripe tomatoes,
   peeled, deseeded
   and roughly chopped

2–3 garlic cloves, roughly
   chopped
225g roasted peppers in olive oil,
   drained and sliced
½ tsp smoked sweet paprika
1½ tsp sherry vinegar
1 tbsp lemon juice
90ml extra virgin olive oil
Sea salt and black pepper

- Rinse the salt cod, then leave it to soak in cold water for about 12 hours, changing the water 4–6 times – this will reduce the saltiness.
- For the sauce, blitz the almonds and bread in a food processor until you have fine crumbs. Add the tomatoes, garlic, peppers, paprika, vinegar and lemon juice and pulse until smooth and vermillion-coloured. With the machine running, slowly drizzle in the olive oil in a steady stream, just as you would for mayonnaise, to give you a thick sauce. Transfer to a serving bowl and clean out the food processor.
- Drain the cod, rinse it well and pat dry with kitchen paper. Place in a saucepan with the milk, garlic and bay leaves. Bring to a simmer over medium heat, then reduce the heat to low and simmer gently for 5 minutes. Drain, discarding the garlic and bay leaves but reserving 55ml of the milk. When the cod is cool enough to handle, put the flesh into the food processor, discarding any skin and bones. Add the olive oil and pulse until the fish is finely chopped, then drizzle in the reserved milk and pulse to emulsify.
- Boil the potatoes in salted water until soft, then drain and press through a ricer or coarse sieve into a bowl. Stir in the fish mixture from the food processor, together with the coriander, lemon zest, ginger and ajwain seeds. Cover and refrigerate until required.
- Fill a large, heavy-based saucepan a third full with the deep-frying oil. Heat the oil to 180°C – if you don't have a thermometer, you will know the oil is ready when a cube of bread turns golden brown in 20 seconds. Use a tablespoon to drop spoonfuls of the salt cod mixture into the hot oil and deep-fry in batches, turning occasionally, until golden brown and crisp, allowing the oil to return to temperature between batches.
- Drain on kitchen paper, then serve hot with wedges of lemon and the romesco sauce on the side.

M'boga na Saladi

Vegetables and Salads

At mid-morning every other day, there'd be a shrill cry of '*Mboga! Mboga!*'[1] Every Nairobi neighbourhood had their own Mama Mboga – a vegetable seller who harvested fresh produce from the few scraps of cultivated land she owned, to peddle door to door. Our Mama Mboga always came to the wrought-iron gate at the back of our house, where she'd stand patiently – some days ushered in, and other days shooed away or ignored.

Her hair was intricately braided, close to her scalp, in neat rows. She carried with her the cow-heavy smell of the village from which she travelled on a stifling *matatu*[2] to our suburb in Nairobi. Her flat, wide feet were swollen in her crude leather *chappals*,[3] her heels cracked like dry earth. She never stopped beaming –

her magnificent, high-wattage smile unleashed several perfect teeth.

The challenges of her life had not marked her face. Sometimes, as well as the basket of vegetables balanced on her head, there'd be a tiny sleeping infant swaddled in a batik *kanga*[4] on her back.

She'd walk, with her knees pointing outwards and her broad hips splayed, to the faucet for a thirsty gulp of water drunk from a cup she made from her hands. Then she'd unfurl a gaudy straw *mkeka*[5] and begin to lay out her wares: delicate *sukuma wiki*[6] wilting in the heat, like the *mzungus*[7] who loitered in air-conditioned hotel lobbies; sharp green *mchungwas*,[8] their thick skin marmalade-bitter; fat, imperfect tomatoes; a few measly okra; and

lush mangoes, which she would cut open to persuade and tempt.

Mama Mboga has remained an inspiration to me – she was the first female entrepreneur I ever really met.

Resilient and full of hope,

she harnessed opportunity and turned it into a business that not only supported her family, but provided our neighbourhood with the freshest fruit and vegetables, which tasted nothing like their over-processed supermarket counterparts. '*Safi,*[9] mama,' she'd say, holding up

a weighty aubergine, its purple skin polished and gleaming.

She may not have made millions, but by peddling vegetables, she created her own prosperity.

She'd chitter-chatter merrily – enquiring after my grandmother's health and checking to see if my baby brother was walking yet – but my mother afforded her no intimacies. She was keen and poised for elaborate bartering. After an unnecessary tussle, she'd always accept that my mother was a sharper, tougher opponent who she could not be bothered to battle. With her shoulders hanging low in defeat, she'd weigh the produce on a rusty-hooked scale and a few shillings would be exchanged. While she packed up her basket, I'd wickedly pilfer a plum the size of a marble or a wrinkled passion fruit. My mother would shout after her to remember to bring bitter gourds and spikier chillies next time, and with that she'd be off to the next house, the load of her basket gradually lightening, and her coin purse filling a little more at each stop.

1 vegetables
2 minibus   6 collard greens
3 sandals   7 foreigners
4 wrap or shawl   8 oranges
5 mat   9 fresh

SERVES 4

500g asparagus, trimmed
70g butter
50g flaked almonds
Juice of ½ lemon

2 preserved lemons, rind only,
   finely chopped
Rapeseed oil
Sea salt and black pepper

For the paneer
1 litre whole milk
Juice of ½ lemon

Asparagus with Smoked Paneer, Brown Butter, Almonds and Preserved Lemon

The smoky paneer in this recipe really accentuates the fresh greeny goodness of the first pencil-thin stalks of spring asparagus. Serve as an appetiser or as part of a dinner-party mezze.

- Begin by making the paneer. Pour the milk into a saucepan and bring to the boil, then take off the heat and slowly pour in the lemon juice, stirring all the time. It should begin to curdle immediately. Leave to stand for 20 minutes.
- Pour the curds into a muslin-lined sieve set over a bowl, letting the whey drain through. Discard the whey. Rinse the curds well under cold running water, then gather the muslin in your hands and squeeze out any excess liquid from the paneer. Turn out the paneer into a large heatproof bowl.
- If you have a gas stove, line the area around one of the burners with foil. Turn the burner on full, place a single piece of lump charcoal directly on it and leave to burn. Alternatively, if you do not have a gas burner, place a sturdy roasting tin on a heatproof surface. Line the tin with foil, followed by some crumpled newspaper. Light the newspaper with a match, then sit a single piece of lump charcoal on top of it and let it burn.
- Once the charcoal is smouldering, pick it up with some tongs and put it in a small heatproof bowl. Sit the bowl of charcoal inside the bowl of paneer, placing it on top of the cheese. Drizzle a little oil over the charcoal – it will begin to smoke immediately. Cover the large bowl tightly with foil or a lid and leave the paneer to smoke for 5 minutes. Discard the charcoal and set the paneer aside.
- Bring a large saucepan of well-salted water to the boil. Add the asparagus and simmer until tender – this should take no more than 2 minutes. Refresh in ice-cold water, then drain thoroughly.
- Meanwhile, heat the butter in a frying pan over medium heat until it begins to turn nut-brown. Add the asparagus and almonds and toss until they begin to colour slightly. Squeeze over the lemon juice and season with salt and pepper.
- Place the asparagus on a plate and crumble over the smoked paneer. Spoon over the brown butter and almonds, then finally sprinkle over the preserved lemon. Serve immediately.

1 × 280g block of firm tofu
1 tbsp rapeseed oil
1 tsp sesame oil
250g asparagus, trimmed
50g cashews, toasted
1 tbsp sesame seeds, toasted
3 spring onions, thinly sliced
1 tbsp coriander leaves

For the chilli oil
350ml groundnut or rapeseed oil
1½ tbsp Sichuan peppercorns
1 cinnamon stick or piece
  of cassia bark
2 bay leaves
3 star anise
2 dried red chillies
2 tbsp coriander seeds
Thumb of ginger, thinly sliced
3 garlic cloves, smashed
6 tsp chilli flakes
2 tsp chilli powder
1¼ tsp sea salt

For the dressing
125ml light soy sauce
60ml mirin
60ml Chinkiang black vinegar
1 tbsp caster sugar
1 tsp sesame oil
Thumb of ginger, finely grated
1 fat garlic clove, very finely
  chopped

Charred Asparagus with Tofu, Cashews, Chilli Oil and Soy Dressing

This block of tofu, custard-soft and served with asparagus drizzled in an umami soy dressing, is a persuasive argument for eating asparagus with a little more than just salt and pepper (although it is wonderful like that too). The chilli oil is positively addictive, and you will soon find yourself using it to perk up everything from rice and noodles to scrambled eggs.

- For the chilli oil, pour the oil into a heavy-based saucepan and add the Sichuan peppercorns, then cover and leave at room temperature for 8 hours, or overnight. Add the cinnamon or cassia, bay leaves, star anise, red chillies, coriander seeds, ginger and garlic and place over very low heat to infuse for 1 hour. Set aside to cool. Put the chilli flakes and chilli powder into a 400ml screwtop jar, then carefully strain over the oil. Add the salt, screw on the lid and leave to stand for at least 6 hours. The chilli oil will keep for at least 3 months at room temperature.
- Place the tofu on a tray or plate lined with kitchen paper or a clean tea towel. Place more kitchen paper or another clean tea towel over the tofu, then put an even weight directly on top of it. I tend to use a cast-iron frying pan, but you could use a stack of plates. Leave to drain in the fridge for at least an hour, or overnight – the tofu will become firmer and more chewy.
- Get a griddle pan good and hot. Mix together the rapeseed and sesame oils. Rub the tofu and asparagus with the oil, then cook on all sides until the tofu is crisp and golden brown and the asparagus is nice and charred.
- For the dressing, simply whisk together all the ingredients.
- To serve, arrange the tofu and asparagus on a platter, pour over the soy dressing and drizzle over chilli oil to taste. Garnish with the cashews, sesame seeds, spring onions and coriander leaves.

150g spelt, rinsed and drained
50g cashews, toasted
3 spring onions, thinly sliced
300g purple sprouting broccoli
1 tbsp rapeseed oil
1 tsp sesame oil
Toasted sesame seeds and
  crisp-fried shallots, to serve

For the dressing
2 tbsp white miso
1 tbsp light soy sauce
2 tbsp rice vinegar
1 tsp mirin
Thumb of ginger, finely grated
1 tsp sesame oil
60ml rapeseed oil

Charred Sprouting Broccoli with Spelt, Cashews and Miso Dressing

Sprouting broccoli can stand up to almost anything you throw at it – its earthy, slightly bitter flavour still shines through. The strong Asian flavours in this salad work particularly well with it, and what's more the whole dish takes no more than 20 minutes to make. Expect rave reviews.

- For the dressing, simply whisk all the ingredients together until they are emulsified.
- Preheat the oven to 180°C/Fan 160°C/Gas Mark 4. Spread out the spelt on a baking sheet and bake for 10–12 minutes. (You can skip this step if you are in a hurry, but I find toasting the spelt before you boil it brings out a rich nuttiness.) Cook the spelt in a saucepan of boiling salted water until tender, but still with a little bite – depending on the variety of spelt you have, this could take anywhere between 10 and 20 minutes. Drain and cool slightly, then stir through the cashews, spring onions and half of the dressing. Transfer to a serving dish.
- Heat a griddle pan over medium–high heat until it is very hot. In a bowl, toss the broccoli in the rapeseed and sesame oils, then cook on the griddle pan for around 8 minutes, until tender and slightly charred. Lay on top of the spelt and drizzle with the remaining dressing. Scatter over the sesame seeds and crispy shallots and serve.

2 heads of broccoli, cut in half
  lengthways
50ml rapeseed oil
Sea salt
Toasted sesame seeds,
  for scattering
1–2 tsp tobiko, to serve –
  optional

For the dashi
75g dried shiitake mushrooms
15g kombu seaweed

For the sauce
75g sesame seeds, toasted
1 tsp caster sugar
2 tbsp light soy sauce
5 tsp mirin
2½ tsp sesame oil
2 tbsp rice vinegar

Dashi Broccoli with Sesame Sauce and Tobiko

Broccoli doesn't always get the love it deserves, but more often than not, that's because of the shoddy way it has been treated. Limp, overcooked florets aren't ever going to convert the broccoli-haters! In this recipe, I first braise the broccoli in Japanese dashi stock for a boost of umami flavour – although you could just use your favourite chicken or vegetable stock if you don't have time to make the dashi (it needs to infuse overnight). Once the broccoli is braised, I roast it with a glaze of nutty sesame sauce, and finally I top it with a mound of glittering tobiko, or Japanese flying fish roe. If you can't find this, feel free to leave it out – but if you're making a trip to the Japanese supermarket for the dashi ingredients, it's worth seeking out for its wonderful pop of texture and delicate citrus flavour.

- To make the dashi, combine the mushrooms and kombu with 2 litres of cold water in a saucepan and leave to infuse overnight. Next day, bring it just to simmering point, being careful not to let it boil or the kombu will give the stock a bitter flavour. Take off the heat and leave to infuse for 30 minutes, then strain, squeezing out any liquid from the mushrooms with the back of a spoon. Discard the solids and set the dashi to one side.
- For the sauce, put the sesame seeds and sugar into a blender and grind to a paste. Add the remaining ingredients and blend again.
- Preheat the oven to 200°C/Fan 180°C/Gas Mark 6. Place the broccoli in a saucepan and pour in the dashi. Set it over low heat and braise gently until the broccoli is tender. Drain the broccoli, reserving the dashi for soup or another recipe, and pat dry with kitchen paper. Transfer the broccoli to a roasting tin, toss in the oil to lightly coat and season with salt. Roast for about 25 minutes, or until it starts to caramelise, then glaze generously with some of the sesame sauce and return to the oven until bubbling.
- Spoon the rest of the sesame sauce onto plates and top with the broccoli. Scatter with sesame seeds and serve at once, with the tobiko, if using.

250g sugarsnap peas
4 baby gem lettuces, cut in half
  lengthways
8 spring onions, thinly sliced
  on the diagonal
1 tbsp rapeseed oil
500g raw prawns, peeled and
  deveined
1 baby cucumber, shaved into
  ribbons with a peeler
1 tbsp black sesame seeds

For the dressing
60ml rapeseed oil
2 tbsp Chinkiang black vinegar
1 tbsp light soy sauce
A few drops of sesame oil
1 small garlic clove, finely grated
Thumb of ginger, finely grated
2 tsp chilli paste
Juice of 1 lime

Charred Gem Lettuce Salad with Prawns and Chilli-ginger Dressing

Gem lettuce tastes wonderful when it is griddled until it softens ever so slightly and begins to char at the tips. The bitterness this creates makes a fine counterpart to the sweetness of grilled prawns and sugarsnap peas.

- For the dressing, simply put everything into a screwtop jar and shake enthusiastically to combine.
- Blanch the sugarsnap peas in a saucepan of boiling water for 45 seconds, then tip into a colander and refresh in ice-cold water. Drain well, then transfer to a bowl and add the lettuce and spring onions.
- Heat a griddle pan until it is very hot. Drizzle a little oil over the lettuce, sugarsnaps and spring onions and toss to coat, then griddle until tiger-striped and charred. Set aside, then drizzle the prawns with a little oil and cook on the griddle until pink and opaque.
- Coarsely chop the lettuce and put into a bowl, along with the sugarsnaps, spring onions, prawns and cucumber. Pour over the dressing and gently toss everything together. Scatter over the sesame seeds to serve.

1 tbsp rapeseed or groundnut oil
500g firm silken tofu
2 garlic cloves, thinly sliced
1 green chilli, thinly sliced
1 red chilli, thinly sliced
4 spring onions, thickly sliced
on the diagonal, including
green parts
100g green beans, cut into
2cm lengths

2 baby cucumbers, cut in
half lengthways and seeds
removed, sliced
Large handful of beansprouts
Large handful of mint leaves
Large handful of coriander leaves
Small handful of Thai basil leaves
Handful of salted roast peanuts,
roughly crushed
1 iceberg lettuce, leaves
separated
Steamed sticky rice, to serve

For the dressing
1 tbsp uncooked jasmine rice
2 tsp fennel seeds
100ml lime juice
4 kaffir lime leaves, shredded
2 lemongrass stalks, white parts
only, roughly chopped
2 tbsp fish sauce
1½ tbsp tamarind concentrate
1 tbsp soft brown sugar
1 tsp Thai roasted chilli powder

Tofu and Green Bean Larb in Lettuce Cups

Larb is a fiery salad, usually made with minced meat, from Thailand's Isan region, in the north east of the country although calling this tongue-tingler a salad doesn't really do it justice. The recipe here uses crumbled tofu instead of meat, fried until crisp and caramelised, then doused in a zingy dressing with an abundance of good stuff: chilli, garlic, spring onions, fragrant herbs and peanuts. I like to serve this with steamed sticky rice to quell the heat.

· To make the dressing, toast the rice in a hot dry frying pan for a minute, until golden, watching it closely and keeping it moving so it doesn't burn. Add the fennel seeds and toast with the rice for a further minute. Using a pestle and mortar, crush the rice and fennel to a fine powder. Transfer to a blender or food processor, add the remaining ingredients and whizz until smooth, then set aside.

· Heat the oil in a frying pan. Pat the tofu dry with kitchen paper, then crumble into the pan and fry until it starts to crisp up and go golden brown. Add the garlic, both chillies and the spring onions and cook until fragrant. Take off the heat, transfer to a large bowl and leave to cool slightly.

· Meanwhile, blanch the green beans in a saucepan of boiling water for 1 minute, until crisp-tender, then tip into a colander and refresh in ice-cold water. Drain well.

· Pour the dressing over the tofu mixture and toss well, then stir through the green beans, cucumber, beansprouts, herbs and peanuts. Serve the larb in lettuce leaves, with sticky rice on the side.

1 Chinese cabbage, roughly
    sliced
1 savoy cabbage, roughly sliced
30g sea salt
180g caster sugar
50g ginger, sliced
15 garlic cloves, roughly
    chopped
75ml tamari sauce

70ml fish sauce
50g Korean chilli powder
75g carrots, peeled and julienned
15 radishes, thickly sliced
5 spring onions, thickly sliced
1 Asian pear, peeled, cored and
    cut into 1cm dice
1 Bramley apple, peeled, cored
    and cut into 1cm dice

Kimchi

*This spicy, funky ferment is the backbone of Korean cookery. It's a versatile
ingredient, and while it is normally served as a condiment, it also gives depth
to everything from stir-fries and soups to noodles and curries. Enjoy it in
a grilled cheese sandwich, stir-fried with rice, shrouded in a fluffy omelette,
in a hot dog, burger or burrito, or with a pork chop to cut through the fat.
The flavour it imparts is magnificent. What's more, kimchi is really good
for you – its probiotic properties help to build immunity and aid digestion.
It is, quite simply, a pickle worth preserving.*

*While you can buy ready-made kimchi, making your own is extremely
rewarding and doesn't have to be too taxing either. This kimchi is good to
eat in just 48 hours, and it only gets better with time.*

- Mix the two kinds of cabbage in a large bowl. Add the salt and 30g of the
  sugar, massaging it into the cabbage, then leave in the fridge overnight.
- Next day, sterilise a 2-litre glass jar by first washing it thoroughly in hot
  soapy water. Rinse well and let it drain on a clean tea towel. Preheat the
  oven to 180°C/Fan 160°C/Gas Mark 4. Place the jar and its lid on a clean
  baking sheet and put in the oven for 10 minutes, then remove and set
  aside until you are ready to use.
- Squeeze out any excess liquid from the cabbage and put it in a large bowl.
  Whizz together the ginger, garlic, tamari, fish sauce, chilli powder and
  the remaining sugar in a food processor. Slowly add 200ml of water –
  you're aiming for a salad-dressing consistency. Pour over the cabbage,
  then mix in the carrots, radishes, spring onions, pear and apple.
- Pack the kimchi into the sterilised jar, ensuring that everything is
  completely submerged. Cover with cling film, piercing it a couple of
  times to allow the air to escape, then leave in a cool, dark place for
  48 hours before using. The kimchi will last for a month in the fridge.

500g Jersey Royals, halved
   lengthways
30g butter
A few drops of sesame oil
300g kimchi (see page 114),
   shredded
30ml tamarind concentrate
1 tbsp light soy sauce
1 tbsp fish sauce

8 tbsp Kewpie mayonnaise
   (or regular mayonnaise
   doctored with a pinch of sugar
   and a squeeze of lime juice)
Large handful of salted roast
   peanuts, roughly crushed
Small handful of sesame seeds,
   toasted

8 spring onions, sliced
Handful of coriander leaves
Handful of broken-up spicy
   prawn crackers

Kimchi Royals

These appear on the menu at Jikoni as soon as the Jersey Royal season kicks in. They are our version of patatas bravas, via Korea. Instead of salsa you have kimchi, there's Japanese mayonnaise rather than allioli – and it's finished off with crunchy peanuts, spring onions, sesame seeds and shards of prawn cracker. It all adds up to a lively little dish that's feistier than the standard patatas bravas.

- Boil the potatoes in salted water until tender. Drain well. In a frying pan melt the butter with the sesame oil over medium heat. Place the potatoes, cut side down, in the hot fat and cook on this side only until crisp and brown. Drain on kitchen paper and keep warm.
- In a small bowl, stir together the kimchi, tamarind concentrate, soy sauce and fish sauce.
- Arrange the potatoes on a platter, cut side up. Top with the kimchi mixture, then drizzle over the mayonnaise. Scatter over the peanuts, sesame seeds, spring onions, coriander leaves and shards of prawn cracker.

Bhel Puri

Here's what I didn't do when I was in Mumbai: I didn't seek spiritual solace at the Haji Ali Dargah, or bow my head in the cool, quiet, sanctuary of Mount Mary Church. Nor did I let love blossom with a sea view at Nariman Point. The sunset came and went at Hanging Gardens without my approving gasps, and the jewelled *Kolhapuri chappals*[1] at Colaba Causeway Market remained unbartered for. My footprints did not even find time to caress the gritty sands of Chowpatty Beach. Because Mumbai is not about the sights, it is about experiences, and you haven't truly experienced the city until you have eaten everything it has to offer, like a mouth on legs. So this is what I did.

[1] Indian handcrafted leather T-bar sandals

> *Armed with the advice that the best mouthfuls are to be found outside colleges and railway stations, I went in search of unpretentious street food.*

[2] a sort of potato fritter served in bread – a typical street food in Maharashtra

It takes someone with a cast-iron constitution and a blind eye to be able to forgive the grubby hands making *vada pav*[2] at lightning speed, or the buzzing flies, happily drunk on tamarind chutney. Service can be surly and you play Russian roulette with E. coli – but who cares when you can fill your belly with the most tantalising food for the equivalent of less than a few pounds?

Sure, there are a clutch of excellent restaurants serving tasty sanitised street food in pristine surroundings, with crockery and cutlery, but you can't beat the appeal of bhel puri, prepared right in front of you with awe-inspiring speed and agility. This street-food snack is best eaten immediately, clumsily and greedily – straight out of the newspaper cone it comes in. Warning: it's addictive! I soon found myself emptying its tangle of puffed rice, tamarind, peanuts, chutney and green mango down my gullet almost every day. I didn't even buy a souvenir. All I brought back was a bhel puri paunch.

2 white-fleshed sweet potatoes
Freshly ground black pepper
1 tsp chaat masala
Drizzle of olive oil
1 × 400g tin of chickpeas,
    drained and rinsed
200g cherry tomatoes, halved
1 Lebanese cucumber, diced
1 green mango, peeled and
    finely diced
1 medium beetroot, peeled
    and grated
200g yoghurt
1 red onion, very finely chopped
250g sev mamra (puffed rice and
    crisp noodles)
Seeds from 1 small pomegranate
50g moong sprouts
Handful of chopped coriander

For the puris
70g plain flour, plus extra
    for dusting
35g fine semolina
Groundnut oil, for deep-frying

For the tamarind chutney
8 pitted dates
1 tbsp grated jaggery or soft
    brown sugar
5 tbsp tamarind concentrate
Chilli powder, to taste
1 tsp toasted cumin seeds,
    lightly crushed
½ tsp ground cinnamon
1 tsp chaat masala
1 tsp black salt (kala namak) –
    optional

For the green chutney
Large handful of mint leaves
Large handful of coriander leaves
1 green chilli, deseeded if you
    don't like too much heat
Juice of 1 lime
½ small red onion
1 tsp cumin seeds, toasted
    and ground
1 tsp chaat masala
1 tsp grated jaggery or soft
    brown sugar

Jikoni Bhel Puri

Bhel puri falls into a category of Indian snacks known as chaat – literally, 'lick'. When you have a good one, and are left with the strong urge to sweep up the remnants with your tongue, the name makes complete sense. A bhel puri is a wildly eventful little snack that people tend to eat on the go. Sold on roadside stands all over India, it is a tantalising riot of flavours and textures: yielding potatoes, crunchy puri (a little like poppadums), crisp puffed rice and savoury noodles known as sev mamra, thrillingly hot sweet-and-sour chutneys and cooling yoghurt.

My version (photographed on the previous page) uses white sweet potatoes for a more East African slant – I find them waxier and less sweet than the orange sort, and more interesting here than ordinary potatoes. Also, rather than mixing everything together as you would for a regular bhel puri, this one is built up in tiers to form a wonderful layered salad.

- Begin by making the puris. Mix together the flour and semolina, then start adding water a little at a time, kneading as you go, until you have a springy and pliable dough. Divide into 6 balls and, on a lightly floured surface, use a rolling pin to roll out to a 2mm thickness. Use a 5cm round pastry cutter to cut out circles, then prick all over with a fork – this will prevent them from puffing up too much as they cook.
- Fill a large, heavy-based saucepan a third full with the deep-frying oil. Heat the oil to 180°C – if you don't have a thermometer, you will know the oil is ready when a cube of bread turns golden brown in 20 seconds. Fry the puris in batches for about 2 minutes, or until golden and crisp, allowing the oil to return to temperature between batches. Drain on kitchen paper and leave to cool. The puris can be made in advance and stored in an airtight container for up to a week.
- Preheat the oven to 200°C/Fan 180°C/Gas Mark 6. Peel the sweet potatoes and cut into bite-sized chunks. Season with black pepper and the chaat masala. Spread out on a baking sheet, drizzle with a little olive oil and roast for 40 minutes or until tender.
- In the meantime, make your chutneys.
- For the tamarind chutney, put the dates and sugar in a saucepan, cover with 250ml of water and bring to the boil, then turn down the heat and simmer for 10 minutes. Stir in the tamarind concentrate, then tip into a blender and whizz until smooth. Strain through a sieve into a bowl (to remove any scraps of date skin), then stir in the remaining ingredients, along with a little water if it seems too thick – it should have the consistency of ketchup. Cool and refrigerate until needed.
- For the green chutney, whizz together all the ingredients in a food processor – it really is as simple as that.
- Now for the fun part: the layering! Crush the puris, then line a serving dish with a layer of them. Next come layers of sweet potato, chickpeas, tomatoes, cucumber, mango and beetroot, followed by dollops of the tamarind and green chutneys and yoghurt, onion, sev mamra, pomegranate seeds, moong sprouts and a sprinkling of coriander, in that order.
- Serve immediately – before it turns into a soggy mush.

9 sheets of filo pastry
150g unsalted butter, melted
40g za'atar
Icing sugar and a pinch of ground
  cinnamon, for dusting

For the filling
670g butternut squash, peeled
  and cut into 2cm chunks
1 tbsp olive oil
100g shankleesh (or feta) cheese
1 tbsp ground cinnamon
Good grating of nutmeg
Sea salt and black pepper

Butternut Squash and Shankleesh M'hencha

M'hencha is a Moroccan pastry that is meant to resemble a coiled snake. It is typically filled with sweet dates and nuts, but my savoury version is stuffed with roasted pumpkin and aged Lebanese cheese. Inspired by another great Moroccan dish, pastilla, it is finished with a snowstorm of icing sugar.

- Preheat the oven to 200°C/Fan 180°C/Gas Mark 6. Line a large baking sheet (ideally a square one) with baking parchment.
- For the filling, put the squash into a roasting tin and drizzle with the olive oil. Roast for about 30 minutes until very tender, then transfer to a bowl and mash coarsely. Add the shankleesh, cinnamon and nutmeg, season to taste with salt and pepper and set aside to cool. Put the cooled filling into a piping bag fitted with a 2cm plain nozzle.
- Lay out 8 of the filo sheets in a single row, overlapping each sheet by 6cm and with one of the short edges facing you. Reserve the final sheet to patch up any tears later. Leaving a 6cm gap at each end, pipe the filling along the length of the pastry sheets, positioning it 3cm in from the edge nearest to you. Gently brush the melted butter over the exposed pastry all around the filling. Fold both ends of the pastry over the filling and tuck them in, then fold over the 3cm border to cover the filling and gently roll the pastry over and over to encase the filling in the filo.
- Gently brush the whole log with melted butter and then, starting from one end, roll it into a snug coil, trying as best you can not to split the pastry – patch any tears or splits with the reserved filo sheet. Brush with melted butter again and sprinkle with the za'atar. Carefully lift the m'hencha onto the baking tray and bake in the oven for 30 minutes or until golden.
- Serve immediately, dusted with a little icing sugar and a pinch of cinnamon. Eat hot or at room temperature.

1kg sweet potatoes
4 tbsp rapeseed oil
Sea salt and black pepper
Nigella seeds and coriander
  leaves, to serve

For the lime pickle and coriander yoghurt
1 heaped tsp hot lime pickle
4 tbsp finely chopped coriander
250g yoghurt

Roast Sweet Potato with Lime Pickle and Coriander Yoghurt

In this recipe, sweet potato gets all dressed up with a spicy, zingy jolt of yoghurt spiked with lime pickle and coriander. The same creamy dressing also makes a wonderful marinade for fish — prawns, in particular — which can then be skewered and barbecued. These sweet potatoes are wonderful served as a side with roast chicken or eaten as part of a mezze.

- Preheat the oven to 200°C/Fan 180°C/Gas Mark 6.
- Peel the sweet potatoes. Cut in half lengthways, then cut each half lengthways again into three. Lay in a roasting tin or baking tray, drizzle over the oil and season well with salt and pepper. Roast for 30–45 minutes until tender and caramelised at the edges.
- In the meantime, whizz together the lime pickle, coriander and yoghurt in a blender until smooth.
- Lay the sweet potatoes on a serving dish and drizzle over the yoghurt. Scatter with nigella seeds and coriander leaves, then serve.

Asian Mushroom Ragout with Sweet Potato Gnocchi

This vegan-friendly mushroom dish takes inspiration from Italian gnocchi with mushroom ragu, but puts an Asian slant on it — no parmesan required. Mushrooms are already deeply umami and make great sponges for the soy-laced broth. Aside from its excellent flavour, this dish is a textural delight, with its fleshy mushrooms, soft pillows of gnocchi, crisp kale and sweet potato crisps. If you want to forego making the gnocchi, simply serve the mushrooms with some springy egg noodles instead.

1kg sweet potatoes (I prefer
    the white variety for gnocchi)
1 tsp chilli flakes
½ tsp ground cinnamon
150g plain flour, plus extra
    for dusting
Rapeseed oil
Sea salt and white pepper

For the ragout
½ onion, thinly sliced
2 spring onions, green parts only,
    sliced
1 tbsp thinly sliced ginger
2 coriander stems, sliced
1 large garlic clove, sliced
2 tbsp dried porcini mushrooms
1½ tbsp light soy sauce
1 tsp caster sugar
350g mixed mushrooms, such
    as shimeji, oyster, shiitake
    and enoki
2½ tsp cornflour, mixed with
    a little water to make a paste

**For the crispy 'seaweed'
and sweet potato crisps**
500g kale
Groundnut oil, for deep-frying
2 orange-fleshed sweet potatoes,
    thinly sliced on a mandoline
1 tsp sugar
1 tsp porcini powder – optional

- Preheat the oven to 200°C/Fan 180°C/Gas Mark 6. Peel the sweet potatoes and cut into wedges. Drizzle with a little rapeseed oil, sprinkle over the chilli and cinnamon, and season with salt and pepper. Roast for about 45 minutes or until very tender, then set aside to cool.
- Once the sweet potatoes are cool enough to handle, press them through a ricer onto a work surface lightly dusted with flour. Add about three-quarters of the flour and knead lightly to make a smooth dough, being careful not to overwork it. Form a 3cm piece of dough into a test gnocchi and cook it in a pan of simmering salted water until it floats – this should take about 2 minutes. Taste to check it doesn't taste too floury – if it does, cook it for a further 30 seconds, then check again. If the gnocchi crumbles apart, add more flour to the remaining mixture, but do not overwork.
- On a lightly floured surface, divide the gnocchi dough into 4 equal pieces. Taking one at a time, shape into a cylinder 1.5cm in diameter, then cut into 2cm lengths, cover with a clean tea towel and set aside. Repeat with the remaining dough.
- For the crispy 'seaweed', wash the kale and remove any tough stems. Dry thoroughly, ideally in a salad spinner, then roll up and shred very finely.
- Fill a large, heavy-based saucepan a third full with the deep-frying oil. Heat the oil to 180°C – if you don't have a thermometer, you will know the oil is ready when a cube of bread turns golden brown in 20 seconds.

M'BOGA NA SALADI

- Deep-fry the sweet potato slices in batches, stirring constantly, until crisp and golden brown, allowing the oil to return to temperature between batches. Drain on kitchen paper.
- Now deep-fry the shredded kale in the same way until it is very crisp. Drain very well on kitchen paper, blotting away any excess oil. Sprinkle with the sugar and porcini powder, if using, then season with salt to taste.
- For the ragout, heat 1 teaspoon of rapeseed oil in a large frying pan over medium–high heat. Add the onion, spring onions, ginger, coriander stems and garlic and fry until golden. Place the dried porcini in a saucepan with 800ml of water and bring to the boil. Add the contents of the frying pan, bring back to the boil and simmer over low heat for half an hour to infuse the flavours. Strain the broth into a bowl, discarding the solids, then stir in the soy sauce, sugar and ½ teaspoon of salt.
- Wipe out the frying pan, then use it to fry the mushrooms in 1 teaspoon of rapeseed oil until they are nutty and caramelised. Drain on kitchen paper. Pour the mushroom broth into the pan and bring to the boil, then return the fried mushrooms to the pan and simmer for 2 minutes, until they have absorbed the liquor. Now slowly add the cornflour mix, stirring gently, until you have a thick glossy sauce. Season with a good pinch of white pepper and keep warm.
- Cook the gnocchi in batches in a large saucepan of simmering salted water for 2–3 minutes, until they float to the surface. Drain and transfer to a plate.
- Heat a little rapeseed oil in a small frying pan and fry the gnocchi until golden brown on all sides, then transfer to a warm serving dish. Serve with the mushroom ragout, sprinkling over the crispy 'seaweed' and sweet potato crisps.

500g parsnips, peeled and
  cut into long quarters
Drizzle of rapeseed oil
½ tsp chilli flakes
1 tsp chaat masala, or to taste
100g yoghurt
50g dates, thinly sliced
  lengthways
1–2 red chillies, thinly sliced
  into rounds and deseeded
  if you like
Handful of coriander sprigs

For the chutney
8 pitted dates
1 tbsp grated jaggery or soft
  brown sugar
5 tbsp tamarind concentrate
Chilli powder, to taste
1 tsp cumin seeds, toasted
  and lightly crushed
½ tsp ground cinnamon
1 tsp chaat masala
1 tsp black salt (kala namak) –
  optional

Roast Parsnips with Dates, Tamarind Chutney and Yoghurt

I love the sweet nutty taste of parsnips, and it intensifies when they are roasted. The addition of dates underlines their sticky sweetness, while the acidity of yoghurt and tamarind chutney brings a balancing fresh sourness. Feel free to invite other roasted roots such as beetroot, salsify, swede and sweet potato to the party.

- Preheat the oven to 200°C/Fan 180°C/Gas Mark 6.
- Put the parsnips in a roasting tin, drizzle over the oil and massage to coat. Sprinkle over the chilli flakes and chaat masala, then roast for 45 minutes or until tender and caramelised.
- Meanwhile, make the chutney. Put the dates and sugar in a saucepan, cover with 250ml of water and bring to the boil, then turn down the heat and simmer for 10 minutes. Stir in the tamarind concentrate, then tip into a blender and whizz until smooth. Strain through a sieve into a bowl (to remove any scraps of date skin), then stir in the remaining ingredients, along with a little water if it seems too thick – it should have the consistency of ketchup. Cool and refrigerate until needed.
- Arrange the parsnips on a serving platter. Beat the yoghurt and, if necessary, add a little milk so it has a pouring consistency. Drizzle over the parsnips, followed by a drizzle of the tamarind chutney. Scatter with sliced dates, chillies and coriander before serving.

Channa Dhal with Wild Garlic Puree

Dhal is as common in India as mashed potatoes are in Britain. The word 'dhal' translates as dried legumes, as in lentils or peas; the stew, soup or porridge cooked from them is also known as dhal – 'LSD' (Life Saving Dhal), as legendary food writer Madhur Jaffrey called it. After all, this is the life-enhancing elixir of the poor in India, who can afford little else. But whether you are a prince or a pauper, dhal is the staple of every meal and it comes in many manifestations.

My earliest memories of food are of dhal – of air damp from the steamy little exhalations of a puffed-out pressure cooker precariously balanced on the stove. To this day, no dhal ever tastes as good as my mother's. Over the years, I have discovered that her secret lies in the unconscionable amount of butter she whips into it. And she always goes in at the end with a 'madhani', a wooden stick that she stands vertically in the pot and rolls between her hands, pureeing some of the lentils to render the dhal velvety and creamy. A masher won't give you exactly the same effect, but it's a pretty good substitute.

Traditionally, the 'tadka' or tempering of spices (which might include cumin or mustard seeds and curry leaves, along with onions, chilli, ginger and garlic) is added at the end, once the pulses have cooked, and it is this that makes the dish explode with fragrance and flavour. In this recipe, mainly to save on the washing up, the tadka is the first step and the dhal is then cooked in the same pot. Once the dhal is done, the texture can be adjusted to your preference: leave it robust and thick, or add water to make it thin and soupy.

1 heaped tbsp ghee
1 onion, finely chopped
2 heaped tsp cumin seeds
Thumb of ginger, finely grated
3 garlic cloves, finely chopped
2 green bird's eye chillies,
    finely chopped
3 ripe tomatoes, peeled and
    blitzed in a blender
1 tsp ground turmeric
250g channa dhal or yellow
    split peas, well rinsed

Juice of 1 lime
Sea salt and black pepper
Steamed rice or chapattis and
    lime pickle, to serve, if you like

For the wild garlic puree
100g wild garlic, roughly
    chopped
6 tbsp rapeseed oil
Juice of ½ lemon

- Heat the ghee in a saucepan over low heat and fry the onion with the cumin seeds for about 10 minutes, until the onion is jammy and caramelised. Add the ginger, garlic and chillies and fry until your nose is full of their scent.
- Add the tomatoes, turmeric and 1.2 litres of water, along with the channa dhal, then bring to the boil. Turn the heat to low and simmer for around 45 minutes until the split peas are soft and tender. (For speedier cooking, invest in a pressure cooker – I don't know an Indian housewife who doesn't own one.)
- While the dhal is cooking, make the wild garlic puree. Put the wild garlic and oil into a blender and blitz until you have a smooth puree. Stir in the lemon juice and season to taste with salt and pepper, then empty into a bowl and set aside.
- When the dhal is cooked, squeeze in the lime juice and season with salt and pepper to taste. Dish out into bowls and top with a dollop of the wild garlic puree. Eat on its own like a soup, or serve with rice or warm chapattis, liberally buttered with ghee. I never turn my nose up at a side of lime pickle either.

The Glee in Ghee

It was my grandmother who bought most of the household groceries when I was growing up in Kenya, partly because she held the family purse strings, but mainly because she could stretch a shilling like nobody else. She would waddle between shops in the heat, huffing and puffing, her body heavy from excessive lunches and long naps in the hot afternoons. She'd compare prices and strategise, before undercutting feeble shopkeepers to purchase burlap sacks of rice and lentils, fat rolls of spinach and fenugreek, foot-long bars of Sunlight soap and primrose-coloured pats of butter to make the most valued commodity: ghee.

According to my grandmother, ghee was more than just clarified butter. It was a precious elixir, the food of the gods.

Food cooked in ghee was far superior to food cooked in oil, and beyond the kitchen it also served as a miracle worker — improving the intellect and aiding digestion, healing cuts and burns and soothing inflammations. She was convinced that her consumption of it during her pregnancies was the reason she had been able to produce four strapping ghee-fed male heirs. If you had told her ghee could make the blind see, she would not have balked. Her regard for it verged on the reverential.

1 case

2 small woven bench

3 coal stove

Butter to make ghee was bought in bulk — in a *pethi*[1] that contained forty pats, each weighing half a kilo. She would sit in the courtyard on a *charpai*,[2] blowing on her tea before slurping it noisily, while the maid lit the *jiko*[3] in preparation. Then she would pretend to pick over lentils, all the while jealously guarding and counting each pat of butter as it was unfurled from its wax paper into a gigantic steel pan. It was a game the maid was accustomed to, but she would graciously feign ignorance.

Ghee, in all its golden, oily sensuality, is not something you can rush. You need to cultivate love and patience when you are making it. The butter has to be melted over low heat until any trace of water in it has evaporated and the impurities have sunk to the bottom. Given that we made ghee with twenty kilos of butter at a time in Nairobi, this process could take an entire afternoon. Once the butter was clear, it would be left to cool until it was just the right consistency – neither free-flowing nor at a standstill, but slow-pouring, with the slightest cling. It was then strained through yards of muslin or clean old cotton *dupattas*[4] into steel canisters to be stored. It was used to make dhal and curries, biscuits and cakes, to fry eggs or the most delicious *gulab jamuns*.[5] It was applied to grazed knees and other such childhood boo-boos, and it was the fuel that kept the *diyas*[6] in our prayer room burning.

4 thin scarves

5 milk dumplings in sugar syrup

6 lamps

My grandmother had married a successful man, and over the years of their union she had become accustomed to many comforts: leather Chesterfield sofas, televisions, servants, fine clothes and jewellery. Despite her status and their burgeoning bank balance, the years of scarcity, scrimping and deprivation that had come before had sunk into her deepest layers, and none of these symbols of material wealth made her feel truly content. 'When I got married, your grandfather's mother was so cruel and tight-fisted,' she'd complain. 'All the ghee and sugar was kept under lock and key. I only got to taste it when I was carrying my sons. Such longing…' She'd sigh and trail off.

But it was that very hunger that had kept my grandparents sharp and ambitious, working hard so that they and their future generations would never have to eat a dry chapatti again.

My grandmother's delight came when she saw the joy of her grandchildren as they ate the chapattis she liberally greased with love and ghee. There was laughter in her voice when she causally doused a pyramid of basmati rice with molten ghee and ground jaggery. She never felt empty if the pot of ghee was full.

125g green lentils
20g dried porcini mushrooms
700ml hot water
4 heaped tbsp ghee
300g wild mushrooms
1 onion, finely chopped
1 tsp cumin seeds
1 black cardamom pod, bruised
1 cinnamon stick, broken up

2 garlic cloves, finely chopped
Thumb of ginger, cut into fine
   matchsticks
1 bay leaf
300g carnaroli rice
Drizzle of truffle oil
Sea salt and black pepper
Thinly shaved truffle, to serve –
   optional

Ghee-fried Wild Mushroom and Truffle Khichdee

Khichdee, the precursor of kedgeree, is one of my favourite comfort foods. Traditionally a peasant dish made with lentils and basmati rice, I wanted this version to feel more luxurious, so I have used wild mushrooms and carnaroli rice for a creamier, more risotto-like texture. The ghee adds silkiness and enhances the sweet, nutty flavour of the mushrooms. If you are feeling flush, go all out with shaved truffle at the end.

- Begin by putting the lentils in a saucepan with enough cold water to cover them generously. Bring to the boil and cook for 8 minutes, until they are half-cooked, then drain. Meanwhile, soak the dried porcini in the hot water for 10 minutes to soften. Drain, reserving the soaking liquid. Finely chop the soaked porcini and reserve. Pour the soaking liquid into a small saucepan and keep warm over low heat.
- Meanwhile, heat half the ghee in a large saucepan over high heat, add the wild mushrooms and fry until tender and golden brown. Set aside. In the same pan, heat the remaining ghee and add the onion, cumin seeds, cardamom and cinnamon stick and fry until the onion is soft. Stir in the garlic, ginger and bay leaf and cook until fragrant, then season with salt and pepper.
- Add the rice and stir to coat and lightly toast. Pour in 100ml of the reserved soaking liquid and stir until reduced by half, then add the lentils and stir to combine. Add the soaking liquid a ladleful at a time, stirring continuously until the stock is absorbed before adding any more. Keep adding ladlefuls of stock and stirring for 15–20 minutes, until the rice is al dente and the lentils are tender. Finally, stir in half of the wild mushrooms and the porcini.
- Serve the khichdee topped with the remaining mushrooms and a drizzle of truffle oil. Shave over the truffle, if using.

Coconut Kadhi with Pea and Potato Pakoras and Tomato and Mint Salsa

Kadhi is a silky buttermilk or yoghurt soup made with chickpea flour. Most Indian states have their own version, and in Punjab, it is traditional to eat kadhi with chickpea-flour dumplings or pakoras floating in it. Here I have taken my mother's basic recipe but used coconut milk instead of the buttermilk and yoghurt, so that my vegan niece can still tuck in to one of our family's favourites!

The pakoras are like onion bhajis, except these contain potatoes and spices such as the aniseed-flavoured ajwain and the tangy dried mango powder called amchur. The recipe won't fall apart without them, but they are an inexpensive investment for your larder next time you are at an Indian supermarket. Do also look out for chaat masala, a deeply savoury and sour powdered spice mix, which is used to give all sorts of dishes a little oomph.

2 tbsp chickpea (gram) flour
1½ tbsp rapeseed oil
1½ tsp brown mustard seeds
¼ tsp asafoetida
20 curry leaves
1 tsp cumin seeds
1 tsp coriander seeds,
  lightly crushed
1 cinnamon stick, broken up
Thumb of ginger, finely grated
2 tbsp chopped fresh
  fenugreek leaves
1 red chilli, thickly sliced into rings
1 green chilli, finely chopped
1 tsp ground turmeric
2 tomatoes, peeled and blitzed
  in a blender
1 tbsp soft brown sugar
400ml coconut milk
Juice of 1 lime
Handful of chopped coriander
Sea salt and black pepper

For the salsa
500g red, orange and yellow
  cherry tomatoes, randomly cut
  into slices, wedges and rings
Large handful of finely
  chopped mint
Large handful of finely
  chopped coriander
½ red onion, very finely chopped
1 heaped tsp chaat masala
Juice of 1 lime

For the pakoras
300g Desiree potatoes,
  peeled and diced
1 red onion, thinly sliced
100g fresh or frozen peas
1 green chilli, finely chopped
Thumb of ginger, finely grated
2 tsp cumin seeds
½ tsp ground turmeric
1½ tsp coriander seeds,
  toasted and lightly crushed
½ tsp ajwain seeds – optional
1 heaped tsp dried mango
  powder (amchur) – optional
Handful of finely
  chopped coriander
Handful of finely chopped mint
100g chickpea (gram) flour
50g cornflour
50ml warm water
Rapeseed oil, for deep-frying

- To make the salsa, simply mix all the ingredients together in a bowl.
- For the pakoras, combine the potato, onion, peas, chilli, ginger, spices and herbs. Stir in both flours and the warm water to make a batter – the consistency should be firm and not too runny. Season with salt and pepper.
- To make the kadhi, put the chickpea flour into a bowl and gradually whisk in 250ml of water until smooth, then set aside. In a saucepan, heat the oil over high heat and add the mustard seeds. When they pop, follow with the asafoetida, curry leaves, cumin seeds, coriander seeds and cinnamon stick and fry for 30 seconds. Next add the ginger, fenugreek, chillies and turmeric. Fry until the ginger is soft, then add the tomatoes and sugar and season with salt. Cook until the tomatoes have turned into a thick sauce, then stir in the chickpea flour mix, coconut milk and 400ml of water. Bring to the boil, then simmer for 30 minutes over low heat, stirring occasionally.
- In the meantime, fry the pakoras. Fill a large, heavy-based saucepan a third full with the deep-frying oil. Heat the oil to 180°C – if you don't have a thermometer, you will know the oil is ready when a cube of bread turns golden brown in 20 seconds. Working in batches, use a dessertspoon to form loose balls of the batter and carefully lower into the oil. Deep-fry, turning occasionally, for about 4 minutes, until golden brown and cooked through, then drain on kitchen paper. Allow the oil to come back to temperature between batches.
- Squeeze the lime juice into the kadhi and stir in the chopped coriander. Pour into bowls and sit the pakoras on top, then spoon over the salsa and serve.

2 large aubergines
3 garlic cloves, roughly chopped
1–2 red bird's eye chillies,
    roughly chopped
2 tbsp palm sugar
2 tbsp fish sauce
Juice of 1 lime
4 spring onions, thinly sliced
Handful of beansprouts

Handful of pea shoots
Handful of mint leaves
Handful of coriander leaves
Small handful of Thai basil leaves,
    torn
2 tbsp crisp-fried shallots
    or onions
3 tbsp roughly crushed salted
    roast peanuts

2 medium-boiled eggs, shelled
Steamed jasmine rice, to serve –
    optional

For the jaggery fox nuts
1 tbsp coconut oil
80g fox nuts (phool makhana)
100g jaggery, grated
Pinch of chilli flakes

Spicy Aubergine Salad with Peanuts, Herbs, Eggs and Jaggery Fox Nuts

In his book How to Pick a Peach, *American food writer Russ Parsons says, 'Let's get one thing straight: most eggplants are not bitter (even though they have the right to be after everything that has been said about them).' Far from being bitter, the eggplant – or aubergine, as it is more commonly known in the UK – is the king of vegetables. Meaty and smoky when fire-roasted, aubergines stand up well to a thrillingly fiery and sharp dressing. Fox nuts are the seeds from a species of waterlily that grows in India, China and Japan. Here they bring crunch and sweetness, but you could use honey-roasted peanuts instead.*

· For the jaggery fox nuts, line a baking tray with baking parchment. Melt the coconut oil in a frying pan over low–medium heat, add the fox nuts and cook for 7–10 minutes until they are crisp. Spread out over the baking tray. In a small saucepan, heat the jaggery until it is golden and molten, then sprinkle in the chilli flakes. Pour the jaggery all over the fox nuts and leave to dry. These are wonderful as a snack in their own right.

· Prick the aubergines all over with a fork – this will stop them exploding! Grill on a chargrill or barbecue, under a hot grill, or over an open gas flame on the cooker. Turn and cook all over until they are really soft and the skin is charred. Leave to cool.

· Using a pestle and mortar, pound the garlic, chillies and palm sugar to a paste. Stir in the fish sauce and lime juice to loosen to a dressing consistency.

· Peel the skin off the aubergines, then cut them lengthways into quarters and lay on a serving platter.

· In a bowl, mix together the spring onions, beansprouts, pea shoots, mint, coriander and basil leaves. Pour in the dressing and toss well, then scatter the lot over the aubergine. Sprinkle with the crispy shallots or onions, peanuts and a handful of the jaggery fox nuts. Halve the eggs and lay on top of the salad, then eat as is – or, to make more of a meal of it, serve with steamed jasmine rice.

5 corn on the cob, 1 left whole,
 and the rest cut crossways
 into 4 chunks
2 tbsp rapeseed oil
1 tsp brown mustard seeds
Pinch of asafoetida
20 curry leaves
1 cinnamon stick
1 star anise
Thumb of ginger, finely grated
4 garlic cloves, finely chopped

1 red chilli, thinly sliced
200g tinned tomatoes
1 heaped tbsp tomato puree
3 tbsp smooth peanut butter
2 tbsp tamarind concentrate
1 tbsp soft brown sugar
Sea salt
Handful each of toasted
 desiccated coconut and
 coriander leaves, to serve

Makkai Paka

Makkai paka is an East African sweetcorn curry that can be served as part of a main meal with rice or chapattis, or eaten on its own as a snack. The original uses crushed peanuts, but I use peanut butter to make a thick, funky creamy sauce spiced up with aromatics, including star anise and curry leaves. Always look out for natural, unsweetened peanut butter.

- Heat a grill to medium and toast the whole corn cob, turning it frequently so it chars all over. Leave to cool, then shuck the sweetcorn kernels from the cob and reserve for later.
- Steam the sweetcorn chunks until tender and set aside.
- Pour the oil into a large frying pan and place over high heat. Add the mustard seeds and, when they pop, follow swiftly with the asafoetida, curry leaves, cinnamon and star anise and fry briefly. Turn the heat down to low, add the ginger, garlic and chilli and cook until fragrant. Stir in the tomatoes, tomato puree, peanut butter, tamarind and sugar and cook for about 8–10 minutes, stirring every so often, until you have a sauce that's thick enough to cling to the sweetcorn. Season with salt to taste.
- Throw in the sweetcorn chunks and stir to coat thoroughly. Finish with the coconut, coriander and reserved sweetcorn kernels.

2 tbsp groundnut or rapeseed oil
1 tsp brown mustard seeds
Pinch of asafoetida
1 stem of curry leaves, picked
1 cinnamon stick, broken up
1 tsp cumin seeds
1 tsp coriander seeds, toasted
  and lightly crushed

Thumb of ginger, finely grated
1 tsp ground turmeric
50g tamarind concentrate
2 tbsp soft brown sugar
6 heirloom tomatoes, randomly
  cut into wedges and rounds
Sea salt

Sweet and Sour Tamarind Tomatoes

This wonderful side dish celebrates the huge variety of tomatoes available in the summer, when they are at their buxom, undiluted tomatoey best. It works particularly well as an accompaniment to grilled or barbecued fish, like sardines, and can be served hot or at room temperature.

- Heat the oil in a frying pan over medium heat. Throw in the mustard seeds. As soon as they pop and crackle, follow with the asafoetida, curry leaves, cinnamon, cumin and coriander seeds. Add the ginger and turmeric and fry until soft and fragrant, then stir in the tamarind, sugar and tomatoes, coating them with the mixture.
- Add 75ml of water and bring to the boil, then turn down the heat and simmer for about 3 minutes, until the tomatoes are soft but still holding their shape. Season with salt to taste.

Paneer Gnudi with Saag
and Cavolo Nero

This dish is inspired by a short film I saw, which documented a crisis in the Italian dairy industry a decade ago, when they were struggling to recruit a workforce. Local people were no longer interested in working the long hours required for such little financial compensation, so the solution had to came from abroad. A programme was set up to bring in Punjabi workers from North India, who were known to be experts at handling livestock such as cows and buffalos.

Marrying Indian and Italian culinary traditions, this dish tells the story of two nations coming together, and is a love letter to those migrant workers. It combines homemade Indian cheese with parmesan to make meltingly light gnudi (a sort of gnocchi without the starchiness of potatoes), which are then served with Italian cavolo nero and Punjabi saag — a spiced spinach puree. You'll need to make the gnudi the day before you want to serve them.

Sea salt and black pepper
1 preserved lemon, rind only,
   finely chopped
Toasted pine nuts and finely
   grated parmesan, to serve

For the gnudi
2 litres whole milk
Juice of 1 lemon
200g fine semolina
50g parmesan, grated
1 large egg yolk
Good grating of nutmeg
25g butter

For the cavolo nero
250g cavolo nero, thick stalks
   removed, leaves roughly
   chopped
60ml extra virgin olive oil
2 garlic cloves, thinly sliced
1 red chilli, finely chopped
Finely grated zest and juice
   of 1 lemon

For the saag
500g baby spinach
40g butter
1 onion, very finely chopped
1 tsp cumin seeds
Thumb of ginger, finely grated
3 fat garlic cloves, finely chopped
1 green chilli, finely chopped

- For the gnudi, pour the milk into a saucepan and bring to the boil, then take off the heat and slowly pour in the lemon juice, stirring all the time. It should begin to curdle immediately. Leave to stand for 20 minutes.
- Pour the curds into a muslin-lined sieve set over a bowl, letting the whey drain through. Discard the whey. Rinse the curds well under cold running water, then gather the muslin in your hands and squeeze out any excess liquid from the paneer.
- Cover a large baking tray with half the semolina. In a bowl, knead the paneer with the parmesan, egg yolk, nutmeg and black pepper to taste, adding about 1 tablespoon of water to make a soft dough. Do not overwork. Roll out into 30 ovals or balls. Lay the gnudi on the baking tray and sprinkle with the remaining semolina. Cover and chill in the refrigerator for 24 hours.
- Next day, put a large saucepan of water on to boil, ready to blanch the greens and cook the gnudi.
- Blanch the cavolo nero in the boiling water for 1 minute, then tip into a colander and refresh in ice-cold water. Drain well, using your hands to squeeze out any excess liquid. Heat the olive oil in a large frying pan over low heat and fry the garlic, chilli and lemon zest until fragrant. Add the lemon juice, then gently fold in the cavolo nero. Season with salt and pepper to taste, then transfer to a bowl and keep warm. Wipe out the frying pan, ready to use for the saag.
- Bring the saucepan of water back to the boil and blanch the spinach for about 10 seconds, then tip into the colander and refresh in ice-cold water. Drain well, using your hands to squeeze out any excess liquid, then blitz in a blender until smooth. Melt the butter in the frying pan over a low—medium heat and fry the onion and cumin seeds until the onion is soft and golden brown. Scatter in the ginger, garlic and chilli and fry until cooked and aromatic. Fold in the spinach puree, season with salt and pepper to taste and cook for a further 5 minutes. Transfer the saag to a bowl and keep warm, then wipe out the frying pan, ready to use for the gnudi.
- Bring the saucepan of water back to the boil. Gently slip in the gnudi and cook for 1 minute, then drain. Heat the butter in the frying pan and fry the gnudi until they are golden brown all over.
- Spoon the saag into the base of warmed bowls and top with the cavolo nero, gnudi, preserved lemon, pine nuts and grated parmesan.

5 garlic cloves, very thinly sliced,
  ideally on a mandoline
400g brussels sprouts, trimmed
  and halved
Knob of butter
100g vacuum-packed chestnuts,
  halved
Vegetable oil
Crisp-fried shallots or onions,
  toasted sesame seeds and
  bonito flakes, to serve

For the dressing
1 garlic clove, finely chopped
2 small red chillies, finely
  chopped
1 tbsp tamarind concentrate
2 tbsp fish sauce
30g palm sugar

Charred Brussels Sprouts and Chestnuts with Hot and Sour Dressing

If you haven't figured out a go-to recipe to make you fall in love with brussels sprouts, may I recommend this one? When I put it on the menu at my restaurant, I was expecting it to be met with ambivalence – but, in fact, it has become one of our most-requested small plates. The combination of charred sprouts, fish sauce and tamarind is already umami, but if you can find Japanese bonito flakes, they will double the intensity of the umami. You'll never cook sprouts any other way again!

· Heat a 3cm depth of vegetable oil in a small saucepan, add the sliced garlic and cook, keeping a close eye on it and stirring frequently, until golden. Drain the garlic chips on kitchen paper.
· Blanch the brussels sprouts in a saucepan of boiling water for 2 minutes, then tip into a colander and refresh in ice-cold water to keep them beautifully green. Drain and set aside. Heat the butter and a splash of oil in a frying pan over high heat. Add the sprouts and chestnuts and cook until they go brown and start to char, then take the pan off the heat.
· To make the dressing, use a mortar and pestle to pound the garlic and chillies to a paste. Add the tamarind concentrate, fish sauce and palm sugar, stirring to dissolve.
· Drizzle the dressing over the sprouts and toss to coat. Serve immediately, topped with the garlic chips, crispy shallots or onions, toasted sesame seeds and bonito flakes.

250g brussels sprouts
1 small pumpkin or round
    squash, such as Delica,
    cut into thin wedges
2 red onions, cut into wedges
4 parsnips, peeled and quartered
    lengthways
1 whole garlic bulb, separated
    into cloves, but left unpeeled
A few sprigs of thyme
A few sage leaves

¼ tsp chilli flakes – optional
Glug of extra virgin olive oil
Sea salt and black pepper
Generous handful of toasted
    hazelnuts or pecans and
    a good handful of grated
    parmesan, to serve

For the dressing
150ml extra virgin olive oil
50ml red wine vinegar
Pinch of sugar

For the croutons
4–5 thick slices of panettone,
    cubed
30g butter
1 garlic clove, finely chopped
1 tbsp finely chopped sage
A few thyme leaves
5 tbsp freshly grated parmesan

Christmas Panzanella with Panettone Croutons

This sustaining salad is perfect for a post-Christmas lunch or dinner, as it uses up the glut of vegetables, such as parsnips and brussels sprouts, that you may have lurking in the fridge, and its cheeriness makes a great antidote to the Boxing Day blues. It also makes terrific use of any leftover Christmas panettone. It may sound strange to use sweet panettone in a savoury salad, but I promise you it adds the most comforting, subtly sweet, festive flavour. If you don't have any left over, just use stale brioche or any other bread you have lying around for the croutons.

·   Preheat the oven to 200°C/Fan 180°C/Gas Mark 6.
·   Blanch the brussels sprouts in a saucepan of boiling water for about 2 minutes, then tip into a colander and refresh in ice-cold water. Drain well, then cut in half.
·   Lay all the vegetables in a roasting tin. Scatter over the garlic cloves, thyme, sage and chilli flakes, if using. Drizzle over the olive oil, then season well with salt and pepper. Roast for 40–45 minutes, until the vegetables are tender and starting to catch and get crispy at the edges.
·   Meanwhile, for the dressing, simply whisk together all the ingredients, seasoning with salt and pepper to taste.
·   For the croutons, put the panettone cubes into a heatproof bowl and line a baking sheet with baking parchment. Melt the butter in a small saucepan, add the garlic and herbs and let them sizzle briefly, then drizzle over the croutons. Mix in the parmesan and season with black pepper. Spread out the croutons on the baking sheet and toast in the oven for 6–8 minutes, or until golden and crisp.
·   Scatter the croutons over the roasted vegetables, then pour over the dressing and gently toss everything together. Finish with the toasted nuts and grated parmesan. Serve at once.

Samaki

Fish and Shellfish

In 1980s Kenyan-Indian society, having an aquarium at home was a bit of a status symbol. My uncle, not wanting to miss out on aquatic decadence, went out and bought one. There were no goldfish, but there was

a beauty pageant of colourful species with glimmering scales,

philosopher's whiskers and great sweeping fins. There was one that looked like a mythical Chinese New Year dragon, and a stern black one that loomed confidently over the rainbow of the others like a shadow. Aquarium is too grand a description – in reality, ours was no more than a yard-long glasshouse filled with twenty cups of water. But there, on the gravel in the middle of the tank, was a sparkling piece of underwater real estate – a Disney-like residence complete with turrets and a drawbridge. It had all the appeal of a dolls' house for me, and suddenly the witless troop of swimmers became my friends and confidantes. I gave them names, ascribed them feelings, thoughts and intentions. I sobbed and sulked when eventually I found one of my fishy pals floating belly-up on the surface of the water.

Eating fish was, of course, out of the question for me. My mother had a repertoire of seafood dishes, which the rest of the family adored and I regarded with revulsion: briny little sprats marinated in ground spices and flour then deep-fried until crisp and almost charred; rich and oily

steaks of kingfish, their meaty flesh clinging to nubs of bone,

poached in a fennel-scented curry with a great thrust of green chilli; clean and delicate *tafi*, a white fish she stuffed with coriander paste, wrapped in banana leaves and roasted. She tried to coax me with battered *Amritsari pakoras*[1] dabbed in tomato ketchup, but still I refused.

My fish boycott, which had been so passionate and unyielding, sputtered and died quickly enough, and quite by accident. One of my sisters had passed an exam, so there was a celebratory dinner at a restaurant.

We went to a pleasant but unremarkable spot that was a favourite of my father's, Hashmi Barbeque — a Nairobi institution still beloved by generations of Kenyans

hooked on the flavour of food cooked in seductive plumes of charcoal smoke.

We took an outside table, where there was a round of *dawas*[2] for the adults and *santara*[3] juice for the children. There was a zesty salad and chips to accompany sharing platters of barbecued meat. However, the spicy white protein I had been tucking into with great gusto turned out not to be chicken, as I thought, but Hashmi's famous masala fish. I made peace with my conscience there and then. Everyone else was eating it, and I always strove to do the right thing and avoid causing hurt intentionally. I have never looked back. And whenever I visit, I am always delighted to find masala fish still on the menu.

Since then, fish and shellfish have become firm favourites: sea bass, salmon, mackerel, scallops, cockles, prawns, oysters, clams and mussels. As a cook, I rave about the fact that these sea creatures outshine every other in terms of ease and speed of cooking and their variety of tastes and textures. The recipes in this chapter demonstrate that whether they are eaten raw, cured, confit, pan-fried or roasted, fish and shellfish are among the greatest and least fussy of culinary pleasures.

1 fish fried in a gram flour batter, a snack from the Indian city of Amritsar

2 popular Kenyan cocktail made from vodka, lime and honey

3 satsuma

Sea salt and black pepper
Extra virgin olive oil, for drizzling
Sumac, small mint leaves and
    pomegranate seeds, to garnish

For the labneh
125g yoghurt
1 small garlic clove,
    finely chopped
Generous pinch of salt

For the pickled fennel
250ml cider vinegar
50g caster sugar
1 tsp fennel seeds
1 tsp yellow mustard seeds
5 black peppercorns
1 fennel bulb, finely shaved
1 small red onion, very
    thinly sliced

For the tartare
500g very fresh salmon fillet,
    skinned and pin-boned
50g bulgur wheat, soaked
    in hot water for 5 minutes
4 spring onions, thinly sliced
1 tsp ground allspice
1 tsp cumin seeds, toasted
    and lightly crushed
1 small red chilli, deseeded
    and finely chopped
2 tbsp extra virgin olive oil

Levantine Salmon Tartare with Pickled Fennel and Labneh

In the power-dressing 1980s, tartare was pretty much a mound of raw, chopped-up beef bound together with mustard, capers and chives, topped with a raw egg yolk. It was the preserve of the showy Wall Street set who liked status symbols and stuffy restaurants. Thankfully, over the years, tartare has been reinterpreted in different ways, with ingredients as varied as tuna and tomatoes. This spiced version is inspired by the Levant, where it is normally made with raw lamb. I've used delicate salmon for a bright, refreshing dish, pairing it with a brazenly acidic pickled fennel and luscious labneh, rather than the traditional egg yolk. You'll need to make the labneh in advance – but if you're short of time, you could just use 4 tablespoons of thick yoghurt or ready-made labneh instead.

- For the labneh, mix together the yoghurt, garlic and salt. Line a bowl with a large square of muslin and spoon in the yoghurt. Gather the corners of the muslin and knot together, then tie to a rack in your refrigerator, placing the bowl underneath to catch any drips. Leave to drain overnight.
- For the pickled fennel, combine the vinegar and sugar in a small non-reactive saucepan and stir over low heat until the sugar dissolves. Stir through the spices, then leave to cool. Add the fennel and onion, pour into a glass bowl or jar and refrigerate for 2 hours or overnight.
- Make the tartare on the day you want to serve it. Use a large sharp knife to finely chop the fish – it may be worth putting it in the freezer for half an hour beforehand to make this easier. In a bowl, combine the salmon with the well-drained bulgur wheat and the remaining ingredients and season to taste with salt and pepper, then cover and refrigerate until chilled.
- Divide the salmon tartare into 6 equal portions. Place a pastry ring on a serving plate and spoon a portion of tartare into it, then remove the ring. Repeat with the rest of the tartare. Top with the pickled fennel and a spoonful of labneh, then drizzle with olive oil. Finish with a scattering of sumac, mint leaves and pomegranate seeds. Serve at once.

2 sea bass fillets, skinned
and pin-boned
Rapeseed oil, for frying
1 tbsp wild or black rice
1 red chilli, thinly sliced
12 yellow and red cherry
tomatoes, thinly sliced
½ green (unripe) mango, peeled
and cut into thin matchsticks
A few coriander leaves
Sea salt and black pepper

For the tomato oil
2 ripe tomatoes
1 red chilli
5 garlic cloves, unpeeled
50ml olive oil, plus extra
for drizzling

For the aam panna
1 green (unripe) mango
Handful of mint leaves
½ tsp cumin seeds, toasted
and ground
1 heaped tsp grated jaggery
or soft brown sugar
Juice of 2 limes
¼ tsp black salt (kala namak) –
optional

Sea Bass Ceviche with Aam Panna and Tomato Oil

*Green mango offers a jolt of acidity that will make your mouth water and
pucker and crave more. It is the main ingredient in aam panna, a drink
known for its refreshing and hydrating properties, and drunk across North
India during the relentless summers. I have used its natural acidity here,
in an untraditional marinade for sea bass, to make a light, summery ceviche.*

- Begin by making the tomato oil. Preheat the grill to high. Place the
tomatoes, chilli and garlic in a small roasting tin, scatter with salt and
pepper and drizzle with a little oil. Grill for 15–20 minutes, or until the
tomatoes and chilli have blackened and the garlic has softened. When
cool enough to handle, squeeze the soft garlic out of its skin, then put
into a blender, along with the tomatoes and chilli. Blitz to a puree, then
strain through a sieve and return to the blender. Add the remaining
50ml of rapeseed oil and whizz briefly. Set aside.
- For the aam panna, boil the unpeeled whole mango in plenty of water for
1 hour, or until it is very soft and almost pulpy. Drain and cool, then peel
the mango and slice the pulpy flesh from the stone. Put the flesh into a
blender with the mint, cumin, jaggery, lime juice and black salt, if using,
and whizz to a smooth puree with the consistency of pouring yoghurt –
if it is any thicker, add a little cold water. Transfer to a large ceramic bowl.
- Slice the fish as thinly as you can, then add to the bowl of mango puree,
making sure the fish is submerged. Cover and refrigerate for 1 hour.
- Meanwhile, pour a 2cm depth of rapeseed oil into a small saucepan.
Heat the oil to 180°C – if you don't have a thermometer, you will know
the oil is ready when a cube of bread turns golden brown in 20 seconds.
Sprinkle in the rice and fry until it begins to puff up, then drain on
kitchen paper, blotting away any excess oil.
- To serve the ceviche, divide the fish between two plates, then spoon over
some of the aam panna. Top with the tomato and chilli slices, mango
matchsticks, coriander leaves and finally the puffed rice. Drizzle over the
tomato oil and serve immediately.

1kg mussels
2 tbsp rapeseed oil
Thumb of ginger, finely grated
Finely grated zest and juice
    of 1 lemon
1 tsp ground turmeric
500g sweetcorn kernels,
    fresh or frozen
1 litre chicken stock
100g basmati rice
A few drops of sesame oil
Sea salt and white pepper
Chopped coriander, to serve

Mussel, Sweetcorn and Rice Soup

This is a cross between a Western chowder and a Chinese sweetcorn soup. The sweetcorn and briny shellfish are given an Asian twist with the inclusion of sesame oil, ginger and turmeric. I add rice to give the broth some body. It tastes like sea air and late summer – bright, spectacular, golden and fleeting. (Happily it can be rustled up during darkest winter too, thanks to the convenience of frozen sweetcorn.)

- Scrub and debeard the mussels, discarding any that are open and do not shut when you tap them. Heat the rapeseed oil in a stockpot or large saucepan. Fry the ginger for a minute or so and, when fragrant, add the lemon zest and turmeric and fry briefly. Stir in the sweetcorn, coating it in the oil.
- Add the stock and rice and cook, uncovered, for around 15 minutes or until the rice is tender. Season with salt and pepper, add the sesame oil and pop in the mussels. Cover and steam the mussels open (this should take 3–4 minutes), then scatter over the coriander, squeeze in the lemon juice, stir and serve. Remember to discard any mussels that have failed to open.

Oysters

My parents weren't generally enthusiastic about prising strange creatures from their shells, so I remained an oyster virgin until after I had graduated from university. My first introduction to them finally came during an internship with a public relations company.

We were schmoozing a client over a fancy dinner, it was the end of the summer and there, on a silver platter, lay a dozen pristine bivalves on the half-shell — full of promise and sexy as hell.

I felt giddy with anticipation and champagne. I lifted an oyster shell and sucked the meat right out. It was like a kiss from the ocean: a pure, primal salty pleasure.

As a gawky, naive 21-year-old, my chief ambition was to be a citizen of a sophisticated and grown-up world. That night, with a swig of ozone, I left behind any childish squeamishness and crossed the threshold into adulthood. Oysters are more than just a delicacy awaiting a drizzle of shallot vinaigrette; they are natural water filters that keep our waters cleaner, have the ability to change sex and can manifest pearls. Connoisseurs are obsessed with their 'merroir', short for marine terroir — meaning that, like wine, each oyster offers unique flavours according to its geographic origin.

When buying oysters, make sure they come from a sustainable source and only buy them if they have closed shells — if they are open, they are dead. Store them in a pan or bowl in the fridge, covered with a damp cloth, and consume within 24 hours. While these sea treasures are ready for slurping au naturel, and are often at their best eaten raw, there are several ways to appreciate their inherent salinity. You can fry them into beignets, roast or grill them, or use them to make sauces for pasta. The world's your... well, you know.

20 oysters
1 quantity tamarind chutney
(see page 128)
½ banana shallot, very finely
chopped
100g sev mamra (puffed rice
and crisp noodles)

For the puris
125g plain flour, plus extra
for dusting
75g fine semolina
Groundnut oil, for deep-frying

Oyster Pani Puris

A pani puri is a crisp cracker made from flour and semolina that puffs up into a crisp orb when deep-fried. Normally served stuffed with chickpeas and potatoes before tamarind water is poured in, it is then downed in one in an undignified, dribbling euphoria. In this recipe I have replaced the traditional filling with briny nuggets of fresh oyster meat for a slurp with a difference.

· Start by checking your oysters over. The shells should be tightly shut – discard any that have even the smallest opening.
· Whisk the tamarind chutney with 500ml of water in a large bowl and refrigerate. This tamarind water can be made up to a week in advance and stored in a screwtop bottle or airtight jar.
· To make the puris, mix together the flour and semolina, then start adding water a little at a time, kneading as you go, until you have a springy and pliable dough. Divide into 6 balls and, on a lightly floured surface, use a rolling pin to roll out to a 2mm thickness. Use a 4cm round pastry cutter to cut out 30 circles (it's always good to have a few extra because there may be some rogue ones that don't puff up).
· Fill a large, heavy-based saucepan a third full with the deep-frying oil. Heat the oil to 180°C – if you don't have a thermometer, you will know the oil is ready when a cube of bread turns golden brown in 20 seconds. Fry the puris in batches for about 2 minutes, or until golden and crisp, allowing the oil to return to temperature between batches. Drain on kitchen paper and leave to cool. The puris can be made in advance and stored in an airtight container for up to a week.
· Shuck the oysters (or ask your fishmonger to do this for you, saving the juices). Crack an opening on one side of a puri and pop in a piece of oyster meat and some of its juices. Sprinkle with some chopped shallot and sev mamra and serve on top of a shot glass filled with tamarind water. To eat, pour some tamarind water into the crack in the puri, then put the whole puri in your mouth and chase with more tamarind water.

Confit Salmon with Mint-Coriander Chutney and Pomegranate-Pistachio Crust

Confit is a classic French technique where fish or meat is submerged in oil over low heat, and cooking salmon in this way means it loses its rawness but remains meltingly soft. Here the fish is first given an injection of flavour with a quick masala-salt cure — this also draws out a little liquid from the fish, firming it up slightly so it doesn't fall apart when it is cooked. It is then smeared with a punchy chutney made from coriander, mint, chilli and lime before having a crust of pomegranate seeds and pistachios pressed onto it. The dish is served at room temperature, so you can cook the salmon up to 4 hours in advance, making it a stress-free option for a summer dinner party. Serve with some French fries or new potatoes.

600g side of salmon, skinned
  and pin-boned
500ml olive oil
Sea salt and black pepper

For the masala salt
1 tsp cumin seeds
1 tsp coriander seeds
1 tsp cardamom seeds
1 tsp fennel seeds
1 tsp black peppercorns
1 cinnamon stick
1 blade of mace
4 tbsp sea salt

For the chutney
Large handful of mint leaves
Large handful of coriander leaves
1 green chilli, roughly chopped
½ tsp cumin seeds, toasted and
  coarsely ground
1 tsp caster sugar
Juice of ½ lime
150g Greek yoghurt

For the crust
100g pistachios, roughly chopped
Large handful of finely chopped
  coriander
1 small red onion, very finely chopped
1 red chilli, deseeded and finely
  chopped
50g moong sprouts
Seeds from 1 small pomegranate
1 tsp chaat masala
Juice of 1 lime
60ml extra virgin olive oil

- To make the masala salt, toast the whole spices in a dry frying pan until fragrant, stirring frequently so they don't burn, then use a pestle and mortar to grind with the salt to a fine powder. The masala salt can be stored in an airtight jar for up to a year.
- Dust the salmon with 1 tablespoon of the masala salt and refrigerate for an hour to lightly cure.
- Rinse the salmon well and dry thoroughly with kitchen paper. Place it in a shallow pan large enough to hold the piece of salmon flat, then pour in the oil – the salmon should be completely submerged. Put the pan over low–medium heat and use a digital thermometer to gauge when the temperature reaches 60°C. Cook for 8 minutes. Remove from the heat and let the salmon rest in the oil for another 2 minutes, then carefully lift out and drain on kitchen paper.
- To make the chutney, in a food processor, blitz the mint, coriander, chilli, cumin, sugar and lime juice to a paste. Fold the paste into the yoghurt so it is well incorporated, seasoning with salt and pepper to taste.
- For the crust, preheat the oven to 180°C/Fan 160°C/Gas Mark 4. Spread out the pistachios on a baking tray and roast for 8 minutes, giving them a shake every so often to make sure they are evenly roasted. Chop the nuts finely, then mix with the remaining ingredients in a small bowl. Season with salt and pepper to taste.
- To serve the salmon, smear the surface with some of the chutney and pack on the crust. Serve with the rest of the chutney on the side.

6 mackerel fillets, pin-boned
60ml fish sauce
1 tbsp rapeseed oil

For the rojak
500g snake beans, cut
    into 6cm lengths
1 small pineapple, peeled,
    cored and thinly sliced
    into semi circles
1 green (unripe) mango,
    peeled and cut into
    matchsticks

4 spring onions, thinly sliced
    on the diagonal
2 Lebanese cucumbers,
    deseeded and thinly sliced
Handful of radishes, thinly sliced
Thumb of ginger, cut into
    ultra-fine matchsticks
Handful each of Vietnamese mint,
    Thai basil and coriander leaves
50g macadamia nuts, toasted
    and roughly chopped
Handful of crisp-fried shallots
    or onions

For the dressing
3 red chillies, finely chopped
2 garlic cloves, finely chopped
2 tbsp palm sugar or grated
    jaggery
200g fresh pineapple
1 tbsp tamarind concentrate
2 tbsp lime juice
2 tbsp fish sauce

Pan-fried Mackerel with Pineapple Rojak

Rojak is a tangy Indonesian salad of fruit and vegetables that varies greatly –
I have had it made with turnips, carrots and papaya – but I love this one with
pineapple and green mango as its sharpness cuts through oily fish. I've used
mackerel here, but I also love it with sea bass or some grilled prawns.

· Dry the mackerel well and place it on a chopping board, skin side
  up. Using a sharp knife, score the skin at 1cm intervals. Combine the
  mackerel and fish sauce in a dish and turn to coat, then set aside at room
  temperature for half an hour.
· In the meantime, make the rojak salad. Put the snake beans into a
  saucepan of boiling water and when the water returns to the boil, tip
  them into a colander, refresh in ice-cold water and drain well. Put
  into a large bowl, along with all the remaining ingredients except the
  macadamias and crispy shallots.
· Make the dressing by simply pounding the chillies and garlic to a paste
  using a pestle and mortar. Add the sugar and pineapple and pound again
  until smooth, then stir in the tamarind, lime juice and fish sauce.
· Just before you are ready to serve, toss the rojak with the dressing and
  scatter with macadamia nuts and crispy shallots.
· Remove the mackerel from the fish sauce and thoroughly pat dry with
  kitchen paper. Heat the oil in a non-stick frying pan over medium–high
  heat, add the mackerel, skin side down, and cook for 3 minutes or until
  the skin is crisp and golden. Turn the fish over, then remove from the
  heat and let it cook through in the residual heat of the pan for 1 minute.
  Serve at once with the salad.

300g baby squid, with tentacles,
  cleaned
500g Jerusalem artichokes
1 tbsp extra virgin olive oil,
  plus extra for drizzling
25g butter
A few sprigs of thyme
1 bay leaf
1 whole garlic bulb, separated
  into cloves and bruised

Juice of 1 lemon
2 heaped tsp smoked sweet
  paprika
Small handful of chopped parsley
1 quantity chorizo crumbs
  (see page 42)
Sea salt and black pepper

For the marinade
60ml extra virgin olive oil
1 tsp Turkish pepper flakes
  (pul biber)
1 tsp caster sugar

Grilled Concertina Squid with Jerusalem Artichokes and Chorizo Crumbs

It really doesn't get any simpler or better than grilled squid. A quick cook on a hot griddle or barbecue and you end up with squid that is crisp on the outside and juicy in the middle. Jerusalem artichokes add a nutty earthiness to this dish, but if they aren't available try La Ratte or Jersey Royal potatoes instead.

· First prepare the squid. To achieve a concertina effect, lay the squid on a chopping board and place a chef's knife flat inside it. Using a second knife, score the squid at 1cm intervals, as if you were cutting it into rings – you won't be able to cut all the way through because of the other knife. Transfer to a shallow dish, then mix together the marinade ingredients and pour over the squid. Season with salt and pepper, then set aside to marinate for at least half an hour.

· Scrub the Jerusalem artichokes well, making sure to get the soil from every ridge and crevice. Cut them in half lengthways. Bring a large saucepan of salted water to the boil, then toss in the artichokes and boil for about 6 minutes until the edges are slightly broken down. Drain well. Heat the olive oil and butter in a large frying pan over medium–high heat and throw in the thyme, bay leaf and garlic (no need to peel the cloves – they're just there to add a subtle background flavour). Once everything is sizzling, add the artichokes, cut side down, in a singer layer. Turn down the heat to medium and let them cook until they are a deep golden brown, then turn and brown on the other side.

· When the artichokes are almost ready, heat a griddle pan over high heat and cook the squid for a minute on each side.

· Using a slotted spoon, fish out the artichokes and arrange on a serving plate, placing the squid on top. Squeeze the lemon juice into the pan and stir in the paprika. Strain the pan juices over the squid and artichokes, then finish with the chopped parsley, a drizzle of extra virgin olive oil and a sprinkling of chorizo crumbs.

1kg cockles
75ml olive oil
1 small onion, very finely chopped
1 large carrot, peeled and
    finely diced
3 sticks celery, finely diced
4 fat garlic cloves, thinly sliced
Generous pinch of saffron threads

Finely grated zest of 1 lemon
A few sprigs of thyme
Large handful of coriander
    leaves, stalks reserved
1 bay leaf
4 vine-ripened tomatoes, peeled
    and finely diced, seeds and
    juices reserved

100ml white wine
500ml fish stock
225ml single cream
Juice of ½ lemon
Sea salt and black pepper

Cockles with Tomatoes, Saffron and Coriander

I love how cockles taste so assertively of the sea – they wash their briny flavour over anything you cook them with. It makes them excellent for recipes with forceful seasonings, like this one, which features garlic, saffron and coriander. Serve with plenty of warm crusty bread to mop up the delicious juices.

- First check over the cockles and discard any that are open. Heat the oil in a large saucepan over low heat and gently fry the onion, carrot and celery until soft but not brown.
- Add the garlic, saffron and lemon zest and fry until fragrant. Tie together the thyme, coriander stalks and bay leaf with kitchen twine, then add this bundle to the pan, along with the tomato seeds and juices. Pour in the wine and let it bubble until reduced by half.
- Now add the stock and bring to a rapid boil. Tumble in the cockles, cover and leave to steam, giving the pan a shake every so often, for 4 minutes or until the cockles have opened. Using a slotted spoon, remove the cockles from the pan. Discard any cockles that have failed to open, along with the herb bundle.
- Pour the cream into the stock and bring to a simmer. Take off the heat, squeeze in the lemon juice and season with salt and pepper to taste, then return the cockles to the pan. Serve in deep bowls, with the diced tomato and coriander leaves scattered over.

Clams Moilee with Lemon Vermicelli Upma

Moilee is a South Indian coconut milk broth that is light, delicate and sophisticated. There is no sinus-clearing heat here, just the sweet mellowness of rich coconut milk and a genteel tempering of nutty mustard seeds and aromatic curry leaves warmed through with cloves and ginger. No lurid day-glo sauce, just the pale sigh of golden turmeric. It's a dish that makes me nostalgic about the time I spent daydreaming on the backwaters of Kerala. This recipe is a favourite holiday souvenir that I share with friends again and again. I love to serve it with lemon vermicelli upma — a sort of lemon noodle stir-fry, but you can equally enjoy it with rice. Feel free to use any type of fish or shellfish in the sauce — prawns, mussels and pieces of monkfish are all delicious options.

1kg palourdes clams

For the broth
2 tbsp rapeseed oil
2 tsp brown mustard seeds
Pinch of asafoetida
15–20 curry leaves
½ tsp cumin seeds
8 cloves, ground to a coarse
   powder
2 red onions, thinly sliced
   into crescents
1 red chilli, thinly sliced
Thumb of ginger, cut into
   fine matchsticks

1 tsp ground turmeric
1 tbsp grated jaggery or soft
   brown sugar
3 tbsp tamarind concentrate
1 × 400ml can of coconut milk
Juice of 1 large lime
Handful of roughly chopped
   coriander
Sea salt

For the upma
200g dried rice vermicelli
2 tbsp groundnut oil
1 tbsp white urid dhal
2 tsp mustard seeds

2 stems of curry leaves, picked
2 green chillies, split lengthways
Thumb of ginger, cut into
   very thin matchsticks
½ tsp ground turmeric
3 tbsp coconut milk
Finely grated zest and juice
   of 1 lemon
2 tbsp desiccated coconut,
   toasted
Handful of peanuts, toasted
Handful of chopped coriander

- Wash the clams well under cold, running water to get rid of any sand or grit. Discard any open ones that won't close when lightly tapped.
- To make the broth, heat the oil in a frying pan over high heat until it is almost smoking, then add the mustard seeds. As soon as they start popping, add the asafoetida and follow swiftly with the curry leaves. Stir briefly, then turn down the heat to low and add the cumin seeds, cloves and onions, along with a good pinch of salt to stop the onions browning. Fry gently until the onions have softened and turned pale pink. Add the chilli and ginger and stir-fry for a few minutes more, then sprinkle in the turmeric and sugar and stir for another minute.
- Whisk the tamarind and coconut milk together, then pour into the pan, along with 400ml of water. Bring to the boil, then let it bubble and reduce for around 10 minutes.
- Meanwhile, for the upma, put the vermicelli in a colander in the sink and pour over plenty of hot water from a freshly boiled kettle. Heat the oil in a wok over medium–high heat and add the urid dhal. Once it starts to go golden, add the mustard seeds and, when they start popping, add the curry leaves, chillies, ginger, turmeric, coconut milk and lemon zest and juice. Stir well, then add the vermicelli and fry for 30 seconds. Remove from the heat and scatter with the coconut, peanuts and coriander.
- Add the clams to the broth, cover and steam for around 3–4 minutes or until they open, giving the pan a gentle shake a couple of times. Discard any clams that fail to open, then squeeze over the lime juice and sprinkle in the coriander. Pour over the noodles to serve.

200g spinach leaves
2 tbsp rapeseed oil
1 onion, finely chopped
1 leek, thinly sliced
2 sticks celery, thinly sliced
2 garlic cloves, finely chopped
1 heaped tbsp Madras
    curry powder
Generous pinch of saffron threads
300ml double cream
2 handfuls of grated mature
    cheddar or parmesan
Juice of 1 lemon

Large handful of chopped
    coriander
450g fillet of cod or other white
    fish, skinned and pin-boned
200g peeled raw prawns,
    deveined
2 hard-boiled eggs, shelled
    and quartered
Sea salt and black pepper

For the topping
40ml whole milk
40ml double cream

1 garlic clove, bruised
½ tsp black peppercorns
1 small onion, studded with
    4 cloves
1 bay leaf
1 tsp ground turmeric
½ tsp smoked hot paprika
750g floury potatoes, peeled
    and diced
75g butter
2 egg yolks

Saffron Fish Pie

Variations of fish pie are endless – but this one, imbued with smoky Madras curry powder, and with a sauce gilded with flecks of saffron in the most luxurious way, is my favourite by far. It's comforting and cosy, yet the flavours are impressive enough for entertaining. Use smoked fish if you like, but I much prefer the clean flavour of fresh fish with sweet chubby prawns and plenty of freshly chopped coriander.

· First make the topping. Put the milk and cream into a small saucepan and pop in the garlic, peppercorns, clove-studded onion, bay leaf, turmeric and paprika. Slowly bring to a simmer, then turn off the heat and leave to infuse while you get on with the potatoes.
· Preheat the oven to 200°C/Fan 180°C/Gas Mark 6.
· Bring a large saucepan of salted water to the boil, add the potatoes and cook until tender. Steam the spinach for the filling in a colander above the pan of potatoes until wilted, then allow to cool slightly and squeeze out any excess moisture with your hands. Chop roughly.
· Drain and mash the potatoes until smooth and lump-free. Beat in the butter and egg yolks. Strain the infused milk and cream, discarding the solids, then slowly pour into the mash and combine thoroughly.
· Heat the oil in a frying pan over low–medium heat. Add the onion, leek and celery and cook, stirring frequently, until pale and translucent. Add the garlic, curry powder and saffron and cook for a further 30 seconds, then pour in the cream and bring to the boil. Remove from the heat and stir in the cheese, lemon juice, coriander and salt and pepper to taste.
· Put the spinach, fish, prawns and eggs into a pie dish and pour over the sauce. Top with the mash and bake for 30 minutes until bubbling and golden on top. Serve at once.

12 scallops, shelled and
  roes removed
1 tbsp rapeseed oil
Ginger matchsticks, thinly
  sliced spring onions, crisp-
  fried shallots or onions,
  coriander sprigs and chilli
  oil (see page 108, or use
  shop-bought), to garnish

For the congee
1 tbsp rapeseed oil
4 fat garlic cloves, crushed
  to a paste
Large thumb of ginger,
  finely grated
350g basmati rice
750ml chicken stock
A few drops of sesame oil
Sea salt and white pepper

Roasted Scallops and Congee with Chilli Oil

*Congee is a savoury rice porridge that is cooked for so long that the grains
of rice disintegrate into a white, toothless slurry, and it makes the MOST
delicious comfort food. Eaten all over Asia, it is delightfully silky and creamy.
While it can be served plain, it is much improved with the addition of tender
swatches of meat or seafood, eggs, spring onions, chilli oil and shards of
ginger. It is hard to go wrong with this recipe, and because it is so gentle in
flavour it makes the perfect canvas for show-stopping ingredients like scallops
to hold their own.*

- To make the congee, heat a little oil in a saucepan over medium–high
  heat, add the garlic and ginger and stir-fry until fragrant. Add the rice,
  chicken stock and 2.5 litres of water, then bring to a simmer. Reduce
  the heat, half cover with a lid and simmer, stirring occasionally, until
  it has a porridge consistency – this will take 1–1½ hours, so it's the kind
  of thing you want to start in the afternoon to eat in the evening. Add the
  sesame oil and season to taste with salt and pepper.
- For the scallops, heat a cast-iron frying pan until it is almost smoking.
  Gently toss the scallops in the oil, season with salt and sear for about
  a minute, before turning and cooking on the other side for 30 seconds.
  The trick is to pan-fry the scallops long enough on the first side so they
  get a burnished, golden top.
- Ladle the congee into shallow bowls and put 3 scallops on top of each
  serving. Garnish with the ginger, spring onions, crispy shallots,
  coriander sprigs and a drizzle of chilli oil.

Fish Fry

1 poppadum
2 deep-fried unleavened bread
3 popular Indian sweet

The Indian penchant for deep-frying knows no bounds — it just makes everything taste so supremely good! Whether it's a *papad*,[1] *puri*[2] or *jalebi*[3] being immersed in hot oil, the result is crisp and dangerously more-ish.

In Nairobi, the long rains always brought with them a craving for the comfort of fried food, accompanied by steaming cups of heady masala chai. The minute guests crossed the threshold of our house, my mother would prop her large cast-iron *kadhai*[4] onto the stove and pour in a litre of oil.

4 wok
5 triangular savoury pastries filled with vegetables or meat
6 spicy deep-fried snacks of vegetables
7 spicy fritter-like snacks

Samosas,[5] *bhajias*[6] and *pakoras*[7] were the most popular deep-fried treats. For the latter, she would whip up a gram-flour batter tinged golden with turmeric and laced with spices, then deftly dip a variety of vegetables in the batter and into the hot oil, producing the most ethereally crunchy snacks. The last drips of batter would be mopped up with triangles of stale white bread, in a sort of spicy homage to the great British greasy spoon — this was always reserved for the cook and the cook's helper as a special treat.

The fryer became a hub around which friends and family would gather.

My mother presented each vegetable individually, like a gift, while chatting affably with everyone as, just like baby birds, they eagerly awaited the next titbit. Although the *fritti* were normally vegetarian, there were the odd occasions when we had little fish *pakoras* served with a fresh tomato and mint chutney. The batter clung to the fish, creating an artificial skin and insulating it from the direct heat of the oil, so the flesh cooked gently, almost steaming. These little parcels were everybody's favourite — irresistible with a squeeze of lime.

Deep-frying can be messy, but this can be mitigated by the simplest of measures: use a wide pot that is broad and deep, like a heavy-based saucepan or a well-made wok. Choose a good oil, such as groundnut or rapeseed, with a high smoke point, and do not overcrowd your pan. If you are not using a cook's thermometer, you must be confident with gauging the oil temperature using a cube of bread. Frying like this is an art and will give you an amazing crunch with no greasiness. You may not have complete success the first time, but as you master the technique, you'll soon be able to deep-fry fearlessly.

SAMAKI

Groundnut oil, for deep-frying
250g squid tubes, sliced
   into rings
12 tiger prawns, peeled and
   deveined, tails intact
400g firm white fish fillets,
   such as cod, haddock or
   pollack, cut into 2cm pieces
100g whitebait

For the chutney
2 tbsp ready-made mint sauce
2 tbsp tamarind concentrate
3 tomatoes, peeled, cut into
   quarters and seeds removed
¾ tsp sugar
Sea salt and black pepper, to taste

For the batter
100g chickpea (gram) flour
40g rice flour
1 tsp bicarbonate of soda
½ tsp sea salt

1 green chilli, finely chopped
2 tsp finely grated ginger
Handful of finely chopped
   coriander
¼ tsp ground turmeric
1 tsp ajwain seeds
1 tsp cumin seeds
1 tsp coriander seeds, toasted
   and lightly crushed
200ml ice-cold sparkling water
Ice cubes

A Sort of Indian Fritto Misto di Mare with Tomato, Tamarind and Mint Chutney

*I can never resist the charms of a 'fritto misto di mare' when it is on a menu –
this assortment of deep-fried seafood is eaten all over the Mediterranean,
usually with little more than a sprinkle of sea salt and a squeeze of lemon.
This version is encased in a batter inspired by my mother's fish pakoras.
It yields the most satisfying first course of crisp bite-sized morsels.*

·   To make the chutney, blend all the ingredients in a food processor until
    smooth. Set aside in a bowl.
·   For the batter, mix both flours and the bicarbonate of soda in a bowl.
    Stir in the salt, chilli, ginger, fresh coriander and all the spices. Whisk
    in the sparkling water, but do not overmix. Add a couple of cubes of ice.
·   Fill a deep saucepan a third full with the deep-frying oil and heat to
    180°C – if you don't have a thermometer, you will know the oil is ready
    when a cube of bread turns golden brown in 20 seconds. Working in
    batches, dip pieces of the seafood and fish into the batter, then carefully
    lower into the oil and deep-fry, turning occasionally, until golden brown
    and cooked through. Drain on kitchen paper. Allow the oil to return
    to temperature between batches.
·   Serve hot with the tomato, tamarind and mint chutney.

Keralan Crab-stuffed Courgette Flowers
with Coriander Chutney

Courgette flowers are the fragile precursors of courgettes. They are so remarkably striking that you'd barely believe they could offer anything to a recipe other than ethereal beauty, but they have a pleasingly subtle flavour and their petals make a handy pocket for stuffing all manner of lovely things, such as this gently spiced crab. Handle them with (metaphorical) kid gloves: remove the yellow stamens from the centre of the flowers carefully so as to avoid damaging the petals and, once stuffed, gently twist the petals together at the ends to contain the filling, making sure none is exposed. Eat these as soon as they are out of the fryer.

10 courgette flowers (male, if possible, as they are bigger)
100g plain flour, seasoned with salt, for dredging
Groundnut oil, for deep-frying
Sea salt and black pepper

For the chutney
1 tsp raw peanuts
½ tsp cumin seeds
2 tbsp frozen grated coconut, defrosted
1 large bunch of coriander, roughly chopped, stalks and all

1 green chilli, roughly chopped
Small thumb of ginger, finely grated
Caster sugar, sea salt and lime juice, to taste

For the stuffing
1 tbsp rapeseed oil
1 tsp brown mustard seeds
Pinch of asafoetida
15 curry leaves
½ tsp ground turmeric
Finely grated zest and juice of 1 lemon

Thumb of ginger, finely grated
1 red chilli, thinly sliced
250g white crabmeat
Handful of chopped coriander
50g frozen grated coconut, defrosted

For the batter
150g rice flour
¼ tsp baking powder
250ml ice-cold sparkling water

- To make the chutney, blitz the peanuts, cumin and coconut in a blender until smooth. Add the remaining ingredients and blend again, adding a little water to make a puree.
- For the stuffing, heat the rapeseed oil in a heavy-based frying pan over medium heat. Add the mustard seeds and, as soon as they start popping, sprinkle in the asafoetida and swiftly follow with the curry leaves. Fry for 5 seconds, then add the turmeric, lemon zest, ginger and chilli, stirring often, for 1–2 minutes or until fragrant. Add the crabmeat and coriander and mix well, seasoning to taste with salt and pepper. Take off the heat and stir in the lemon juice and coconut. Set aside to cool.
- Make a little cylinder of crab mixture and stuff into the centre of a courgette flower, then gently twist the petals together at the ends, making sure there is no exposed filling. Repeat with the rest of the crab mixture and courgette flowers.
- Make the batter just before you're ready to fry. Sift the rice flour and baking powder into a bowl and whisk in the sparkling water, being careful not to overmix. Roll each courgette flower in seasoned flour and then dip into the batter to coat lightly – you want a thin, delicate coating.
- Fill a large, heavy-based saucepan a third full with the deep-frying oil. Heat the oil to 180°C – if you don't have a thermometer, you will know the oil is ready when a cube of bread turns golden brown in 20 seconds. Carefully holding each courgette flower by the stem, dip its head into the oil for a few seconds to set the batter before releasing. Fry in batches until golden brown and crisp. Drain very well on kitchen paper, letting the oil return to temperature between batches.
- Serve immediately, with the chutney alongside.

16 scallops, on the half-shell
1 tsp rapeseed oil
1 tsp sesame oil
Sea salt

For the crispy 'seaweed'
150g kale
Groundnut oil, for deep-frying
½ tsp shichimi togarashi

For the avocado-yuzu puree
2 avocados
1 tbsp yuzu juice
1 tsp sambal oelek
    (or other Asian chilli sauce)

Pan-fried Scallops with Avocado-Yuzu Puree and Crispy 'Seaweed'

In their beautiful shells, scallops are among the most desired seafood. As with most luxurious ingredients, cooking them simply is often best: I especially love to grill them or sear them in a hot pan to intensify their flavour and give them a crisp, burnished exterior. I first made this dish for a dinner party one balmy summer's evening, and found the buttery lusciousness of avocado spiked with yuzu and chilli made an excellent partner for the sweet scallops.

- For the crispy 'seaweed', wash the kale and put through a salad spinner to make sure it is thoroughly dried. Cut out any tough stems, then roll up and shred very finely. Fill a large, heavy-based saucepan a third full with the deep-frying oil. Heat the oil to 180°C – if you don't have a thermometer, you will know the oil is ready when a cube of bread turns golden brown in 20 seconds. Briefly fry the kale, stirring constantly, until crisp. Drain well on kitchen paper, blotting away any excess oil if necessary. Season with salt and the shichimi togarashi and set aside.
- To make the avocado-yuzu puree, put all the ingredients in a blender with a little salt and blitz till smooth.
- Cut the scallops from their shells, but keep the half-shells for serving. Put a large frying pan over high heat and add the rapeseed and sesame oils. Season the scallops with salt, then add to the pan and cook for 2 minutes without moving them. Turn the scallops over and cook for a minute on the other side.
- To serve, spoon the avocado puree onto the half shells, then top with the scallops. Garnish with the 'seaweed' and serve straightaway.

2 skate wings
75g unsalted butter
1 tbsp rapeseed oil
1 heaped tbsp lime pickle,
    pounded with a pestle and
    mortar until smooth
Juice of 1 lemon

2 tbsp finely chopped coriander
Sea salt and black pepper

For the tempura samphire
2 sheets toasted nori
80g plain flour

1 heaped tbsp cornflour,
    plus extra for dredging
Ice-cold sparking water
Groundnut oil, for deep-frying
200g samphire

Skate with Lime Pickle Brown Butter, Tempura Samphire and Nori

*Skate has a beautifully refined flavour and all the springiness of lobster.
Its flat, diamond shape offers two fan-shaped fillets that look like ribbed angel
wings. It is one of the easiest fish to cook, as long as you cook it on the bone
to stop it falling apart. I always used to eat skate pan-fried and doused with
brown butter and capers, then this variation came about when I had no capers
to hand, so I reached for a jar of lime pickle instead. I have ONLY cooked it this
way ever since. The pickle adds both sharpness and saltiness, enhancing the
skate's delicate flesh. Serve with a pile of tempura samphire, as here – or simply
blanch the samphire in boiling water, drain well and then pan-fry in butter.*

· Preheat the oven to 110°C/Fan 90°C/Gas Mark ¼.
· Rinse the skate wings and dry thoroughly with kitchen paper, then
  season with salt and pepper. Melt 25g of the butter and the rapeseed oil
  in a large frying pan. When the butter is sizzling, add the skate wings,
  fleshier side down, and fry for 5 minutes until the flesh is opaque and
  the skin is golden brown. Gently flip over and cook on the less-fleshy
  side for 3 minutes. Transfer to a baking tray and keep warm in the oven.
· Wipe out the frying pan, add the remaining butter and melt over high
  heat. When it starts to go brown, quickly stir in the lime pickle and follow
  with the lemon juice. Take off the heat and stir through the coriander.
· For the tempura samphire, using scissors, cut the nori into pieces and
  blitz to a powder in a blender or spice mill. Tip into a large bowl, add
  both flours and mix well. Gradually whisk in just enough sparkling water
  to make a thin batter, being careful not to overmix. Fill a large, heavy-
  based saucepan a third full with the deep-frying oil. Heat the oil to 180°C
  – if you don't have a thermometer, you will know the oil is ready when
  a cube of bread turns golden brown in 20 seconds. Working in batches,
  dredge the samphire in cornflour, then dip in the batter and deep-fry in
  the hot oil for about 3 minutes or until crisp and golden, allowing the oil
  to return to temperature between batches. Drain on kitchen paper.
· Put the fish onto serving plates and spoon over the lime pickle brown
  butter. Serve with the tempura samphire.

Kuku na Nyama

Poultry and Meat

My paternal grandmother Ranjit Kaur, who we lovingly called *mama*,[1] had married early and married well. She wore a stack of gold bangles and a prominent pendant to announce to the world that her husband was a man of means. Even without all the gilt, she was noticeable – at four and a half feet tall, she was a whisper to my grandfather's six feet. She was portly and round and, in shadow, it was hard to tell if she was facing you or standing in profile. She slicked her hair with coconut oil that stained and fragranced her pillow, and she wore pale austere colours. She had a reputation as a battle-axe, and was devout, superstitious and ritualistic in equal measure. I simply adored her.

Mama always rose at dawn and bustled about, getting ready for prayers in the small temple my grandfather had built on the upper floor of our house. She'd pleasure the air with incense, light *diyas*[2] made from cotton-wool wicks dipped in ghee, mumble her prayers at speed and screech *shabads*[3] to the oompah of the old harmonium. Three times a day she'd lay out a platter of fruit or *prashaad*[4] for God to bless and eat.

God had the power to answer prayers, but he also had an appetite,

and *mama* never ate a meal without feeding him first. A baptised Sikh, my grandmother never ate meat. She believed that indulging in animal flesh fed and fanned our beastlier instincts and desires, though for a woman who had never so much as cracked an egg, she had quite the frightful, snarling temper in an argument. As the steely matriarch she had strict rules that nobody dared challenge: food, as much as possible, should be homemade; eating restaurant food or fast food was frowned upon; beef was forbidden; no alcohol or meat was to be consumed on religious days or on saints' days, which were every Tuesday and Sunday. Any meat-guzzling on those days was done covertly by my father and uncle, who were staunch carnivores, at Hashmi Barbeque or the aptly named Carnivore in Langata. Still, my grandmother could sniff out ripe animal odour or beer stench at ten paces, and there was always an ugly fight, followed by a fire-and-brimstone lecture as they digested their *nyama choma*[5] and whisky dinner.

Given her anti-meat stance, most of the food we ate at home was vegetarian, and it was always delicious. Chickpeas cooked with a hint of *anardana*,[6] *kadhi*,[7] *sarson ka saag*,[8] which sweltered all day on the *jiko*,[9] *maragwe*[10] and all manner of lentils – *maha*,[11] *masoor*,[12] *moong*,[13] *toor*,[14] all garnished with heart-clogging amounts of butter. On meat days, we enjoyed silky *keema*,[15] made rich with tobacco-smoky black cardamom, *murgh mussalam*,[16] stuffed with mince and boiled eggs, and intense curries of goat with marrow-rich bones. There were barbecues too, where *seekh kebabs*[17] and goat *mishkaki*[18] were rolled in doughy naan and eaten like sandwiches.

Sundays were for socialising, and there was always a party to attend. I'd seethe with resentment as I passed up

plates of tandoori chicken, glistening with ghee,

for *aloo tikkis*[19] under my granny's watchful, judgy eye. Still, I am eternally grateful to her for setting an ideal that has only recently gripped the conscience of those of us who are seeking healthier, more sustainable and environmentally sound diets. While I rarely skip a Sunday roast (sorry, *mama*), my diet remains mainly vegetarian, and when I do buy meat, I try to look for the most humane choices. Yes, organic and free-range costs more, but it means I buy and eat less of it that way. I never ate a Happy Meal as a child (despite my protestations), but as an adult I certainly never want to eat an unhappy one!

1 Swahili for mother	10 Kenyan kidney beans
2 lamps	11 black gram
3 religious songs	12 split red lentils
4 semolina halva	13 green gram
5 barbecued meat	14 split red gram
6 pomegranate powder	15 minced lamb
7 buttercup-yellow gram-flour and yoghurt curry	16 Mughal-style whole roast and stuffed chicken
8 Punjabi dish of stewed mustard greens	17 minced lamb kebabs
	18 barbecued meat skewers
9 outdoor coal stove	19 spicy potato cakes

4 quail, spatchcocked
225g giant couscous (maftoul)
500g watermelon
1 tsp rosewater, plus
    a few drops extra
60g pomegranate seeds
50g chopped pistachios
Handful of mint leaves, torn
Handful of chopped parsley

1 tsp sumac
1 tbsp pomegranate molasses
60ml extra virgin olive oil
100g feta cheese, crumbled
Sea salt and black pepper

For the marinade
1 tbsp rapeseed or groundnut oil
5 tbsp pomegranate molasses

1 tbsp clear honey
1 tsp ground allspice
1 tsp coriander seeds,
    lightly crushed
1 tsp ground cinnamon
1 tsp ground ginger
2 garlic cloves, crushed

Pomegranate Quail with Giant Couscous, Feta and Rose Watermelon

While most people are happy to feast on quail at restaurants, they would rarely think of cooking it at home. But if you can roast a chicken, quail should be no problem at all, and it is ready to serve in a quarter of the time. The meat is delicious, more deeply flavoured than most chicken, and it can wear any flavour profile from Middle Eastern to Asian with panache. In this recipe, it is sticky with pomegranate molasses and fragrantly spiced like the Arabian nights.

· Make the marinade by mixing together all the ingredients. Smear over the quail and leave to marinate in the fridge for at least 1 hour, but the longer the better – overnight is ideal.
· Meanwhile, cook the giant couscous in a saucepan of boiling salted water for about 10 minutes (or according to the instructions on the packet), then drain and set aside to cool.
· Cut the watermelon into 2cm cubes, sprinkle over the rosewater and leave to infuse.
· Fluff up the cooled couscous with a fork and mix in the pomegranate seeds, pistachios, herbs, sumac and season with salt and pepper. Whisk together the pomegranate molasses and olive oil to emulsify, then stir through the couscous. Scatter over the feta.
· Preheat the oven to 200°C/Fan 180°C/Gas Mark 6. To cook the quail, heat a griddle pan until very hot and sear the quail, skin side down, for 3–4 minutes or until crisp and well browned, then turn and cook on the other side for 2 minutes. Transfer to the oven and roast for 8–10 minutes or until cooked through.
· Remove the quail from the oven and sprinkle with a little extra rosewater, then cover with foil and leave to rest for 5 minutes. Serve with the couscous and rosewater-infused watermelon.

Chicken

I did not have the sort of childhood where meat came wrapped in neat packages that concealed the violence committed on the diner's behalf. Growing up surrounded by goats and chickens, animal slaughter was plain to see, and I understood there wasn't anything savage about the act. I once watched John, our house helper, chase a clutch of chickens, catch and tuck one under his arm, and decapitate it with one swoop of his *fanga*.[1] I looked from his bloody hands to the chicken's head, which had landed next to my shiny patent-leather Mary Janes, its eye resembling a tiny dark bead. My stomach fluttered a little… in anticipation of my mother's chicken curry.

1 machette

Chicken, in its many manifestations, has always found a way onto my plate. I have fond memories of family trips to the Bellevue drive-in cinema. All of us children would be crammed into the back of my father's Citroen, eating tandoori chicken from a downtown Nairobi joint called Minar, which has long since closed its doors, sadly. The meat was as tender as the night, spicy enough to fill your eyes with tears, but cleverly cooled down by a yoghurt with a pouring consistency and a sweet-and-sour date and tamarind chutney.

There was also the occasional treat of kikapu chicken (fried chicken in a basket) at Carnivore restaurant — no fried chicken I have tried since can shine a light to its off-the-Richter-scale crunch.

Then there was my mother's repertoire of homemade curries and spicy roast birds, and at Eid a delicately fragrant tray of chicken biryani that our genial Pakistani neighbours shared with us.

Chickens have had a pretty rough ride. They look and sound comical and have no natural defences against wily foxes or hungry people. As meat, they are often seen as the bland option, but they are just about the perfect creature to roast and devour whole. A good-quality chicken should have a slightly gamier flavour and needs little more than salt, butter and heat, but its tender meat also makes the perfect blank slate for skilled cooks to flavour any way they like.

KUKU NA NYAMA

There may not be anything pioneering about poultry, but it's almost impossible to tire of it and the zillion ways you can make it truly delicious. Importantly, if you don't want to waste a scrap (and you shouldn't, as good chickens aren't cheap), keep the carcass to gently simmer for a few hours, along with some chicken wings and vegetables such as fennel, carrots and celery, to make a golden savoury broth that you can make a multitude of soups with. And if you are pan-frying it, don't discard the golden fat it leaves in your pan. With skin-on and bone-in thighs or breasts, render the fat over medium heat without moving them – this will take some time and you'll have to be patient, but your reward will be a pool of deeply flavourful fat in the bottom of your pan that you can use for cooking potatoes, beans or croutons.

Kikapu Chicken with Plantain Chips

The best fried chicken I have ever had the pleasure of knowing was the one I had as an occasional Sunday treat in my childhood, at Carnivore restaurant in Nairobi. The juicy, dark, almost gamy meat came with a crisp and craggy crust and a subtle hit of spice that made you gnaw it right down to the brittle bones. I always washed it down with a Krest bitter lemon (I may have been the only child in the world who enjoyed the slightly medicinal flavour of bitter lemon — the gateway to a healthy appreciation of Negronis in adulthood). It came served in a kikapu — a woven basket. This is exactly how we serve it at Jikoni now: it's nostalgia in a basket. I haven't managed to get my mitts on Carnivore's secret recipe, but this one makes a pretty honourable contender. The buttermilk tenderises the meat and leaves it juicy and succulent, while the addition of crushed cornflakes in the crust adds a hefty crunch. Serve with a green salad or some colcolaw.

1 × 284ml tub buttermilk
3 garlic cloves, crushed
1 tsp mustard powder
¼ tsp cayenne pepper
1 tsp smoked sweet paprika
1 tbsp dried oregano
2 stalks of rosemary, leaves picked
8 bone-in chicken thighs, skin on
Groundnut oil, for deep-frying
Sea salt and black pepper

For the crust
350g plain flour
125g cornflakes, crushed
50g cornflour
2 tbsp garlic powder
1 tbsp onion powder
1 tbsp sea salt
1 tbsp sweet paprika
1 tsp cayenne pepper
½ tsp freshly ground black pepper

For the chips
4 green (unripe) plantains
1 tsp sea salt
½ tsp garlic powder
½ tsp chilli powder
½ tsp ground coriander
1 tsp ground cinnamon

- In a large bowl, mix the buttermilk with the garlic, mustard powder, cayenne, paprika, oregano and rosemary, and season well with salt and pepper. Add the chicken thighs, making sure they are completely covered. Refrigerate for at least half an hour, but preferably overnight. The buttermilk will help to tenderise the meat and the spices will really penetrate its flesh.
- To make the crust, simply mix all the ingredients together in a bowl.
- For the chips, cut the plantains into 2cm-thick slices on the diagonal. Boil in a saucepan of salted water until the edges are giving way, then drain and dry well. Cool and refrigerate until you are ready to fry.
- Preheat the oven to 200°C/Fan 180°C/Gas Mark 6.
- Fill a large, heavy-based saucepan a third full with the deep-frying oil. Heat the oil to 180°C – if you don't have a thermometer, you will know the oil is ready when a cube of bread turns golden brown in 20 seconds.
- Working in batches, lift the chicken thighs from the spiced buttermilk and roll in the cornflake mix, then fry for 7 minutes, or until golden and crisp, allowing the oil to return to temperature between batches. Drain on kitchen paper, then transfer to a baking tray and bake for 7 minutes.
- Meanwhile, deep-fry the plantain chips in the hot oil until golden and tender – this should take around 5 minutes. In a small bowl, combine all the remaining ingredients for the plantain fries to make a spice mix. Drain the chips on kitchen paper, then season with the spice mix. Serve at once with the chicken. Baskets optional!

800g bone-in, skin-on chicken
  breasts or thighs
6 tbsp olive oil
1 heaped tsp harissa
3 flatbreads, roughly torn
  into 2cm pieces
2 heads cos lettuce, torn into
  large pieces

Handful of parsley leaves
Handful of coriander leaves
2 small preserved lemons,
  rind only, finely chopped
100g feta cheese
100g pitted black olives
Sea salt and black pepper

For the dressing
Small handful of roughly
  chopped parsley
Handful of roughly chopped
  coriander
1 garlic clove, finely grated
Juice of 1 lemon, or to taste
40g tahini
40ml extra virgin olive oil
2 tbsp Greek yoghurt

Roast Chicken Salad with Chicken-fat Croutons and Green Tahini Dressing

Think of this salad as a sort of North African take on a Caesar salad. What makes it extra special is the punchy herb-laced tahini dressing and the chicken fat and harissa flatbread croutons – it's worth cooking it just for those!

- Heat the oven to 190°C/Fan 170°C/Gas Mark 5.
- Season the chicken generously with salt and pepper. Heat 1 tablespoon of the olive oil in a large cast-iron frying pan over medium heat. Add the chicken, skin side down, and cook without moving for 8 minutes or until golden brown and crisp. Turn the chicken and cook for another 8 minutes until it is browned on the other side. Remove the chicken with tongs and put on a plate. Add the harissa to the chicken fat and juices in the pan, along with another 2 tablespoons of the olive oil, and swirl around so the harissa amalgamates with the oil.
- Toss the flatbread into the pan, tossing it through the juices. Put the chicken back in the pan and roast in the oven for 15 minutes until it is cooked through and the croutons are golden brown and crisp.
- Meanwhile make the dressing. Place the parsley and coriander in a blender, along with the garlic, lemon juice and tahini, and whizz to a smooth paste. With the blender running, drizzle in the extra virgin olive oil. Transfer to a bowl and then fold in the yoghurt. Season to taste with salt and pepper.
- Place the lettuce, herbs and preserved lemon on a platter and dress with some of the green tahini dressing. Crumble over the feta and scatter with the olives. Drizzle over the remaining 3 tablespoons of olive oil.
- Remove the chicken from the oven and let it rest for a few minutes, then slice it off the bone and place on top of the salad, along with the croutons. Serve with more dressing on the side.

6 poussins, spatchcocked
3 tbsp rapeseed oil

For the marinade
Large thumb of ginger, grated
5 garlic cloves
2 lemongrass stalks, sliced
Large handful of roughly chopped
  coriander, leaves and stalks
50g light brown sugar or
  palm sugar
250ml light soy sauce

For the dressing
½ red chilli, finely chopped
1 garlic clove, grated
Small thumb of ginger,
  finely grated
1 tbsp clear honey
2 tbsp fish sauce
2 tbsp light soy sauce
2 tbsp groundnut or rapeseed oil
A few drops of sesame oil
Juice of 1 lime
1 tbsp rice vinegar
1 small shallot or ½ red onion,
  finely chopped

For the salad
2 red bird's eye chillies, finely chopped
1 garlic clove
2 tbsp soft brown sugar
2 tbsp fish sauce
2 tbsp rice vinegar
2 tbsp lime juice
3 green (unripe) mangoes, peeled
  and cut into matchsticks
100g mixed cherry tomatoes
1 small red onion, very thinly sliced
Handful of Thai basil leaves
Handful of coriander leaves
Handful of mint leaves, torn
75g peanuts, roughly crushed

Lemongrass Poussin with Green Mango and Peanut Salad

This wildly flavourful roast poussin is inspired by the fragrant and punchy flavours of Thailand. If the weather permits, throw it on the barbecue and cook it in the seductive plumes of its smoke. Serve with steamed jasmine rice.

- To make the marinade, put the ginger, garlic, lemongrass, coriander and sugar in a food processor and blitz to a paste. Transfer to a large bowl and stir in the soy sauce. Add the poussins and massage well, using your fingers to gently loosen the skin so you can get some of the marinade underneath it. Cover and leave in the fridge for 2 hours or overnight.
- Take the poussins out of the marinade and set aside. Strain the marinade into a saucepan and bring it to the boil, then let it bubble and reduce for about 10 minutes until you have a lovely glaze.
- Preheat the oven to 200°C/Fan 180°C/Gas Mark 6.
- Pour the oil into a large ovenproof frying pan over medium–high heat, add the poussins and fry, skin side down, until crisp and well browned. Brush over the glaze, then transfer to the oven and roast for 30–45 minutes, glazing again halfway through the cooking time.
- Meanwhile, make the dressing by shaking together all the ingredients in a screwtop jar. For the salad, use a mortar and pestle to pound the chillies, garlic and sugar to a smooth paste. Stir in the fish sauce, vinegar, lime juice and 2 tablespoons of warm water. Taste and adjust the flavours as necessary with more sugar, fish sauce, vinegar or lime juice until you have that classic Thai balance of hot, sweet, salty and sour, then transfer to a large bowl. Lightly pound the mango with the pestle and mortar to tenderise, then add to the bowl and pour in the dressing. Crush the tomatoes with the mortar and pestle, then add to the bowl, along with the red onion. Just before serving, add the herbs, toss to combine and scatter with the peanuts. Serve the poussins with the salad on the side.

1 tbsp ghee
1 red onion, finely chopped
Thumb of ginger, finely grated
4 garlic cloves, crushed
2 green chillies, finely chopped
1 tsp ground turmeric
100g chopped tinned tomatoes
6 chicken drumsticks
400ml coconut milk
Juice of 1 lime

Piece of lump charcoal – optional
2 hard-boiled eggs, shelled
   and cut in half
Sea salt
Small handful of chopped
   coriander, to serve

For the masala
2 tbsp coriander seeds
2 tbsp cumin seeds

1 tbsp fennel seeds
1 dried red chilli
1 tsp green cardamom pods
¼ tsp cloves
1 star anise
1 tsp black peppercorns
1 cinnamon stick
1 tsp hot paprika
1 tsp ground ginger
¼ nutmeg, finely grated

Kuku Paka

This is an East African–Indian hybrid of a chicken curry that has its roots in coastal Mombasa, a port on the Indian Ocean where many immigrants from India, the Middle East and other parts of Africa arrived. My own grandfather was one of those immigrants who came in search of better prospects in the 1940s.

Kuku paka is now an iconic dish eaten in homes all over Kenya. Every family has their own version of it – the spices differ and some may not include tomatoes – but what they all share is the use of coconut milk in all its weighty creaminess. Here is my version. I smoke it after cooking, to recreate the memory of eating it cooked over a coal 'jiko' (outdoor stove). Serve with saffron rice.

- Begin by making the masala. Heat a dry frying pan over medium heat and toast all the whole spices until they are aromatic, stirring frequently and being careful not to scorch them. Pop the spices into a spice grinder and whizz to a fine powder. Stir in the paprika, ginger and nutmeg.
- Put the ghee in a large frying pan over low heat. Add the onion and cook, stirring occasionally, for about 20 minutes or until dark and caramelised, then add the ginger, garlic and chillies and fry until fragrant. Next add 2 tablespoons of the masala and the turmeric and cook for a few minutes until your kitchen is full of the fragrance of the spices. Now tip in the tomatoes and season with salt. Cook for 10 minutes, then add the chicken and coconut milk. Mix well, then cover and simmer for 25 minutes or until the chicken is tender and toothsome. Squeeze in the lime juice.
- If you want to smoke the dish, sit the piece of charcoal directly on a gas burner or barbecue, letting it catch light and burn. When it is smouldering and grey, use tongs to carefully transfer it to a small heatproof bowl. Nestle the bowl inside the pan with the chicken and drizzle a little oil over the charcoal – it will start smoking immediately. Cover the pan with a tight-fitting lid and leave to smoke for half an hour.
- Serve the kuku paka topped with hard-boiled egg halves and scattered with chopped coriander.

2 tbsp rapeseed oil
1 stem of curry leaves, picked
3 heaped tbsp chickpea
    (gram) flour
400ml coconut milk
1 red chilli, thickly sliced
750g boneless, skinless
    chicken thighs, cut into
    bite-sized pieces
2 tbsp fish sauce
1 tbsp soft brown sugar
Juice of 1 lime
500g dried flat rice noodles

For the curry paste
5 dried Kashmiri chillies
1½ tbsp coriander seeds
2 tsp cumin seeds
½ tsp black peppercorns
½ tsp ground turmeric
5 fat garlic cloves, roughly
    chopped
Large thumb of ginger, roughly
    chopped
1 green bird's eye chilli,
    roughly chopped
2 small red onions, roughly
    chopped
1 tbsp cashew nuts

For the garnishes
Medium-boiled eggs, shelled
Finely chopped coriander
Crisp-fried shallots or onions
Garlic cloves, thinly sliced and
    deep-fried until golden
Green chillies, finely sliced
    and steeped in rice vinegar
Roasted peanuts, roughly crushed
Lime wedges
Crisp noodles (sev)
Thinly sliced spring onions
Beansprouts
Chilli oil

Indian-style Khao Suey

Khao suey is simply rapture in a bowl. This Burmese noodle soup of hot coconut broth, springy noodles and a madness of garnishes — from boiled eggs to peanuts or crispy shallots — is hugely popular in India due to its trading history with Burma. The versions cooked in Indian households, like this one, are not always authentically Burmese. The broth can be made with poultry, vegetables and tofu or seafood such as prawns, and it makes for extremely satisfying slurping.

· Begin with the curry paste. Toast the Kashmiri chillies, coriander and cumin seeds and peppercorns in a dry frying pan over medium heat until fragrant. Tip into a blender and blitz to a fine powder. Add the turmeric, garlic, ginger, bird's eye chilli, onions and cashew nuts and blend, adding just enough water to give you a smooth curry paste.

· Heat the oil in a large saucepan over low heat and scatter in the curry leaves. Fry briefly, then add the curry paste and cook, stirring constantly, for about 10–15 minutes until it smells rich and is darker in colour. Next add the chickpea flour and stir for 5–6 minutes to cook out its rawness. Whisk in 250ml of water to get rid of any lumps, then add the coconut milk, red chilli and another 250ml of water. Bring to the boil and then reduce the heat to low and let it simmer for 10 minutes.

· Now add the chicken and simmer for 10–15 minutes or until cooked through and tender. Season with the fish sauce, sugar and lime juice and set aside while you cook the noodles according to the instructions on the packet.

· To serve, half-fill six large bowls with noodles, then top with the chicken and broth. Finish with garnishes of your choice — I like all of them!

Duck and Pistachio Pierogi with Hot Yoghurt Sauce and Pul Biber Butter

As Jikoni has evolved and our wonderful team has grown, they have had the opportunity to influence the menu with their own culinary heritage. This recipe came about when I asked one of our chefs from Poland to teach me to make pierogi. At the time we stuffed the pierogi with freshly made paneer and served them with a Turkish-inspired yoghurt sauce, but I later developed this rich confit duck version. Admittedly, the recipe is time-consuming (if you want to skip a step, you could just shred the meat from ready-made confit duck legs for the filling), but the results are totally worth it. It mixes three traditions — French, Polish and Turkish — and it is exactly the kind of border-blending dish the restaurant has become well known for.

50g butter
1 heaped tbsp Turkish pepper
   flakes (pul biber)
1 heaped tbsp dried mint
Finely grated zest of 1 lemon
2 tbsp pine nuts
Sea salt and black pepper

For the duck confit
4 duck legs
1 tsp coriander seeds
1 tsp cumin seeds
1 tsp allspice berries
50g sea salt
3 sprigs of rosemary
1 whole garlic bulb, halved
   crossways
500g duck fat
2 bay leaves
1 tsp black peppercorns

For the filling
1 tbsp rapeseed oil
1 onion, finely chopped
3 garlic cloves, finely chopped
1 tsp ground cinnamon
1 tsp ground allspice
2 tbsp very finely chopped
   pistachios
2 tbsp golden raisins, finely
   chopped
40ml double cream
Handful of finely chopped mint

For the pierogi dough
700g plain flour
50g butter, melted and
   cooled slightly
80g soured cream
Pinch of salt
1 egg, lightly beaten
About 200ml warm water

For the sauce
1 tbsp rapeseed oil
1 onion, finely chopped
2 garlic cloves, finely chopped
500ml hot chicken or vegetable
   stock
500g Greek yoghurt
1 egg, beaten
40g plain flour, mixed with
   40ml water to make a paste

- The day before, start on the duck confit. Place the duck legs in a bowl. Put the coriander and cumin seeds and the allspice berries in a dry frying pan and toast until slightly coloured and aromatic. Tip into a mortar and crush lightly with the pestle, then stir in the salt. Rub all over the duck, then add the rosemary and garlic to the bowl, cover and marinate in the fridge for 24 hours, turning three or four times.
- Next day, preheat the oven to 150°C/Fan 130°C/Gas Mark 2. Pat the duck dry with kitchen paper, then put into a heavy-based flameproof casserole and cover with the duck fat. Add the bay leaves and peppercorns and cook in the oven for about 3½ hours, or until the meat is falling off the bones.
- Meanwhile, make the pierogi dough. Pile the flour onto a clean work surface. Make a well in the centre and add the butter, soured cream, salt and egg. Start flicking in the flour, first with a fork and then using your hands, bringing everything together until you have a crumble. Start adding the warm water, a little at a time, kneading well and adding just enough water to give you a smooth, elastic dough. Put the dough into a clean bowl, cover with a damp tea towel and set aside to rest for at least half an hour, or up to 4 hours.

- To make the filling, lift the duck legs out of the fat using tongs, pull away the skin and discard it, then finely shred the tender meat. Pour off the duck fat and wipe out the casserole. Set the casserole over medium heat, pour in the oil and fry the onion until golden brown. Add the garlic and cook, stirring, until fragrant, then follow with the cinnamon and allspice and fry briefly for another minute. Now fold in the shredded duck, pistachios and raisins, then pour in the cream and season with salt and pepper to taste. Cook for a further 3 minutes, then take off the heat and stir in the mint. Tip into a bowl and leave to cool.
- For the sauce, put the oil in a saucepan over low heat and sweat the onion until soft but not brown. Add the garlic and fry, stirring, until fragrant, then pour in the stock and bring to a simmer. In a bowl, mix together the yoghurt, egg and flour paste. Add a ladleful of the hot stock to the bowl and stir to combine, then pour into the pan. Whisk constantly until it just comes to a simmer – do not let it boil or it will curdle.
- Take half the pierogi dough and roll it out until it is 2mm thick, then use a 5cm round cutter to cut out circles of dough. Repeat with the other half of the dough. Place 1½ teaspoons of the filling on each circle of dough, then gently fold the dough over to form a semi-circle. Pinch the edges of the pierogi to seal, then press with the prongs of a fork.
- At this point the pierogi can be frozen for up to 4 weeks, refrigerated overnight, or cooked right away in a large stockpot of boiling salted water. Only cook about 10 at a time, so they have room to float without sticking. The exact cooking time will vary, depending on whether the pierogi are fresh or frozen – but if you give them 4 minutes from when they float to the surface, they'll be done perfectly.
- While the pierogi are cooking, make the pul biber butter. Melt the butter in a small frying pan over low heat and, when it is foaming, add the Turkish pepper flakes, mint and lemon zest. Cook until the butter has turned nutty brown, then add the pine nuts and remove from the heat.
- Gently reheat the sauce, taking care that it doesn't boil.
- Drain the pierogi and put into a serving bowl. Spoon over the yoghurt sauce and drizzle with the pul biber butter. Serve at once.

4 duck legs
400ml coconut milk
3 tsp palm sugar, or to taste
2 tbsp fish sauce
Juice of 1 lime

For the curry paste
15 dried Kashmiri chillies
15 dried bird's eye chillies
1 red onion, roughly chopped
50g ginger, roughly chopped
25g galangal, roughly chopped
4 fat garlic cloves, roughly chopped

2 stalks lemongrass,
    roughly chopped
8g fresh turmeric,
    roughly chopped
3 tsp shrimp paste
2 tbsp rapeseed oil

Duck Rendang

Rendang is an aromatic, dry braised curry from Malaysia. It is normally made with tough cuts of beef that require lengthy cooking, but I like to use duck legs, which also become luscious with a long, slow braise. The duck is first seared to render any excess fat and then simmered for hours in a lip-tingling chilli-spiced coconut sauce that turns the meat into a meltingly tender, flavourful sludge. Serve with steamed rice.

· First make the curry paste. Break up the chillies and soak in hot water for 2 hours, then drain. Roughly chop the chillies and put into a small food processor or blender, along with the onion, ginger, galangal, garlic, lemongrass, turmeric, shrimp paste and oil. Process to a coarse paste.
· Heat a large, deep non-stick frying pan over medium–high heat. Add the duck legs, skin side down, and fry, without turning, until the fat renders and the skin is golden brown, about 2–4 minutes.
· Set the duck legs aside, reserving 1 tablespoon of the fat in pan. Add the curry paste and fry over medium heat, stirring constantly, until the colour deepens and the onion becomes fragrant – it will take around 10 minutes to cook out the rawness of it and tease out all the flavours. Add the coconut milk and 375ml of water and bring to a simmer. Add the duck legs and return to a simmer, then reduce the heat to low, cover and simmer gently for 1½ hours, stirring occasionally, until the duck is very tender and the sauce is thick and deepened in colour.
· Finally, add the palm sugar to the sauce, stirring to make sure it all dissolves, then stir in the fish sauce and lime juice.

4 goose legs
3 tbsp ghee
2 red onions, thinly sliced
into crescents
6 tbsp yoghurt
3 tbsp double cream
Pinch of saffron threads,
crushed and steeped in
2 tbsp warm water

¼ tsp garam masala
A few drops of kewra water
(screwpine essence) – optional
Toasted flaked almonds, crisp-
fried shallots and chopped
coriander, to garnish

For the curry paste
30g almonds, soaked in hot
water for at least 1 hour
or overnight
1 tbsp coriander seeds
1 tsp chopped red chilli
1 red onion, roughly chopped
5 garlic cloves, roughly chopped

Goose Leg Qorma

Qorma tends to be dismissed as a safe curry option for those who are spice-shy, but in fact its history is as rich as its sauce. It once graced the tables of the Mughal emperors and was famed for its use of luxurious ingredients, such as cream, nuts and expensive spices. This version, cooked with the rich meat of goose legs, takes it back to its days of pomp and circumstance, and a final dash of kewra water makes the dish opulently fragrant. Serve with rice or naan.

· First make the curry paste. Drain the almonds and slip them out of their skins. Put into a food processor or blender, together with the coriander seeds, chilli, onion and garlic, and whizz to a paste. (You could also do this using a pestle and mortar.)

· Heat a large, non-stick saucepan over medium–high heat and fry the goose legs in two batches, skin side down, without turning, until the fat renders and the skin is golden brown. Remove the goose legs from the pan and set aside.

· Pour off the fat from the pan and wipe it out. Add the ghee and fry the onions over low heat until they are soft and golden brown. Remove from the pan using a slotted spoon and set aside.

· Now add the curry paste to the pan and cook slowly, stirring constantly, until it is sticky and caramelised. Add the goose legs and stir to coat with the curry paste, then add just enough water to cover. Put a lid on the pan and braise over very low heat until they are tender – this should take around 1½ hours.

· Briefly whisk the yoghurt, then add to the pan, along with the fried onions. Keep cooking until the sauce is dry and sticky, then add the cream, saffron and garam masala – and the kewra water, if using. Garnish with toasted flaked almonds, crispy shallots and chopped coriander.

500g turnips, peeled and
  quartered
3 tbsp rapeseed oil
2 tbsp ghee
1 cinnamon stick, broken up
1 bay leaf
8 green cardamom pods, bruised
2 black cardamom pods, bruised

2 red onions, finely chopped
5 garlic cloves, finely chopped
Thumb of ginger, finely grated
2 tsp Kashmiri chilli powder
1 tsp ground turmeric
1 heaped tsp ground fennel
2 tsp ground coriander
1½ tsp hot paprika

1kg lamb shoulder, cut into
  bite-sized chunks
200g blitzed tinned tomatoes
  or passata
Sea salt and black pepper
Chopped coriander, to garnish

Shalgam Gosht

*A sturdy bowl of this Kashmiri curry is the solace I seek in late autumn,
when there are wet winds and fallen leaves. Lamb and turnips may not
seem like a classic pairing, but their marriage is far lovelier than you would
expect. Turnips have a dowdy reputation but, once cooked, they offer a sweet,
uncomplicated pleasure that is very underrated. The spicy sauce here adds
some friction to the union of two otherwise mellow mates. Serve with rice or
hot buttered chapattis or parathas.*

· Put the turnips in a colander, sprinkle over 1 teaspoon of salt and
  massage in well. Leave for 1 hour, then rinse thoroughly and pat dry with
  kitchen paper.
· Heat the oil in a frying pan over medium heat and fry the turnips until
  they are golden brown all over. Drain on kitchen paper.
· In a large, heavy pot, melt the ghee over low–medium heat and add the
  cinnamon stick, bay leaf and black and green cardamom pods. Fry,
  stirring constantly, until fragrant, then add the onions and turn down
  the heat to low. Fry the onions for 15 minutes or until they are well
  caramelised and sticky, then add the garlic and ginger. Fry, stirring
  frequently, until the ginger and garlic have softened, then add the chilli
  powder, turmeric, fennel, coriander and paprika and keep frying for
  another 2 minutes.
· Now add the meat and stir well, then cover and cook for 10 minutes.
  The meat will start to release its juices. Take off the lid and cook over low
  heat, taking the time to really turn the meat so it sears all over and the
  spices get properly cooked. Pour in the blitzed tomatoes or passata and
  season well with salt and pepper. Pour in 300ml of water, cover and leave
  to simmer for 45 minutes.
· Finally add the turnips, cover again and cook for 10–15 minutes or until
  the turnips and the meat are tender. Garnish with coriander and serve.

Massaman Pork and Peanut Curry with Pineapple Relish

Thai curries do not have to be searingly hot. The mild massaman curry, traditionally belonging to the Thai Muslim community, is often given to Thai children before they take their chilli stabilisers off. Aromatic spices from the Indian subcontinent are mixed with fragrant Thai ingredients to make a powerfully addictive dish. It is generally made with beef or lamb, but is equally good with pork, chicken or robust vegetables such as pumpkin. This one always tastes even better the next day, so I tend to make it a day in advance. Serve with steamed jasmine rice.

1 tbsp coconut oil
1kg diced pork neck
1 star anise
3 green cardamom pods
A few curry leaves
1 cinnamon stick, broken up
300ml coconut milk
3 potatoes, peeled and diced
3 shallots, peeled and halved
1 tbsp fish sauce
2 tbsp tamarind concentrate
1 tbsp palm sugar
Handful of roasted peanuts
Sprigs of Thai basil, to garnish

For the curry paste
4 dried Kashmiri chillies
2 tsp coriander seeds
2 tsp cumin seeds
7 green cardamom pods
1 cinnamon stick
1 star anise
1 tbsp rapeseed oil
2 banana shallots, roughly
  chopped
6 garlic cloves, roughly chopped
1 tsp shrimp paste
100ml coconut milk
2 lemongrass stalks, roughly
  chopped
Thumb of ginger, roughly chopped

For the relish
½ small pineapple, finely chopped
70g jaggery, grated
3 tsp basil seeds – optional
4 tsp fish sauce
2 tbsp rice wine vinegar
2 tbsp lime juice
1 red chilli, finely chopped
1 banana shallot, very thinly
  sliced into crescents
2 kaffir lime leaves, stalks
  removed, very thinly sliced
Handful of finely chopped mint
Handful of coriander leaves

- For the curry paste, put the chillies, coriander and cumin seeds, cardamom pods, cinnamon stick and star anise into a dry frying pan and toast over medium heat, stirring frequently, until aromatic. Transfer to a spice grinder or pestle and mortar and grind to a powder.
- Pour the oil into the frying pan, add the shallots and garlic and fry until caramelised, then add the shrimp paste and the ground spices and fry, stirring constantly, until fragrant. Tip the contents of the frying pan into a food processor, add the coconut milk, lemongrass and ginger and blend to a smooth paste.
- In a large frying pan, fry the pork in the coconut oil with the star anise, cardamom pods, curry leaves and cinnamon stick until the meat is lightly sealed. Add the coconut milk, then fill the empty tin with water and add that to the pan as well, along with the curry paste. Bring to a simmer, cover and cook for 1½ hours or until the pork is butter-soft.
- Meanwhile, make the relish. Place the pineapple in a bowl. Put the jaggery into a small pan with 100ml of water and stir over medium heat until the jaggery dissolves, then bring to the boil and simmer for 2 minutes or until syrupy. Remove from the heat and leave to cool completely. If you are using basil seeds, put them into a small bowl and soak in just enough water to cover for 10 minutes – they will puff up. Pour the cooled syrup over the pineapple, then follow with the soaked basil seeds, if using, and the remaining ingredients except the mint and coriander. Refrigerate until needed. Just before serving, toss through the herbs.
- Add the potatoes, shallots, fish sauce, tamarind concentrate and palm sugar to the curry and simmer, uncovered, for 30 minutes, or until the potatoes are tender, then stir through the peanuts. Garnish with Thai basil leaves and serve with the pineapple relish.

4 × 100g boneless lamb loin fillets
3 tbsp olive oil, plus extra for
  brushing
3 red onions, thinly sliced
3 sprigs of thyme, leaves picked
1 tsp soft brown sugar

100ml red wine
150g feta cheese, well-drained
  and crumbled
2 tsp sumac
40g pine nuts
Handful of chopped mint

1 x 375g sheet of ready-rolled
  all-butter puff pastry
2 egg yolks, lightly beaten
Sea salt and black pepper

Lamb Wellington with Feta, Pine Nuts and Sumac

When it comes to dinner parties, cooking a leg or shoulder of lamb is always a good idea – but for a special occasion, such as Easter Sunday lunch, I like the more refined lamb fillet. It has little fat and is ideal for cooking either whole or cut into thick noisettes. This recipe fulfils my personal fantasy of lamb loins individually wrapped in a flaky, buttery, burnished pastry. The stuffing of lactic feta and mouth-puckering sumac borrows flavours from Greece and Lebanon, which are tart enough to cut through the richness of the red meat. Serve with new potatoes and wilted spinach.

- Brush the lamb fillets with a little olive oil and season with plenty of salt and pepper. Pour 2 tablespoons of the oil into a frying pan over high heat, add the lamb and sear on all sides, including the ends, until the meat has a lovely golden brown crust. Remove from the pan and leave to cool to room temperature.
- Wipe out the pan and fry the onions in the remaining 1 tablespoon of olive oil over medium heat until softened, then add the thyme and sugar and cook, stirring frequently, until the onions are caramelised. Pour in the red wine and let it bubble and reduce until syrupy. Transfer to a bowl and set aside to cool.
- Stir the feta, sumac, pine nuts and mint into the cooled onions. On a flour-dusted surface, cut the pastry sheet into 4 rectangles, each large enough to enclose a lamb fillet, leaving a 1cm border at each end. Cut lengthways along each loin to make a pocket, being careful not to go all the way through. Divide the onion mixture evenly between the pockets, then pop a stuffed lamb fillet on each pastry rectangle. Brush the edges of the pastry with beaten egg yolk and fold over the pastry to wrap the lamb, pressing the edges of the pastry with the prongs of a fork to seal. Place the lamb wellingtons, seam side down, on a baking sheet lined with baking parchment. Glaze with beaten egg yolk, then use the back of a knife to mark each parcel with long diagonal lines, being careful not to cut into the pastry. Chill for at least 1 hour to firm up.
- When you're ready to cook the wellingtons, preheat the oven to 200°C/ Fan 180°C/Gas Mark 6 and bake for 25–30 minutes – the pastry will be crisp and golden, and the meat should be cooked to medium.

Lamb and Aubergine Fatteh

Fatteh is a layered feasting dish. This one features lamb, aubergine and pulses, ladlefuls of garlic-spiked tahini yoghurt sauce and spicy tomato salsa, all topped off with fried shards of flatbread, pine nuts and almonds – and that most iconic Middle Eastern ingredient, pomegranate. This is a great recipe for a crowd. With every bite, your guests will luxuriate in different flavours.

4 tbsp olive oil
4 lamb shanks
1 cinnamon stick, broken up
2 tsp allspice berries
2 tsp coriander seeds
6 green cardamom pods, bruised
1 tsp black peppercorns
2 red onions, unpeeled, cut into quarters
1 whole garlic bulb, halved crossways
2 aubergines, thinly sliced into rounds
1 × 400g tin chickpeas, drained
2 Lebanese flatbreads

Groundnut oil, for deep-frying
1 tbsp ghee
2 tbsp flaked almonds
2 tbsp pine nuts
Seeds from ½ large pomegranate
1 tbsp black sesame seeds
1 tsp sumac
Handful of parsley leaves
Sea salt and black pepper

For the sauce
250g yoghurt
1 tbsp tahini
Juice of 1 lemon
1 garlic clove, crushed

For the salsa
1 heaped tsp Turkish pepper paste (biber salcasi) or good-quality harissa
2 tbsp olive oil
Juice of 1 lemon
4 tomatoes, peeled and finely chopped
1 red onion, finely chopped
1 green pepper, finely chopped
Large handful of finely chopped parsley
1 tsp sumac
1 tsp Turkish pepper flakes (pul biber)
½ tsp dried mint

- Preheat the oven to 180°C/160°C Fan/Gas Mark 4. Pour 2 tablespoons of the oil into a large flameproof casserole over high heat and sear the lamb shanks all over. Add the cinnamon, allspice, coriander seeds, cardamom pods, peppercorns, onions and garlic and fry for 1 minute. Pour in 1.5 litres of water, then cover and cook in the oven for 2 hours.
- In the meantime, place the sliced aubergine on a lined baking sheet, drizzle over the remaning 2 tablespoons of oil and season with salt and pepper. Roast in the oven for 45 minutes or until soft, then set aside.
- Make the sauce by simply mixing all the ingredients together.
- For the salsa, put the paste, oil and lemon juice into a bowl, season with salt and pepper and stir until well combined, then add the tomatoes, red onion, green pepper, parsley, sumac, Turkish pepper flakes and dried mint.
- Take the lamb out of the oven and add the chickpeas, then cover again and return to the oven for a further 30 minutes.
- Using scissors, cut the Lebanese bread into bite-sized shards. Fill a large, heavy-based saucepan a third full with the deep-frying oil. Heat the oil to 180°C – if you don't have a thermometer, you will know the oil is ready when a cube of bread turns golden brown in 20 seconds. Fry the flatbread for 1 minute, or until golden and crisp, then drain on kitchen paper.
- Heat the ghee in a frying pan over medium heat and fry the almonds and pine nuts until golden and toasty, keeping a close eye on them as they can quickly burn. Drain on kitchen paper.
- To serve, lift the lamb shanks out of the casserole and onto a chopping board. Shred the meat with two forks, then lay over a serving dish. Fish out the chickpeas with a slotted spoon and tumble over the lamb, along with a few ladlefuls of the stock to moisten the lamb. (Keep the rest of the stock to make soup another time.) Cover the lamb and chickpeas with the aubergines, arranging them in a single layer, followed by the tomato salsa and dollops of the yoghurt sauce. Finish with the fried flatbread, almonds, pine nuts, pomegranate seeds, sesame seeds, sumac and parsley.

4 double lamb cutlets
Sea salt and black pepper
Za'atar, for sprinkling

For the marinade
100g yoghurt
25ml olive oil
3 fat garlic cloves, finely chopped
Finely grated zest and juice
    of 1 lemon
3 tsp za'atar
1½ tsp coriander seeds, toasted
1½ tsp cumin seeds, toasted

For the tzatziki
2 large courgettes, grated
500g Greek yoghurt
1 fat garlic clove, crushed
½ tsp ground cardamom
Handful of finely chopped mint
Juice of 1 lemon
Piece of lump charcoal – optional
2 tbsp extra virgin olive oil
Sprinkle of cayenne pepper

Za'atar Lamb Cutlets with Courgette Tzatziki

Even on the rainiest days, this dish has all the flavour of a summer barbecue. It is also one of the many good reasons to buy a jar of za'atar, the versatile Middle Eastern spice mix bursting with bold, earthy flavours. Serve with a fresh green salad.

- First make the marinade by mixing together all the ingredients. Massage over the lamb, then set aside to marinate in the fridge for at least half an hour, but preferably overnight.
- In the meantime, make the tzatziki. Put the grated courgette into a large bowl. Sprinkle with 1 teaspoon of salt and leave in the fridge for 30 minutes – this will draw excess liquid from the courgette to give it texture and crunch. Drain in a colander, using your hands to squeeze out as much liquid as possible, then return to the bowl. Add the yoghurt, garlic, cardamom, mint and lemon juice and season with salt and pepper.
- If you want to smoke the tzatziki, which I would highly recommend, sit the piece of charcoal directly on a gas burner or barbecue, letting it catch light and burn. When it is smouldering and grey, use tongs to carefully transfer it to a small heatproof bowl. Nestle the bowl inside the bowl of tzatziki and drizzle a little oil over the charcoal – it will start smoking immediately. Cover the bowl tightly with foil and leave to smoke for half an hour, then take out the small bowl and discard the charcoal.
- Drizzle the olive oil over the tzatziki and finish with a sprinkling of cayenne pepper. Refrigerate until needed.
- Preheat the oven to 200°C/Fan 180°C/Gas Mark 6. Heat a griddle pan over high heat, add the lamb and sear all over. Transfer to the oven and roast to your liking – 7 minutes for medium rare. Sprinkle with za'atar and serve with the tzatziki.

8 pork chops
Sea salt
Lime wedges, to serve

For the marinade
1 tsp cumin seeds
1 tsp coriander seeds
Seeds from 3 green cardamom
    pods
Seeds from 1 black cardamom
    pod
1 blade of mace
½ tsp black peppercorns

Handful of roughly chopped
    coriander, stalks and leaves
Handful of mint leaves
Thumb of ginger, roughly chopped
4 garlic cloves, roughly chopped
2 green chillies, roughly chopped
250g yoghurt
1 tsp ground turmeric
½ tsp chilli powder
1 tsp hot paprika
1 tsp chaat masala
1 tsp ground cinnamon
Fat pinch of salt
Juice of 1 lime

For the sambol
1 tbsp rapeseed oil
1 stem of curry leaves, picked
2 green chillies, finely chopped
45g tamarind concentrate
150g frozen grated coconut,
    defrosted
1 tbsp Maldive fish or anchovies
1 small onion, finely chopped
2–3 garlic cloves
Juice of 1 lime
2 tsp soft brown sugar

Tandoori Pork Chops with Coconut Sambol

Strictly defined, tandoori meat is marinated in spiced yoghurt and then cooked in a tandoor oven – a sort of clay oven that reaches ferocious temperatures. My pork chops use the same marinade but are cooked on a barbecue or griddle. The yoghurt helps to tenderise the pork, but also acts as a carrier for the dominant flavours of ginger, garlic, chillies and aromatic spices. The coconut sambol recipe is a souvenir I brought home from a trip to Sri Lanka, and it makes an excellent relish to smear over the juicy meat. If you can't find Maldive fish for the sambol, you can use dried anchovies or regular tinned anchovies – just drain well and blot off any excess oil with kitchen paper. Serve these juicy chops with some roast sweet potatoes or a crisp salad.

- First make the marinade. Heat a dry frying pan over medium heat and toast all the whole spices until aromatic, tossing them frequently and keeping a close eye on them to make sure they don't burn. Tip into a spice grinder and grind to a fine powder. In a food processor or blender, whizz the coriander, mint, ginger, garlic and chillies until you have a puree, adding a little water to help things along if necessary. Tip into a large bowl, then stir in the yoghurt and all the remaining ingredients.
- Put the pork chops in a bowl, spread the marinade liberally all over them, then leave to marinate for at least 1 hour, but ideally overnight in the fridge.
- For the sambol, heat the oil in a small frying pan and add the curry leaves and chillies. As soon as the curry leaves crackle, take off the heat and put them into a food processor, along with all the remaining ingredients and salt to taste. Blitz to a paste, then transfer to a bowl and refrigerate until needed.
- When you're ready to cook the chops, put a griddle pan over medium heat. Scrape away the excess marinade from the chops and grill for 8 minutes, turning occasionally, until they are just cooked through. Leave to rest for 6 minutes, then serve with the coconut sambol and lime wedges.

1kg pork ribs, cut into
   double ribs
Juice of 2 limes

For the pickle
1 large carrot, peeled and grated
   or julienned
1 large mooli (daikon), peeled
   and grated or julienned
3 tsp sea salt
115g caster sugar
350ml white vinegar

For the caramel sauce
250g caster sugar
1 star anise
½ tsp black peppercorns
1 small cinnamon stick, broken up
60ml fish sauce
30ml tamarind concentrate
1 tbsp Chinkiang black vinegar
4 garlic cloves, finely chopped
3 red bird's eye chillies, finely
   chopped

Vietnamese-style Caramel Pork Ribs with Pickled Daikon and Carrot Salad

I inherited my love of pork from my father, who devoured the meat in all its incarnations from sausage to chop. I often think about how much he would have savoured this dish. The wow factor comes from making a sweet and spicy caramel to lacquer the pork ribs with – once they are glazed, cook them slowly for an irresistibly sticky and tender bite. The pickle adds a welcome sharp note to cut through the pork's inherent fattiness. Serve with steamed rice.

- For the pickle, begin by sterilising a 500ml glass jar. First wash the jar thoroughly in hot soapy water. Rinse well, then let it drain on a clean tea towel. Preheat the oven to 180°C/Fan 160°C/Gas Mark 4, place the jar and lid on a clean baking sheet and bake for 10 minutes. Set aside.
- Put the carrot and mooli in a muslin-lined colander. Sprinkle with the salt and massage it in really well. Leave for 20 minutes, then rinse and drain, using your hands to squeeze out excess liquid. Put the carrot and mooli into the sterilised jar. Make a brine by combining the sugar, vinegar and 300ml of water in a non-reactive saucepan over low heat, stirring until the sugar has dissolved. Leave the brine to cool until it is lukewarm, then pour into the jar. Let the vegetables pickle for at least an hour before eating. They will keep in the fridge for 4 weeks.
- Preheat the oven to 150°C/Fan 130°C/Gas Mark 2.
- For the caramel sauce, put the sugar and 50ml of water in a large saucepan over low–medium heat and swirl to dissolve the sugar. Add the spices and keep swirling until you have a deep amber caramel. Carefully (it will spit!) pour in another 50ml of water, then add the fish sauce, tamarind, vinegar, garlic and chillies and simmer for 3 minutes over low heat.
- Add the ribs and stir to coat in the caramel, then transfer to a roasting dish. Cover with foil and cook for about 2½ hours, basting once or twice and removing the foil for the last 15 minutes. When done, the ribs should be sticky and tender. Squeeze over the lime juice and serve with the pickle.

Fragrant Pulled Goat Shoulder with Burnt Aubergine, Pine Nuts and Barberries

Goat has been a staple in Asia, Africa, the Caribbean and some parts of the Mediterranean for centuries, but has recently trotted into yuppier climes and become quite fashionable. It is lower in fat than chicken and can be cooked just like lamb, though you will find it has an earthier, gamier flavour. Marinating it in this way and slow-cooking it will give you delicious pulled meat which is soft and tender throughout, but irresistibly crisp and caramelised around the edges. Serve with steamed rice or a bulgur salad. If you can't find goat, lamb shoulder works equally well in this recipe.

1.5kg goat shoulder
Seeds from 1 pomegranate
50g pine nuts, toasted
50g barberries, soaked in
　hot water for 30 minutes,
　then drained
Small handful of mint leaves, torn
Sea salt and black pepper

For the marinade
1 star anise
1 small blade of mace
½ tsp cloves
1 tsp coriander seeds
1 tsp cumin seeds
1 tsp fennel seeds
Seeds from 3 green
　cardamom pods
½ tsp sweet paprika
½ tsp ground turmeric
1 tsp ground cinnamon
Generous pinch of saffron threads
1 tbsp dried rose petals
Good grating of nutmeg
½ tsp salt
6 fat garlic cloves, crushed
Finely grated zest and juice
　of 1 lemon
125ml olive oil

For the burnt aubergine
2 large aubergines
60ml olive oil
40g tahini
Juice of 1 lemon
1 tsp cumin seeds, toasted
　and coarsely ground
1 tsp sumac
Large handful of chopped
　coriander
Large handful of chopped mint

- For the marinade, heat a dry frying pan over medium heat and toast the whole spices until they are aromatic, tossing them frequently and keeping a close eye on them to make sure they don't burn. Tip into a spice grinder (or use a pestle and mortar) and grind to a powder. Transfer to a bowl and stir in all the remaining ingredients to make a lavish marinade.
- Using a sharp knife, score the goat shoulder all over. Place it in a shallow dish and pour over the marinade, then massage into the meat, making sure you get into the crevices and under the skin if possible. Cover and refrigerate overnight.
- Next day, preheat the oven to 160°C/Fan 140°C/Gas Mark 3. Place the goat in a deep roasting tin, pour in 250ml of water, cover with foil and roast for 4 hours or until the meat falls off the bone easily.
- Meanwhile, make the burnt aubergine. Roast the aubergines over an open gas flame or under a hot grill, turning frequently, until they are charred on the outside and really soft on the inside. When they are cool enough to handle, peel off the skins and chop the flesh finely. Put the flesh into a bowl and add the olive oil, tahini, lemon juice, cumin, sumac and herbs. Mix well, seasoning with salt and pepper to taste.
- To serve, coarsely shred the meat and spoon over some cooking juices. Smear a plate with the burnt aubergine, top with the pulled goat and scatter over the pomegranate seeds, pine nuts, barberries and mint leaves.

2 tbsp rapeseed oil
1kg scrag end of lamb
2 red onions, finely chopped
2 carrots, peeled and finely
  chopped
2 sticks celery, finely chopped
8 green cardamom pods, bruised
1 black cardamom pod, bruised
2 tsp cumin seeds

1 tsp ground cinnamon
200g tinned chopped tomatoes
2 tbsp tomato puree
6 garlic cloves, finely chopped
Thumb of ginger, finely grated
2 green chillies, finely chopped
200g frozen peas
2 tbsp red wine vinegar
Sea salt and black pepper

For the topping
40ml whole milk
40ml double cream
1 small onion, studded with 4 cloves
½ tsp black peppercorns
1 bay leaf
1 garlic clove, bruised
1 tsp ground turmeric
½ tsp smoked hot paprika
750g floury potatoes, peeled and diced
75g butter
2 egg yolks

Spicy Scrag End Pie

When the temperature nose dives and the world is looking grey, few things provide more comfort than shepherd's pie. Our version at Jikoni is made with scrag end of lamb – that's the neck – rather than mince. The long, slow cooking this cut requires results in a deep, hearty flavour and intensely soft meat. A whack of spices will warm you right through to your shivering bones – and, of course, there is still the thick insulating layer of buttery mashed potatoes. This is foodie anti-freeze!

- Heat the oil in a large, heavy-based saucepan over medium heat, add the scrags and brown well, then set aside. Add the onions, carrots and celery to the pan and fry, stirring regularly, until they are soft and golden brown. Add the cardamom pods, cumin seeds and cinnamon and fry for a few minutes until they're beautifully fragrant. Pour in the tomatoes and the tomato puree, then add the garlic, ginger and chillies. Season with salt and pepper, then bring to the boil and let it bubble away for 8 minutes. Return the lamb to the pan and pour in enough water to cover. Put on the lid and leave to cook over very low heat, stirring every so often, for about 3 hours or until the meat is falling off bones.
- For the topping, put the milk and cream into a small saucepan and pop in the clove-studded onion, peppercorns, bay leaf, garlic, turmeric and paprika. Bring to a simmer, then take off the heat and leave to infuse while you get on with the potatoes.
- Boil the potatoes in a saucepan of salted water until tender. Drain and mash until smooth and lump-free, then beat in the butter and egg yolks. Strain the infused milk and cream, discarding the solids, then slowly pour into the mash and mix well. Season to taste with salt and pepper.
- Preheat the oven to 200°C/Fan 180°C/Gas Mark 6.
- Transfer the lamb to a bowl and, when it is cool enough to handle, pull the meat off the bones in chunky shreds. Return the meat to the pan and mix in the peas and vinegar, then pour the whole lot into an ovenproof dish. Smother with the mash, scraping it into peaks in places – these bits will go lovely and crisp. Bake in the oven for 25–30 minutes until bubbling and golden, then serve.

Biryani:
A Love Story

1 term of endearment that means child

'Everyone gets old. Everyone gets their heart broken, and eventually everyone dies. So you see, *beta*,[1] there are no happy endings. There are just these small moments, blessings of food, shelter and friends, and we should be content with that.' My university friend's 77-year-old father was sharing some pearls of wisdom while polishing off the third helping of his wife's biryani.

I had watched him eat his first plate, then a second helping and now a third, just as quickly, in a trance of comforting carbohydrate bliss.

For a man of such heavy stature, with bristly hair sprouting wildly from his ears and nostrils, he wore an expression of innocent, youthful joy.

2 lamb and turnip curry
3 excellent

I visited the Khans often. On some days Mr Khan would return home from an afternoon of reading the free newspapers at the library, excitedly sniffing the air and trying to decipher what his wife had cooked for dinner. 'Ah-ha-ha, *shalgam gosht*[2] – *bohat badhiya*!'[3] he'd exclaim. He'd always find Mrs Khan in the kitchen, perched on a stool set close to the stove, puffing up chapattis over the naked gas flame. He'd open up the cooking pots and peer in, and she'd giggle with surprising girlishness, shooing him away, while giving him a little taste on a wooden spoon.

4 headscarf

Their terraced townhouse was as neat as a pin, and Mrs Khan lovingly prepared meals for large family get-togethers in a kitchen that had barely changed since they moved in, thirty years ago. She had stopped dyeing her hair, and loose grey strands fell loose from under her *hijab*.[4] Though she was frail and her mouth drooped (the legacy of a stroke), you could see his heart visibly melting as she smiled and buttered another chapatti for him. He still saw in her the shy 17-year-old girl he'd married in Uttar Pradesh some fifty years ago.

So this is what contentment feels like, I thought. A house that seems unremarkable to most, but is overflowing with happiness and loved ones and laughter. A kitchen that is cluttered and worked in, a refrigerator covered in magnetic souvenirs and photos of children and grandchildren. A larder stocked full and plates that are never allowed to remain empty. That, and a pot of Mrs Khan's exceptional biryani.

Biryani is a humble dish of rice and meat, yet the slightest adjustments in ingredients and technique can arouse passionate culinary fisticuffs.

5 noble There is no doubt that its origins are *nawaabi*,[5] but its thrifty use of meat, fleshed out with starchy grains, means it's economical and perfect for large gatherings. There are several versions of biryani, hailing from regions as diverse as Hyderabad and Sindh, but for me Mrs Khan's version of it best represents the warm, secure embrace of family and is the epitome of Indian home cooking. I remember its saturation of fragrance and flavour – dark tender meat, heady smoky spices, an egg gilded ochre, a tangle of crisp onions, perfumed rice and fragrant coriander giving chase to chilli. But most of all I remember the feeling of ethereal contentment after polishing off a plate of it. Mr Khan was right – all you really need to get through life is shelter and sustenance, kith and kin.

Mughlai Paigham Biryani

There are so many versions of biryani, but this is perhaps one of the more unusual ones. Rather than joints of chicken, fillets of fish or cubes of lamb, it contains rolled-up cabbage leaves stuffed with delicious minced meat. The word 'paigham' means a message or a letter, so perhaps the cabbage rolls represent the scrolls used to invite guests to the lavish feasts the Mughal nobility was known for. There are no shortcuts to making a good biryani — it is a labour of love and completely worth persevering with!

400g basmati rice
2 tbsp ghee
1 tbsp cumin seeds
4 cloves
1 cinnamon stick
6 black peppercorns
4 green cardamom pods
2 bay leaves
800ml boiling water
½ tsp saffron threads
50ml whole milk, warmed
Sea salt
Chopped coriander, toasted
    flaked almonds, crispy onions
    and raisins or sultanas, to serve

For the cabbage rolls
3 tbsp ghee
2 red onions, finely chopped
2 tsp cumin seeds
5 green cardamom pods
1 black cardamom pod
1 tsp ground cinnamon
1 tbsp pomegranate powder
    (anardana)
4 garlic cloves, finely chopped
Thumb of ginger, finely grated
2 green chillies, finely chopped
3 tomatoes, peeled and chopped
1 tsp ground turmeric
2 tbsp dried fenugreek
    (kasoori methi)

2 tbsp Greek yoghurt
500g minced mutton or lamb
Handful of chopped coriander
Juice of ½ lime
1 small savoy cabbage

For the tomato masala
2 tbsp ghee
2 onions, finely chopped
1 tsp cumin seeds
4 garlic cloves, finely chopped
Thumb of ginger, finely grated
2 green chillies, finely chopped
300g tinned chopped tomatoes
250g yoghurt

- Start with the filling for the cabbage rolls. Heat 2 tablespoons of the ghee in a large frying pan over low heat and slowly fry the onions, stirring occasionally, for about 20 minutes or until caramelised. Add the cumin seeds and the green and black cardamom pods and fry, stirring, for a minute. Next add the cinnamon and pomegranate powder and fry for a further minute, then add the garlic, ginger and chillies and fry until they have softened. Add the tomatoes and cook until they have broken down, then stir in the turmeric and dried fenugreek. Tip the contents of the frying pan into a bowl and leave to cool, then fold in the yoghurt and mince. Leave to marinate in the fridge for a minimum of 3 hours, or preferably overnight.

- Heat the remaining 1 tablespoon of ghee in a large flameproof casserole over medium heat and add the mince. Turn the heat down to low and stir continuously for 5 minutes or until browned. If it seems watery, turn up the heat to evaporate the liquid. Season with salt and stir through the coriander and lime juice. Empty the filling into a bowl and set aside to cool. Wipe out the casserole, ready for the tomato masala.

- Rinse the rice in several changes of water, then cover with water and leave to soak for half an hour.

- Meanwhile, to make the tomato masala, melt the ghee in the casserole over medium heat and fry the onions with the cumin seeds, stirring frequently, until they are dark, sticky and caramelised. Add the garlic, ginger and chillies and fry for 3 minutes, then pour in the tomatoes and cook for 5 minutes. Take off the heat and stir in the yoghurt to give you a lovely creamy sauce. Season with salt.
- Put the whole cabbage in a saucepan of boiling salted water and simmer for 5 minutes. Carefully fish it out with a couple of spatulas and plunge into ice-cold water. The leaves should have softened slightly, but not be overcooked. Separate all the leaves and lay them out on a clean benchtop.
- Place a tablespoonful of the filling in the centre of each one. Fold in the ends, then roll up tightly so you end up with securely wrapped cigar shapes about 10cm long. Carefully slip them into the tomato masala, making sure they are submerged. Cover and cook over low heat for 15 minutes or until the cabbage leaves are cooked and the mince filling is heated through.
- To cook the rice, melt the ghee in a heavy-based saucepan over medium heat. Add the whole spices and bay leaves and fry, stirring, until fragrant. Add the drained rice, then pour in the boiling water and season with salt. Turn down the heat to very low, cover and cook for 8–10 minutes or until the rice has absorbed all the water and is beautifully fluffy.
- Meanwhile, use a pestle and mortar to crush the saffron, then steep it in the warm milk. Spread out the cooked rice over a large plate, then drizzle the saffron milk unevenly over it – the aim is to get contrasting patches of crocus-stained rice and pearly white rice.
- Preheat the oven to 180°C/Fan 160°C/Gas Mark 4.
- To assemble the biryani, take a large casserole and spoon in a third of the rice, spreading it out evenly. Add a layer of stuffed cabbage leaves and sauce, then another layer of rice, followed by another layer of stuffed cabbage and sauce and the final layer of rice. Cover and warm through in the oven for 20 minutes. Sprinkle with chopped coriander, toasted flaked almonds, crispy onions and a handful of raisins or sultanas, then serve.

100g butter
Generous pinch of saffron threads
1 × 5kg free-range turkey
500ml chicken stock
30ml sherry vinegar
50ml olive oil
Sea salt and black pepper

For the stuffing
300g freekeh
1 tbsp olive oil
1 red onion, finely chopped
4 garlic cloves, finely chopped
1 heaped tsp ground allspice

Large handful of finely chopped
  coriander
3 preserved lemons, rind only,
  finely chopped
90g toasted pine nuts, finely chopped
100g currants

Saffron-roasted Turkey with Freekeh, Pistachio and Preserved Lemon Stuffing

Luxurious saffron adds a festive golden hue, as well as an exquisite fragrance, to this exceptionally flavoursome bird. This makes a really special centrepiece for your Christmas or Thanksgiving table. Serve with the usual roast dinner sides or the Christmas panzanella with panettone croutons on page 150.

· Melt the butter in a small saucepan over low–medium heat. Using a pestle and mortar, crush the saffron, then sprinkle it into the butter. Turn off the heat and leave to infuse.

· To make the stuffing, boil the freekeh in plenty of salted water for 10–15 minutes or until tender. Drain and leave to cool. Meanwhile, heat the oil in a frying pan, add the onion and fry until soft. Add the garlic and cook briefly until fragrant, then sprinkle in the allspice and cook for 2 minutes. Fold in the freekeh, coriander, preserved lemon, pine nuts and currants. Season well with salt and pepper.

· Preheat the oven to 180°C/Fan 160°C/Gas Mark 4. Season the turkey inside and out with salt and pepper. Gently ease your fingers under the skin over the breast of the turkey, being careful not to tear it, then put some of the saffron butter under the skin and massage the rest all over the turkey. Fill the cavity with the freekeh stuffing, then truss the legs and place the bird in a large roasting tin. Pour the stock into the tin, cover the breast with foil and roast the turkey, basting frequently, for 3 hours, replenishing with more stock or water to stop the juices from drying out.

· Remove the foil and roast for a further 30 minutes, basting occasionally, until golden brown and cooked through. Test by inserting the tip of a small knife into the thickest part of the thigh – the juices should run clear.

· Carefully lift the turkey out of the tin onto a large warmed serving platter, then cover loosely with foil and leave to rest in a warm place for 15 minutes.

· Meanwhile, spoon any excess fat from the juices in the roasting tin and discard. Place the roasting tin over medium heat and add the sherry vinegar and olive oil, whisking to emulsify. Season with salt and pepper to taste and serve with the turkey.

Tamu Tamu

Sweet Things and Desserts

My foodie memory lane is paved with sugar. First there was

a ransacked bag of Fox's fruit-flavoured boiled bonbons,

stained-glass oblong tablets with a slightly gooey centre pilfered from my grandmother's cupboard, each sugary detonation sucked and chewed until I felt quite sick. Then there were the English chocolates my father brought home as souvenirs that started the early rot of my milk teeth. Ice cream and ice lollies, toffees, cream puffs, Victoria sponges, Swiss rolls and gigantic tins of homemade biscuits all contributed to my sugar highs.

My first clumsy foray into baking was alongside one of my elder siblings, who would occasionally make a cake or a latticed apple tart in the early days of acclimatising to our new home in England. It was the sponge cakes I loved the most,

as round as a full moon and just as full of promise.

They would disappear into the oven as pale as sand and come out burnished golden when the batter had stopped jiggling. We liked to eat them while they were still a little warm and not quite sturdy, every sweet buttery crumb gathered up with the padded tip of an index finger. Even now, the cosy fragrance of vanilla emanating from an oven still conjures up feelings of coming in from the cold.

There was a glut of ice cream too. An occasional cone dipped in the thinnest film of melted milk chocolate that froze immediately at Sno Cream, or vanilla ice cream in a cup from the Lyons Maid vendor who rode his tricycle of frozen assets around the suburbs at weekends.

He also peddled Red Devils, a racy sort of ice lolly that dyed your mouth red and gave five-year-old girls the grown-up thrill of lipstick-ed pouts. Predictably, my mother forbade these.

Desserts are aspirational.

They're the one part of the meal you don't really have to eat – but you do.

They're the most indulgent and greedy part.

When the waiter comes around with the pudding menu, the sugar fascists are the ones who'll refuse to even sneak a peek. I'm likely to say, 'I'll have a bite if you order something,' when really I don't intend to share at all. Yes, everything in moderation, and sugar is now the enemy when it comes to healthy eating, but in the toughest of times, sweets give an unfailing sense of happiness. And if you make them for people you love, they'll know you are gifting them a piece of luxury, as you've lavished such time and effort on something so fleeting, destined never to last very long.

Banana Cake with Miso Butterscotch and Ovaltine Kulfi

To confine your use of miso to just soup would be to miss out on a multitude of exciting gastronomic opportunities — one of the best of which would have to be the miso butterscotch that goes with Jikoni's famous banana cake. This dessert has such a cult following that certain die-harders will call ahead to make sure we have a portion saved for them.

The banana cake is based on the idea of a sticky toffee pudding, although it is much less dense. Then there's that dizzyingly luxurious miso butterscotch with its compelling mix of sweet and salty flavours. To top it all off, we have the 'nostalgia in a bowl' of Ovaltine kulfi, a condensed-milk ice cream that has an almost chewy texture. And if that wasn't enough to make you fall in love with this dessert, making it is a piece of cake!

1 tbsp black tea leaves
200ml boiling water
200g pitted dates
110g unsalted butter
350g dark muscovado sugar
1 tbsp treacle
1 tbsp date syrup
400g self-raising flour

4 eggs
1 tsp vanilla extract
1 tbsp bicarbonate of soda
200g peeled bananas

For the kulfi
50g Ovaltine
450g condensed milk
300ml double cream

For the butterscotch
500ml double cream
175g demerara sugar
175g unsalted butter
1 tbsp golden syrup
60g white miso

- The kulfi will take at least 6 hours to set, so make it ahead of time. In a large bowl, mix the Ovaltine into the condensed milk until there are no lumps. In a separate bowl, whip the cream to soft peaks, then fold it into the condensed milk mixture. Pour the kulfi into a tub and freeze until set. It really is as simple as that!
- Preheat the oven to 190°C/Fan 170°C/Gas Mark 5. Line a 24cm square cake tin with baking parchment.
- Put the tea leaves in a heatproof jug or bowl, pour over the boiling water and allow to infuse for a minute. Strain the tea, discarding the tea leaves, then soak the dates in the hot tea for 10 minutes.
- In a large bowl, beat together the butter and sugar until smooth. Stir in the treacle and date syrup, followed by the flour, and mix well. Mix the eggs in one at a time.
- Tip the soaked dates and tea into a blender or food processor, along with the vanilla extract, and blitz to a puree. Add the bicarbonate of soda and pulse briefly, then add to the bowl and mix thoroughly.
- Wipe out the blender, add the bananas and blend until smooth, then add to the cake batter and stir in well. Pour into the tin and bake for 1 hour or until a skewer inserted in the centre of the cake comes out clean.
- Meanwhile, to make the butterscotch, put the cream in a saucepan over low heat. Add the sugar, butter and golden syrup and whisk until the sugar has dissolved and the butter has melted. Finally whisk in the miso, then remove from the heat.
- Turn the cake out on to a wire rack and leave to cool a little.
- To serve, cut into 12 portions, then serve warm with the hot miso butterscotch and the Ovaltine kulfi.

200g raspberries
200g strawberries
1 tbsp rosewater
Creme de framboise, for drizzling
500g good-quality vanilla custard
300ml double cream,
  lightly whipped
100g pashmak
75g Turkish delight, chopped
Seeds from 1 pomegranate

2 tbsp finely chopped roasted
  pistachios
Dried rose petals, to serve

For the jelly
300ml pomegranate juice
Juice of ½ lemon
1 tsp rosewater
125g caster sugar
5 gelatine leaves

For the sponge
150g unsalted butter, softened
150g caster sugar
3 eggs
1 tsp vanilla extract
150g self-raising flour
½ tsp baking powder
100g finely ground pistachios

Turkish Delight Trifles with Pashmak

This ethereal trifle is scented with the delicate perfume of rosewater and showcases luscious summer berries and pomegranates. You can find pashmak, a magical candyfloss-like spun sugar confection, at Turkish or Middle Eastern supermarkets — it will give your trifle a good measure of jolliness and whimsy.

· The jelly will take up to 6 hours to set, so you'll need to make it in advance. In a bowl or jug, combine half the pomegranate juice with the lemon juice, rosewater and 150ml of water. Put the other half of the juice into a small saucepan with the sugar and heat gently, stirring to dissolve the sugar. Once it has come to a simmer, remove from the heat.
· Soak the gelatine leaves in cold water for 5 minutes, then squeeze out the excess water. Stir the gelatine into the hot juice until it has completely dissolved. Mix the two juices together and pour through a fine sieve into a 500ml container. Leave to cool, then chill until set, about 4–6 hours.
· To make the sponge, preheat the oven to 180°C/160°C Fan/Gas Mark 4. Line a 26cm square cake tin with baking parchment. In an electric mixer fitted with the beater attachment, cream together the butter and sugar until light and fluffy. Add the eggs one at a time, beating each one in well before adding the next, then mix in the vanilla extract. Gently fold in the flour, baking powder and ground pistachios, then pour the batter into the tin and bake for 20–25 minutes or until a skewer inserted in the centre comes out clean and dry. Leave the sponge to cool in its tin.
· Meanwhile, combine half the berries and the rosewater in a small bowl and mash with a fork, then strain the berry puree into a bowl, discarding the solids. Hull and slice the remaining strawberries and set aside, along with the remaining raspberries, to decorate the trifles.
· Cut the sponge into 2cm cubes and divide between 6 glasses, then drizzle with creme de framboise. Turn out the jelly, cut into cubes and divide between the glasses, then top with custard and whipped cream. Chill until needed. To serve, spoon some of the berry puree over each trifle, then top with pashmak, Turkish delight, sliced strawberries, raspberries, pomegranate seeds, chopped pistachios and rose petals.

The Guava Tree

I was ill during my first summer in England, and I won't forget it. It was the fuzzy dried-up end of the season and autumn had already begun to displace the sultry haze of the evening sun with its detached violet hue. There had been numerous visits from the doctor, but no treatment seemed to work. I had no strength and, as I lay in bed, pushing my mother's runny *khichdee*[1] around the bowl, and sipping but barely swallowing drops of weak squash, it felt like I had no will to recover either.

1 A simple soup made from rice and lentils

My bedroom was not furnished in the usual pretty style of a girl aged eight — it was chaste and impassive, like the clear vowels of someone just beginning to learn the English language. There was the tired yellowing wallpaper, some windless drapes, and a small vase of mute dried flowers that seemed to have even less bloom than me. The silence spread over my sheets like a stain, weighing me down — I can't even remember hearing the sound of my mother's voice, only the faintest dull thud every now and then, which must have been my slow, wary heart.

The days and nights stretched out ahead of me: my mother bringing in a tray of food three times a day, a sponge bath, the see-saw sound of a comb passing through my matted hair, but nothing else — just a numb, woozy stillness. In the mid-afternoon, when the sun threw the frieze of a tree across my wall, I would exhaust myself by counting each bud, each leaf, noting the numbers decreasing every day. I lay in that milky bed, without the faintest desire to get up, talk, walk, read or eat until one day, quite suddenly, I awoke from a dream and was stunned to hear the sound of my own voice, calling out for my mother.

I'd been dreaming of home: of a red-earthed garden perfumed with the scent of wet marigolds, flamboyant bougainvillea and sprawling leopard orchids — but it was the narcotic aroma of the guava tree that had leapt through my sleepy wonderland and filled my room like a giant balloon.

My mother pattered in, her gold bangles jangling, and touched the back of her hand to my forehead. '*Bakhaar*,'[2] she noted.

2 fever

I laughed out loud. 'Mum, I want a guava.' It was the only thing I had asked for in weeks, 'Can you cut one for me?' I was drooling now, as the fragrance of the fruit seemed to deepen in my room.

My mother seemed aghast. She held up her hands to question me. 'And where am I supposed to find a guava? This is England, *beta*,'[3] she reasoned.

3 term of endearment that means child

'But there is a guava tree outside – just ask the neighbours,' I pleaded. 'They'll know – I can smell it.'

She unfolded her limbs and sank into the bed next to me and whispered, 'Tomorrow…'

I couldn't sleep. I was tantalised by the hope of sinking my teeth into that pink-fleshed fruit, just like the ones we had eaten with such casual gluttony at our house in Nairobi. Sometimes they were so ripe that they almost blazed fuchsia-pink through their paper-thin pistachio skins. As I thought of them, my heart palpitated in my empty hands. I pined for their fragrant juice just as much as I yearned for the beloved grandmother we had left behind in our hasty voyage to England. I imagined her there – alone – surrounded by the tree's harvest, and I burned.

The next day, my mother brought in china plates piled high with papaya, mango and passion fruit, but my heart rebelled against them. All I wanted was a smooth-skinned guava, warming nicely in the cup of my small palm. Some days later, my mother announced that she had a surprise. She carried in a small cardboard box and laid it on my lap. 'Open it,' she said.

Carefully I lifted off the top, and there, perfect as the fingers of a newborn, were eight tiny guavas, nestled in shredded paper. They were expensive, out of season and unripe, but it didn't matter. 'They're still not ripe,' she said. 'You'll just have to wait for a few days, and then you'll see how delicious they are.'

She set them out, carefully and precisely, on my windowsill to ripen. I looked at them with contentment, enjoying the pleasure of anticipation. Then I walked to the window and squashed my nose against the glass. I closed my eyes – I was home again.

8 ripe guavas
450g condensed milk
300ml double cream

For the chilli salt
30g Himalayan salt
½ tsp chilli powder

Guava Kulfi with Chilli Salt

One of the fondest memories of my childhood in Nairobi is of the dry, hot afternoons when my eldest sister (who, when I was four years old, was already twenty) would pick me up from Aunty Daisy's nursery school in her tiny lipstick-red Renault. Halfway home, she'd pull over at the fruit shack and treat me to a guava or an unripe mango, which the vendor would sprinkle liberally with a mixture of salt and chilli. I liked the mangoes, but it was the custardy, aromatic orbs of guava that really held my heart, as their sweetness set off the chilli salt that left my lips thrillingly numb. The fruits of my childhood were a deep pink inside, but it is more common in the UK to find the cream-coloured Asian varieties — either works for this kulfi recipe. The chilli salt is essential to counterbalance the guava's sweetness.

- First make the chilli salt. Using a pestle and mortar, grind the salt and chilli powder to a fine powder.
- To make the kulfi, peel 6 of the guavas, then blitz the flesh in a blender until smooth. Pass the guava puree through a sieve into a bowl, discarding the seeds, then mix in the condensed milk.
- In another bowl, whip the cream to soft peaks, then fold in the guava mixture. Pour the kulfi into six ramekins or kulfi moulds and freeze for 6 hours or until set.
- To serve, turn the kulfi out of the moulds onto serving plates — the best way to do this is to briefly dip the moulds in hot water to loosen the frozen cream. Peel and slice the remaining guavas and divide between the plates, then liberally sprinkle with the chilli salt for an unusual treat.

Meringue Roulade with Poached Stonefruit and Orange Blossom Cream

*Meringue is the miracle that comes from whisking egg whites with sugar.
I like it as a pavlova or broken up in an Eton mess, but a meringue roulade
is my favourite showstopper. You can change the fruit filling according to the
seasons — try strawberries with lemon verbena, rhubarb with rose, cooked
apples with brandy creme patissiere and toasted oats and nuts. This summer
version celebrates the honeyed ripeness of peaches, nectarines and apricots.*

150g mascarpone
80g creme fraiche
150ml double cream
1 tbsp icing sugar
1 tbsp orange blossom water
A few basil or mint leaves, torn

For the poached fruit
350ml Sauternes or similar
    dessert wine
100g caster sugar
150g apricots, stoned and
    cut into 4 wedges
150g peaches, stoned and
    cut into 6 wedges
150g nectarines, stoned
    and cut into 6 wedges

For the pistachio sugar
100g shelled pistachios
50g icing sugar

For the meringue
4 egg whites
200g caster sugar
1 tsp vanilla extract
1 tsp white vinegar
2 tsp cornflour, sifted

- For the poached fruit, bring the wine and sugar to the boil in a large frying pan over medium–high heat, stirring to dissolve the sugar. Add all the fruit and cover with a round of baking parchment, then reduce the heat to low–medium and simmer until the fruit is tender, about 10 minutes. Strain the fruit, reserving the liquid. Return the liquid to the pan and reduce over high heat for 5 minutes until thick and syrupy. Add the fruit and cook for a further 2 minutes or until it is well glazed. Cool and refrigerate until needed.
- To make the pistachio sugar, blitz the pistachios and icing sugar in a blender until you have a fine powder. Set aside.
- For the meringue, preheat the oven to 200°C/Fan 180°C/Gas Mark 6. Line a 32cm x 24cm baking tray with baking parchment and lightly grease with oil. Whisk the egg whites in an electric mixer until soft peaks form, then gradually add the caster sugar, a little at a time, and continue whisking until thick and glossy. Quickly fold in the vanilla extract, vinegar and cornflour. Transfer the meringue to the baking tray, spreading it out evenly, and bake for 10 minutes, then reduce the oven temperature to 170°C/Fan 150°C/Gas Mark 3½ and cook for a further 10 minutes.
- Remove the meringue from the oven and leave to cool for 2–3 minutes on the tray. Dust a sheet of baking parchment with half the pistachio sugar. Carefully invert the baking tray to turn out the meringue onto the pistachio-sugared baking parchment. Let it cool for a further 5 minutes, then carefully peel off the baking parchment from the top of the meringue. Starting from one of the long sides, and using the baking parchment underneath to help you, gently roll up the meringue to form a log and set aside.
- To make the filling, beat together the mascarpone and creme fraiche. In another bowl, whip the double cream with the icing sugar until you have soft peaks, then fold in the mascarpone and creme fraiche, along with the orange blossom water.
- Carefully unroll the meringue and spread with the filling. Drain the poached fruit, discarding the liquid, and lay it evenly over the filling, then sprinkle with the basil or mint leaves and roll up, again using the paper to help you.
- Refrigerate the roulade for an hour to set, then serve in slices, dusted with the remaining pistachio sugar.

750g rhubarb, cut into 1cm chunks
80g honey
3 tbsp pink peppercorns,
  roughly crushed
50g brown sugar
150g golden caster sugar
Finely grated zest and juice
  of 3 oranges
Seeds from 1 pomegranate

For the ice cream
1 vanilla bean, split and
  seeds scraped
400ml double cream
1 tsp ground cinnamon
125g golden caster sugar
6 egg yolks
200ml buttermilk

For the crumble
150g plain flour
150g brown sugar
150g cold unsalted butter, diced
150g ground almonds
75g rolled oats
Fat pinch of sea salt

Rhubarb, Pomegranate and Pink Peppercorn Crumble with Buttermilk Ice Cream

Before the fashion for continental desserts like panna cotta and creme brulee, there was the reliable English crumble – a frugal way of using up fruit that was past its best. Like a favourite old cashmere jumper, it has been neglected but brings delight when rediscovered. This crumble is still rustic, but I have dressed it up a little with the addition of pink peppercorns and a scoop of buttermilk ice cream, rather than the more traditional custard. The crumble on top has rolled oats and nuts in it, together with just enough sugar and butter to keep it crisp long after baking, and a little salt to balance the tartness of rhubarb and pomegranate.

- For the ice cream, put a large bowl in the fridge to chill. Meanwhile, put the vanilla pod and seeds into a saucepan with the cream and cinnamon and heat gently – do not let it boil. In a heatproof bowl, whisk together the sugar and egg yolks until pale, then slowly pour in the infused cream (discarding the vanilla pod), whisking constantly. Pour the custard back into the saucepan and stir over low–medium heat until it is thick enough to coat the back of a wooden spoon. Pour into the chilled bowl and whisk in the buttermilk, then refrigerate until completely cold. Transfer to an ice-cream maker and churn according to the manufacturer's instructions.
- For the crumble, put the flour and sugar into a bowl, add the butter and briskly rub between your fingertips until you have a rough crumble texture. Add the ground almonds, rolled oats and salt and gently rub together for a few seconds.
- Preheat the oven to 200°C/Fan 180°C/Gas Mark 6.
- Put the rhubarb, honey, peppercorns, both sugars and the orange zest and juice into a non-reactive saucepan. Place over medium heat and simmer for about 10 minutes or until the rhubarb is tender. Stir in the pomegranate seeds, then pour into a baking dish. Scatter the crumble over the top and bake for 20–25 minutes until golden and bubbling.
- Serve with scoops of buttermilk ice cream for a taste of utter joy!

75g basmati rice
2 carrots, peeled and grated
675ml whole milk
250ml double cream
100g golden caster sugar,
  plus extra for sprinkling
Seeds from 5 cardamom pods,
  crushed
1 vanilla bean, split and
  seeds scraped
4 egg yolks

Carrot, Cardamom and Vanilla Kheer Creme Brulee

This soothing pudding is inspired by my mother's delicious kheer (Indian rice pudding), which she always cooked with grated carrots and cardamom. I whisk egg yolks into the strained rice-cooking liquid to make a custard, then fold the rice back into it before baking. What you end up with is a pool of just-set silky cream studded with chewy rice grains, under a thin burnt-sugar crust – a rice pudding and a creme brulee rolled into one.

- Put the rice, carrots, milk, cream, sugar, cardamom and vanilla pod and seeds into a heavy-based saucepan and bring to the boil over low heat, stirring constantly. Turn the heat down to low and simmer very gently for about 20 minutes, then remove from the heat.
- Preheat the oven to 140°C/Fan 120°C/Gas Mark 1.
- Strain the rice and carrots, reserving the liquid (discard the vanilla pod). Leave the liquid to cool slightly, then gently mix the egg yolks into the warm liquid until well combined. Return the rice and carrots to the mixture and stir well, then divide between six ramekins. Pop the ramekins into a roasting tin, then pour in enough hot water to come halfway up the sides of the ramekins. Transfer to the oven and bake for 45 minutes.
- Remove the ramekins from the water bath and leave to cool, then chill the kheer in the fridge for about 1 hour or until set.
- To serve, sprinkle the tops with the extra caster sugar and brulee with a blowtorch or under a hot grill until bubbling and well browned.

225g caster sugar
350ml double cream
200ml whole milk
¾ tbsp orange blossom water
Tiny pinch of saffron threads,
  crushed into 1 tbsp warm milk
2 eggs, plus 4 egg yolks
Chopped pistachios, to garnish

For the rhubarb
400g rhubarb, chopped
  into 7cm lengths
300g caster sugar
6 green cardamom pods,
  bruised
Finely grated zest of 1 orange
125ml orange juice

Saffron and Orange Blossom Creme Caramel with Cardamom and Orange Rhubarb

Creme caramel requires bravery and an inner steeliness from the cook, as the caramel must be cooked past golden stage and all the way through amber and mahogany until it is a whisker away from burnt. That edge of dark, bitter caramel against the rounded sweetness of the creamy custard makes for the most delightful flavour combination. Sometimes it's best not to mess with the classics, but I have found that a good custard base lends itself well to the introduction of unusual flavours – I've taken the liberty of adding a Middle Eastern flourish to this one.

- For the rhubarb, preheat the oven to 200°C/Fan 180°C/Gas Mark 6. In a baking dish, combine the rhubarb with the sugar, cardamom pods, orange zest and juice. Roast for about 12 minutes or until the rhubarb is just tender. Leave to cool, then cover and refrigerate.
- For the caramel, have ready six ramekins (or a ring-shaped mould). Combine 150g of the sugar with 100ml of water in a saucepan and heat gently until the sugar dissolves, swirling the pan to help it along. Hold your nerve until the caramel goes past the golden stage and turns a deep brown. Pour into the ramekins or mould, tilting to coat the base and sides evenly. Set aside to cool.
- Preheat the oven to 140°C/Fan 120°C/Gas Mark 1. Whisk together the cream, millk, orange blossom water and saffron. In another bowl, whisk the eggs and yolks with the remaining 75g sugar, then slowly whisk in the cream mixture. Sit the caramel-lined ramekins in a roasting tin and pour the custard into them, stopping 5mm short of their rims. Fill the tin with enough hot water to come halfway up the sides of the ramekins, then bake for 1 hour or until just set. Remove the creme caramels from the water bath and leave to cool, then refrigerate for at least an hour to chill.
- When you are ready to serve, briefly dip the bases of each ramekin into hot water to loosen the creme caramel, then invert onto a plate. Serve with the rhubarb and some chopped pistachios.

1 bunch of holy basil,
  leaves picked
250ml double cream
150ml whole milk
25g caster sugar
250ml coconut milk
125g white chocolate
4 gelatine leaves, soaked in cold
  water for 10 minutes
A few Thai basil leaves, torn
Freshly ground black pepper

For the pineapple carpaccio
500g caster sugar
1 lemongrass stalk, bruised
1 vanilla bean, split
1 star anise
1 cinnamon stick
1 small pineapple, peeled and
  thinly sliced into discs

Coconut, White Chocolate and Holy Basil Panna Cotta with Pineapple Carpaccio

A good panna cotta should be a confection of cream, milk, prayers and as little gelatine as you can possibly get away with, if you want a seductive wibble. This one is inspired by the fragrant flavours of Thailand and makes an impressive, light and refreshing finale to an Asian meal.

- To make the pineapple carpaccio, put the sugar, lemongrass, vanilla bean, star anise and cinnamon into a saucepan with 1 litre of water and stir over medium heat until the sugar has dissolved. Bring to the boil, then simmer for 10 minutes until you have a syrup. Pour this over the sliced pineapple, then refrigrate until needed.
- Blanch the basil leaves in hot water for 15 seconds, then refresh in ice-cold water. Squeeze out any excess water and chop finely.
- Pour the cream and milk into a saucepan and place over medium heat. When it is simmering, add the sugar, stirring to dissolve.
- Put the coconut milk into a heatproof bowl set over a pan of simmering water – the water should not touch the base of the bowl. Add the chocolate and stir to melt.
- When the chocolate has completely melted, pour the mixture into the saucepan of cream and mix until well combined. Squeeze out the soaked gelatine leaves and stir into the mixture. Once the gelatine has dissolved, pour the mixture into a blender, along with the basil leaves, and blitz. Strain through a fine sieve, discarding the solids, then pour into six 6cm dariole moulds and refrigerate for 5 hours or until set.
- Turn out the panna cottas onto plates, serve with the pineapple carpaccio and garnish with torn Thai basil leaves. A good grating of black pepper will really make the pineapple sing.

150g caster sugar
Zest of 1 orange, peeled in strips
(use a potato peeler)
5 gelatine leaves
75ml gin
75ml Campari
75ml sweet vermouth

For the granita
1 litre freshly squeezed
orange juice
200g caster sugar
3 stalks of rosemary
A few drops of orange bitters

For the citrus salad
1 ruby grapefruit, segmented
1 pink grapefruit, segmented
2 oranges, segmented
250g strawberries, hulled and
cut into quarters
Seeds from 1 pomegranate
2 tsp icing sugar
50ml moscato

Negroni Jelly with Orange Granita and Citrus Salad

The Negroni is a classic Italian cocktail made from bittersweet Campari, gin and vermouth, and is best sipped while lounging on a sun-dappled Italian veranda and living la dolce vita. Riffing on the same ingredients, this dessert is about as refreshing as it gets, and the colour makes for a stunning centrepiece. Don't skimp on the gin — I love Sacred gin, from London. Be warned, Negronis are notoriously strong; post-pudding Vespa rides are not recommended!

- For the citrus salad, sprinkle the citrus segments, strawberries and pomegranate with the icing sugar, then pour over the moscato. Mix well to combine and then leave in the refrigerator to macerate.
- For the granita, put the orange juice, sugar and rosemary into a non-reactive saucepan and stir over low heat until the sugar has dissolved. Pick out and discard the rosemary, then stir in the orange bitters. Pour into a shallow 2-litre container and leave to cool, then freeze for at least 6 hours, using a fork to scrape the semi-frozen granita every few hours to form delicious ice crystals.
- To make the jelly, put the sugar and 500ml of water into a saucepan over medium heat and whisk gently until the sugar starts to dissolve. Add the strips of orange zest and bring to the boil, then reduce the heat to low and simmer for 5 minutes. Take off the heat and strain to remove the zest.
- Soak the gelatine leaves in cold water for 5 minutes, then squeeze out and add to the sugar syrup, whisking until the gelatine has completely dissolved. Stir in the gin, Campari and vermouth and leave to cool. Pour into a jelly mould or six individual cocktail tumblers. Refrigerate for 6 hours or until set — the jelly should still have a little wibble.
- If you've set the jelly in a mould, turn it out onto a serving plate. Scoop generous helpings of granita over the jelly, spoon over the citrus salad and serve immediately.

Tahini Ice Cream with Honeyed Quince
and Rose and Pistachio Crisps

This ice cream welcomes the caramel nuttiness of tahini, giving it an almost savoury note that will have the freezer beckoning you at midnight. If you want to serve it with something other than quince, it works well with coconut caramel bananas (see page 18), shop-bought sesame brittle and a drizzle of chocolate sauce too. The rose and pistachio crisps are a bit like a tuile and add another level of fancy — they can be made ahead as they will keep well for several days.

250ml whole milk
250ml double cream
75g caster sugar
6 egg yolks
5 tbsp good-quality tahini

For the honeyed quince
4 quince
320g honey
220g caster sugar
Thinly peeled zest and juice
   of 1 orange
Thinly peeled zest and juice
   of 1 lemon
1 vanilla bean, split and
   seeds scraped

For the crisps
60g unsalted butter
100g caster sugar
50g liquid glucose
50g plain flour, sifted
5 tbsp ground pistachios
5 tbsp dried rose petals

- Pour the milk and cream into a saucepan and bring to a simmer. In a heatproof bowl, whisk together the sugar and egg yolks until pale, then slowly add the milk and cream, whisking constantly. Return the custard to the saucepan and stir over low–medium heat until it is thick enough to coat the back of a wooden spoon. Pour into a blender, add the tahini and blitz until the tahini is well amalgamated. Pour into a 1-litre bowl and refrigerate until completely cold, then transfer to an ice-cream machine and churn according to the manufacturer's instructions.
- Meanwhile, for the honeyed quince, preheat the oven to 120°C/Fan 100°C/Gas Mark ½. Peel, core and quarter the quince, reserving the peel and trimmings. Put the honey, sugar, the citrus zests and juice and the vanilla pod and seeds into a large ovenproof saucepan. Pour in 750ml of water and stir over medium–high heat until the sugar dissolves, then remove from the heat and add the quince, peel and trimmings. Lay a circle of baking parchment directly on the surface of the liquid and place a plate on top to keep the fruit submerged, then cover with foil and cook for 3 hours or until the quince is tender and pale pink. Remove the quince with a slotted spoon and set aside, then strain the cooking liquid into a clean saucepan and simmer over medium–high heat for 25 minutes until syrupy and reduced by half. Pour the syrup over the quince and set aside.
- To make the crisps, put the butter, sugar and glucose into a saucepan over low heat, stirring until melted and well combined. Take off the heat and gently fold in the flour, being careful not to overwork the mixture. Leave to set for 45 minutes.
- Preheat the oven to 180°C/Fan 160°C/Gas Mark 4. Line a baking tray with baking parchment or a silicone mat.
- Roll the mixture into gobstopper-sized balls, place on the baking tray and bake for 10 minutes until golden. Sprinkle with the pistachios and rose petals while still warm. If you want to tidy the edges of the crisps, immediately use a biscuit cutter to score each one into a neat indented round – they will then come away easily once they are completely cool and set. If not using straightaway, store the crisps between sheets of baking parchment in an airtight container.
- Serve balls of the tahini ice cream with the honeyed quince, pouring over a little of the syrup, and finish with the rose and pistachio crisps.

4 sharp apples, such as
  Granny Smiths
Rapeseed oil, for deep-frying
Cornflour, for dredging
2 tbsp crushed pistachios
1 tbsp fennel seeds, toasted
  and lightly crushed

For the ice cream
450ml double cream
150ml whole milk
2 tbsp fennel seeds, toasted
  and lightly crushed
120g caster sugar
6 egg yolks

For the jalebi batter
250g cornflour
25g plain flour
¼ tsp bicarbonate of soda
1 tsp saffron threads, steeped
  in warm water for 2 minutes
325g yoghurt

For the syrup
500g caster sugar
1 tbsp lemon juice
2 tbsp rosewater

Apple Jalebis with Fennel Ice Cream

Although they are made from simple ingredients like milk, sugar, butter and nuts, Indian sweets (also known as 'mithai') take on vibrant forms and colours. None more so than jalebis — sticky spiral fritters dunked in rosy sugar syrup. These untraditional ones are like a cross between an apple fritter and a jalebi, and the fennel in the ice cream cuts through the rich, saccharine fritters.

- To make the ice cream, put the cream and milk into a saucepan and stir in the fennel seeds. Bring to a simmer over low heat, then remove from the heat and leave to infuse for 1 hour.
- Meanwhile, in a heatproof bowl, whisk together the sugar and egg yolks until pale. Slowly strain in the cream and milk, whisking constantly. Pour the custard back into the saucepan and stir over very low heat until it is thick enough to lightly coat the back of a wooden spoon. Pour into a bowl and refrigerate until completely cold, then transfer to an ice-cream maker and churn according to the manufacturer's instructions.
- For the jalebi batter, sift the cornflour, plain flour and bicarbonate of soda into a bowl. Mix together the saffron and yoghurt, then tip into the flour mixture and whisk until smooth. Leave the batter to rest for 1 hour.
- Next, make the syrup by putting the sugar into a saucepan with 250ml of water. Bring to the boil, then simmer for 10 minutes until syrupy. Take off the heat and stir in the lemon juice and rosewater.
- Peel and core the apples, then cut into 3mm rings. When everything is ready, fry the jalebis. Fill a large, heavy-based saucepan a third full with the deep-frying oil. Heat the oil to 180°C — if you don't have a thermometer, you will know the oil is ready when a cube of bread turns golden brown in 20 seconds. Working in batches, dredge the apple rings with cornflour, then dip into the jalebi batter and fry until golden and crisp, about 5 minutes.
- Lift out the apple jalebis and plunge them into the syrup for a couple of seconds, then retrieve and drain on a wire rack. Sprinkle with crushed pistachios and fennel seeds and serve at once, with a scoop of ice cream.

200g strawberries, hulled
3 tbsp icing sugar
1 heaped tsp sumac
500g Greek yoghurt
Micro basil cress or small basil
   leaves, chopped pistachios
   and sumac, to garnish

For the fruit salad
250g strawberries, hulled
   and sliced
125g raspberries
15 cherries, halved and pitted
Seeds from 1 small pomegranate
1 tbsp icing sugar
1 tbsp rosewater

Sumac and Strawberry Shrikhand with Strawberry, Raspberry Pomegranate and Cherry Salad

*When my husband, Nadeem, tried to convince me of the charms of shrikhand —
a sweetened hung yoghurt from his ancestral state of Gujarat — I was dubious.
At breakfast, I love the lactic tang of yoghurt dolloped over granola, but still
I didn't hold out much hope for it as a bona fide pudding. So my first spoonful
surprised me: I was seduced by the rich, creamy heft that comes from hanging
the yoghurt until it is dense and fudgy. We have since had shrikhand in various
incarnations — mango and passion fruit with saffron is one of my favourites —
but I especially love this one, with the sherbet-like astringency of sumac and
a summery fruit salad.*

- Blitz the strawberries in a blender or food processor, then pass through
  a sieve to extract the seeds. Mix the strawberry puree, icing sugar and
  sumac into the yoghurt.
- Wash and dry the sieve, line it with muslin and set it over a bowl. Spoon
  the yoghurt into the sieve, then leave to drain in the fridge for at least
  4 hours or overnight.
- When the shrikhand is ready, make the fruit salad. Mix the strawberries,
  raspberries, cherries and pomegranate seeds with the icing sugar and
  rosewater. Divide between serving plates, then top with quenelles or
  dollops of the shrikhand. Garnish with basil, chopped pistachios and
  more sumac.

3 blood oranges
75g unsalted butter
125g caster sugar
2 large eggs

1 tsp vanilla extract
150g plain flour, sifted
3 tbsp fine polenta
1½ tsp baking powder
150ml whole milk

For the caramel
150g caster sugar
2 tbsp Cointreau

Cointreau Caramel and Blood Orange Upside Down Cake

I was four or five years old when I saw my first Christmas pudding. It was a tantalising sight — a chocolate-brown bomb wearing a jaunty fascinator of holly and berries. But my greedy milk teeth had bitten off more than they could chew, and my infantile tastebuds immediately rejected the overpowering bite of dried fruits and brandy. Luckily for me, we had a reason to dodge the dense shot-put of a pud that Christmas threw at us. My late father shared Jesus's birthday, so we always had a fancy cake complete with candles instead.

This was the last cake I baked for him: the melting stickiness of the boozy caramel and soft blood oranges evoke the British marmalade he was so fond of. I have decided that his spirit will live on through our tradition of baking a cake every Christmas — both to celebrate his life, and because after all these years I still hate Christmas pudding!

- Cut 2 of the unpeeled oranges into thin circles, discarding the ends. Finely grate the zest of the remaining orange.
- To make the caramel, put the sugar and 250ml of water into a heavy-based or cast-iron saucepan — I use a 25cm tarte tatin tin. Place over medium heat and swirl the pan until the sugar melts and the caramel turns dark amber in colour. Do not be tempted to stir it, as this will cause the sugar to crystallise. Swirl in the Cointreau and take off the heat.
- Carefully place the sliced oranges directly onto the caramel in the pan, overlapping them slightly.
- Preheat the oven to 180°C/Fan 160°C/Gas Mark 4.
- In a large bowl or an electric mixer fitted with the beater attachment, cream the butter, sugar and orange zest together until light and fluffy. Beat in the eggs, one at a time, mixing them in well, then stir in the vanilla extract. Gradually fold in the flour, polenta and baking powder. Finally, stir in the milk, being careful not to overmix.
- Pour the batter over the caramel and oranges in the pan and bake for 30—35 minutes, until the sponge is springy and a skewer inserted into the centre of the cake comes out clean. Leave the cake to cool a little before carefully turning it out onto a serving plate.

The Audacity
of Rasgullas

By the time she came home from the hospital, there were already thirty mourners who had descended like ants into her modest living room. They sat drinking pale, sugary chai. Aside from a few sniffles from the toothless old ladies she knew from the local *Gurudwara*[1] *satsang*[2] group, the room was still. When she had her audience, she wrenched off her gold bangles, letting them drop to the floor.

[1] Sikh temple
[2] musical congregation

Her face crumpled like a flower and she began to wail like a siren.

The mourners shuffled in their seats awkwardly and said nothing. Two of the women stood up to comfort her, cupped her face as in prayer and pulled a thin white mourning shroud over her head. They led her away from the cloudy eyes of the rubberneckers to drink a glass of water and to wash her face. With empathy hanging on my shoulders like a damp heavy coat, I held onto her *kameez*[3] and followed her.

[3] tunic

In the kitchen, I noted that everything had been organised. A pragmatic neighbour had cooked savourless rice and dhal, as is appropriate for such occasions. Sitting at the kitchen table, she considered her late husband. She had married him when she was barely out of her teens, having met him only once, and with a chaperone present. She had been instructed by her mother not to be so bold as to even look up at him, but vaguely remembered a flash of bottle-green velvet suit and the reek of spray-on macho. Within a short few weeks of marrying him, she realised he was a drunk, neglectful of his work, and violent.

She recalled their first quarrel – the raised hand, the insistent clutch of hair that left a bald patch, the fist in the face, the alarm, the cowering and the rage. Afterwards he calmly stepped over the wreck of her, and vanished for the next few days. Soon enough, she discovered he had a mistress, a pretty woman with large breasts who wore ornate gold toe-rings. Once the profound humiliation had congealed, she accepted the bleak cards fate had dealt her. She cleared out any naive illusions of romantic love, instead making room for the absence of tenderness. She buried her pain deep, never to be excavated again.

TAMU TAMU

Now a lifetime of unshed, briny tears flowed freely. I passed her the box of Kleenex and rubbed her back. She was crying not for the misfortune of losing her 52-year-old husband to the misery of liver failure, but for her own lost girlhood, for the many solitary nights, for the gobstopper-eyed child bride in the fuchsia-pink *salwar kameez*[4] who had dreamt that life would be as pretty as the black-and-white Bollywood films she watched at the drive-in. She wiped her eyes and blew her nose loudly. Then she got up and steadied herself, walked over to the refrigerator and opened it. Inside she found a small white Corelle bowl, which she pulled out. She helped herself to a spoon from the cutlery drawer and sat back at the table.

[4] Indian tunic and trousers

At any other time, the two small *rasgullas*[5] suspended like pearls in sugar syrup would have been just that – a happy encounter between milk, sugar and rosewater – but at that moment her act of eating them seemed absurd, perverse even. The women who had led her, heaving with tears and sighs, into the kitchen, watched her uneasily. She lowered the spoon into the first spongy ball, pierced it, cut off a piece and brought it to her lips.

[5] dessert of spongy balls made from paneer soaked in sugar syrup

She ate it, turned the spoon upside down and licked its interior curve.

Then she brought it back down to the *rasgulla* and sliced into it again. She quietly polished off the last bite and didn't bother to drink up the dregs of syrup. Sated, she wiped the stickiness from the corners of her lips, which seemed to curl up in a half smile. I picked up the bowl and started washing up.

The women were visibly shocked. Born just half a generation after a time when widows were stripped of their property, had their heads shaved and lived out their remaining years like mere dust, they couldn't work out whether she had gone mad, was wicked and possessed, or whether this was just an insolent act of grief. I remember well those cruel murmurs about her that spread like hospital sheets to the living room, where the mourners were still drinking tea. Inside the kitchen, she belched loudly, appreciating the sweetness of a new life and new beginnings.

SWEET THINGS AND DESSERTS

Coffee Rasgullas with Mascarpone Ice Cream and Espresso Caramel

Rasgullas are sweet milk-and-cheese dumplings from Bengal that are poached in sugar syrup. If you ask a Bengali what they like – aside from famed poet Rabindranath Tagore – they are likely to say rasgullas. Purists should avert their eyes now, as I have taken great liberties with the traditional recipe. But if, like me, you love the boozy caffeinated flavours of tiramisu, you will love this dessert.

SERVES 4 (MAKES 12)

1 litre whole milk
2 tbsp lemon juice
500g caster sugar
2 tsp instant espresso
  granules, mixed with
  100ml boiling water

For the ice cream
1 litre whole milk
90ml marsala
1 vanilla bean, split and
  seeds scraped
250g caster sugar
8 egg yolks
750g mascarpone

For the caramel
300g caster sugar
100g liquid glucose
70ml brewed espresso coffee
80ml double cream
70g unsalted butter, diced

280   TAMU TAMU

- First make the ice cream. Put the milk, marsala and the vanilla pod and seeds into a saucepan and bring to a simmer, then remove from the heat. In a heatproof bowl, whisk together the sugar and egg yolks until pale, then slowly add the milk mixture, whisking constantly. Pour the custard back into the saucepan and stir over low–medium heat until it thinly coats the back of a wooden spoon. Strain back into the bowl. In another bowl, whisk the mascarpone to soften, then gradually add the custard, whisking until smooth and well combined. Refrigerate until completely cold, then transfer to an ice-cream machine and churn according to the manufacturer's instructions.
- Meanwhile, make the caramel. Put the sugar, liquid glucose and 100ml of water into a saucepan and stir over medium–high heat until the sugar dissolves. Bring to the boil and cook, without stirring, until you have a dark caramel. Take off the heat, then carefully (it will spit!) add the espresso and 50ml of water and return to the heat. Add the cream and butter, whisking to combine, then simmer until you have a thick syrup. Set aside.
- Next make the paneer for the rasgullas. Pour the milk into a saucepan and bring to the boil, then take off the heat and slowly pour in the lemon juice, stirring all the time. It should begin to curdle immediately. Leave to stand for 20 minutes. Tip the curds into a muslin-lined sieve set over a bowl, letting the whey drain through. Discard the whey. Rinse the curds well under cold running water, then gather the muslin in your hands and squeeze out any excess liquid. Place the curds in a bowl and knead for 6 minutes or until they start to clump together into a mass.
- Now you need to make two syrups for the rasgullas. For the espresso syrup, place half the sugar and the espresso mixture in a small saucepan, along with 150ml of water. Place over medium heat, stirring to dissolve the sugar, then simmer for 10 minutes or until thickened. Remove from the heat and set aside. For the sugar syrup, put the remaining 250g of sugar into a shallow saucepan with 500ml of water. Place over medium heat and simmer for 10 minutes, stirring to dissolve the sugar.
- Divide the curds into 12 equal balls of around 10g each. Roll each one between your palms until it is tight and very smooth, ensuring there are no cracks in the surface.
- Lower half the rasgullas into the pan of gently simmering sugar syrup, cover with a lid, and cook for 12 minutes or until spongy – they will expand. Remove using a slotted spoon and place in a dish, making sure they are not touching. Repeat with the rest of the rasgullas. Once they are all cooked, pour over the espresso syrup and leave to cool, then refrigerate for a minimum of 4 hours.
- Gently reheat the espresso caramel, then serve the rasgullas with the mascarpone ice cream and the warm espresso caramel.

SWEET THINGS AND DESSERTS

Edible Christmas Wreath

*I'm not remotely qualified to be a pastry chef, so if I can do this so can you!
Making choux pastry is simply a matter of bringing water and butter to the
boil, then dumping in flour and stirring until a mass forms, which takes only
a minute or two. You let the steaming dough cool for a moment, then beat in
some eggs, one at a time. That's it! You can use it to make profiteroles or eclairs,
but I'm giving my choux pastry a festive twist by turning it into a beautiful
piped ring, ready to be stuffed with a salted caramel filling and festooned with
chocolate and cheery decorations to make it look like a Christmas wreath.
This really is one to impress your guests at Christmas.*

2 clementines, unpeeled, thinly
sliced into rings, sprinkled with
caster sugar and caramelised
with a blowtorch
Handful of edible flowers
1 small punnet of redcurrants
1 tbsp toasted flaked almonds
Icing sugar, for dusting

For the filling
250g caster sugar
500ml whole milk
Big pinch of sea salt
1 vanilla bean, split and
seeds scraped
5 egg yolks
50g cornflour
75ml double cream, whipped
to soft peaks

For the choux pastry
100g unsalted butter
Pinch of salt
200g plain flour
4 eggs
1 egg yolk, lightly beaten

For the glaze
75g caster sugar
40ml double cream
75g dark chocolate

- For the filling, put 150g of the sugar and 75ml of water into a saucepan over medium heat and cook, swirling to dissolve the sugar, until you have a dark caramel. Remove from the heat and carefully stir in the milk, salt and vanilla pod and seeds, then return to the heat and bring to a simmer. In a heatproof bowl, whisk together the egg yolks and the remaining 100g sugar until pale. Add the cornflour and whisk again, then slowly strain in the milk mixture, whisking constantly. Return to the pan and whisk over medium heat until the mixture comes away from the sides of the pan. Transfer to a bowl, cover with cling film, pressing it onto the surface to prevent a skin from forming, and leave to cool. Once it is completely cold, fold in the whipped cream and refrigerate until needed.
- To make the choux pastry, put the butter and salt into a saucepan with 250ml of water and bring to the boil. Remove from the heat, then tip in all the flour at once and beat with a wooden spoon – and plenty of elbow grease – until it is smooth and lump-free. Return to a medium heat and stir for a few minutes until it comes away from the sides of the pan and forms a mass. Leave to cool for 15 minutes, then beat in the eggs one at a time, mixing well, until you have a glossy choux pastry. Transfer to a piping bag fitted with a 15mm plain nozzle.
- Preheat the oven to 200°C/Fan 180°C/Gas Mark 6.
- Draw a 20cm-diameter circle onto a sheet of baking parchment and pipe the pastry carefully around the circle to make a ring. Pipe a second ring inside the first one, so they are touching, then pipe a final ring along the seam between the two rings. Brush with egg yolk and bake in the oven for 15 minutes, without opening the door – not even for a little peek! Lower the oven temperature to 180°C/Fan 160°C/Gas Mark 4 and cook for another 30–35 minutes until golden and puffy. Switch off the oven and prop the door open, then leave the choux ring to cool down inside.
- Meanwhile, make the glaze. Put the sugar and 50ml of water into a small saucepan, place over medium heat and swirl to make a light caramel. Remove from the heat and carefully add the cream and another 50ml of water. Add the chocolate, return to the heat and stir until smooth and well combined. Keep warm.
- Once the choux ring is completely cold, use a serrated knife to slice off the top. Put the salted caramel filling into a piping bag fitted with a 10mm nozzle and generously pipe onto the base of the ring, making sure you create height. Pour the chocolate glaze over a large plate, dip the top of the ring into it and place over the filled base. Working quickly, while the glaze is still wet, decorate with the clementines, flowers, redcurrants and flaked almonds. Finish with a dusting of icing sugar, then serve to whoops of delight!

Ingredients

Most of these ingredients are becoming easier to find in larger supermarkets, but those that aren't are still worth seeking out. Introduce them to your larder and they will be transformative, giving your cooking light, shade and delight. Once they have found a home in your kitchen, embrace them, riff with them and really get to know what they are all about – they will expand your culinary toy box and give you more to play with.

INGREDIENTS

AJWAIN SEEDS
Available in Indian food shops, these seeds have a subtle aniseed flavour that works really well with seafood.

ASAFOETIDA
A pungently scented spice that is also known as devil's dung or hing, asafoetida is available as resin blocks or an easier-to-use powder form. It comes from the dried gum of a rhizome native to Asia and mimics the flavour of garlic and onions – which is useful, since many Jain and Hindu sects do not eat either for religious reasons. Given the amount of beans and pulses consumed in India, its anti-flatulence properties are also very handy!

BLACK SALT (KALA NAMAK)
Also known as kala loon, this is a skunky-scented, dark pink or almost black salt. It is harvested in the Himalayas and has a sulphurous scent not dissimilar to eggs, with a deeply savoury flavour that makes it ideal for seasoning Indian salads, chutneys and raitas. It is also a component of chaat masala.

CHAAT MASALA
This more-ish spice mix is made up of various spices, including cumin seeds, black salt and coriander seeds. Zingy, salty, sweet and hot all at once, it is used as a spice in cooking and as a garnish for salads, savoury Indian snacks and even drinks like Indian lemonade.

CHANNA DHAL
Also known as split Bengal gram, channa dhal is produced by splitting black chickpeas that have had their outer shell removed. It is popular for making dense and hearty dhals.

CHICKPEA (GRAM) FLOUR
A gluten-free flour made from ground chickpeas, this is used in Mediterranean, Middle Eastern and Indian cooking, as well as in some other Asian cuisines, such as Burmese. It makes great pancakes, batters and fritters.

CHINKIANG BLACK VINEGAR
Also known as Zhenjiang black rice vinegar, this comes from the eastern Chinese city of Zhenjiang, or Chinkiang. With a complex flavour that is sweet, sour and slightly smoky, it is perfect for making dipping sauces.

CURRY LEAVES
Curry leaves are a part of the same family as citrus fruit. Their glossy green leaves are very fragrant and have a unique flavour. I would always recommend buying them fresh and stashing any leftover leaves in the freezer, as the dried ones have barely any flavour at all.

DASHI
This is a classic stock used in Japanese cuisine to lend an umami flavour to soups and other dishes – it can be made from kombu (a type of seaweed), dried fish flakes or shiitake mushrooms.

DRIED MANGO POWDER (AMCHUR)
Made from dried green mangoes, this tangy powder has a lemony sharpness.

FENUGREEK
When most people think of fenugreek, what usually comes to mind are the light brown oblong-shaped seeds, which have a distinctive bitter flavour, but its clover-like leaves (also known as methi) are also widely used. While the ground seeds are added to a variety of spice mixes such as garam masala, the leaves are cooked down like spinach and added to sauces, stews and curries across India, parts of Africa and the Middle East. When dried, the leaves are called kasoori methi, and they are added to curries to give them pungency and depth of flavour.

FOX NUTS
Fox nuts, or phool makhana, are the seeds from a species of waterlily that grows in India, China and Japan. They are available to buy in Indian supermarkets.

FROZEN GRATED COCONUT

Available in Indian and other Asian shops, this is just shredded coconut flesh that has been frozen. It is a really convenient product to have in your freezer and makes a good alternative to grating fresh coconut.

GHEE

A staple in Indian kitchens, ghee is clarified butter – butter which has had it milk solids and water removed. This means it can withstand heat for a longer period than ordinary butter without burning.

HARISSA

This spiky North African chilli paste is made from dried chillies, spices, garlic and oil; recipes for harissa vary widely across Tunisia and Morocco.

HIMALAYAN SALT

Mined from the salt mountains of North India, this is used to flavour food, much like table salt or sea salt. It has a pinkish hue and some claim it has health benefits, though these remain unproven.

JAGGERY

This unrefined cane sugar is full of antioxidants – while it may be healthier than refined sugar, it's still got the same amount of calories, gram for gram! You should be able to find jaggery at Asian shops and larger supermarkets.

KEWRA WATER

This is the extract of pandanus or screwpine flowers, and it has been used in Indian perfumery and cookery for many years. Kewra water isn't expensive, lasts forever and is worth searching out in good Indian supermarkets.

LIME PICKLE

A delicious condiment that can be hot, sweet or sour, this is made by pickling lemons or limes with spices, salt and sugar.

MALDIVE FISH

Essentially dried and cured skipjack tuna, Maldive fish is to Sri Lanka what shrimp paste is to South East Asia – it is full of umami flavour and a little goes a long way. It is an essential ingredient in many sambols and curries and can be found in speciality Sri Lankan shops.

MIRIN

This subtly sweet and slightly syrupy Japanese rice wine adds a mellow sweetness to teriyaki and other sauces.

MISO

Miso paste is made by fermenting grains and/or soybeans with salt and koji fungus. All miso is salty, but the light varieties – white (shiro), yellow and some light brown varieties – are sweet as well. White miso, made with rice, barley and a relatively small proportion of soybeans, is the mildest tasting; the more soybeans that are used in a miso, the darker its colour and the stronger its flavour.

PAANCH PHORAN

A Bengali five-spice mix made up of equal quantities of fennel, fenugreek, nigella, cumin and brown mustard seeds. The whole seeds are heated in oil until they pop, giving a rich, distinctive flavour to curries, pickles and chutneys.

PANKO BREADCRUMBS

These Japanese-style breadcrumbs are made from a special crustless loaf of white bread. The loaf is ground into fine slivers, which are then dried to make the crunchiest breadcrumbs.

PICKLED CHILLIES

These are fairly mild chillies pickled in brine, not dissimilar to the ones found in Turkish kebab restaurants. They are available in Turkish and Middle Eastern food stores, although I have also spotted them in larger supermarkets.

PICKLED GINGER

A wonderful accompaniment to sushi, but also lovely chopped up and added to anything that needs a tart, pickle-y, ginger-y flavour, such as salads and salad dressings. This ginger is traditionally pickled in a mixture of sugar and rice vinegar, and I have been known to eat it straight out of the jar!

POMEGRANATE POWDER (ANARDANA)

Made from ground sun-dried pomegranate seeds, this is used in Indian and Persian cookery as a souring ingredient similar to sumac or dried mango powder (amchur). It brings a welcome touch of acidity to sauces cooked with rich meats like lamb, but is equally lovely added to salads or drinks.

PUFFED RICE (MAMRA)

This plain puffed rice is sold in Indian food shops and can be stir-fried in a little oil with turmeric, red chilli powder and mustard seeds to make a quick snack.

ROASTED DARIA (SPLIT GRAM)

Made by roasting channa dhal (split black chickpeas), this is often added to chutneys for texture or ground into minced-meat kebabs to give them density and help bind them together.

SEV MAMRA

This more-ish Indian snack is a mixture of spicy dry ingredients such as puffed rice, savoury noodles and peanuts; it is often used to top Indian snacks like bhel puri.

SHICHIMI TOGARASHI

This blend of spices includes dried red chillies, Japanese sansho pepper, roasted orange peel, seaweed, sesame seeds and more. It is ideal for sprinkling over dishes you want to add a little heat to, such as salmon or udon noodles.

SUMAC

This ground condiment is made from dried red berries and has an acerbic sherbet tang. It is wonderful sprinkled over salads and roasted meat such as lamb. It is readily available in Middle Eastern grocery shops.

TAMARIND CONCENTRATE

Tamarind is used in Asian cooking for its sweet/tart flavour. Tamarind concentrate is also sometimes called tamarind paste. It comes from the pulp of the fruit from a tamarind tree. It is fantastic for adding a rich sweet/sourness to curries and chutneys.

TURKISH PEPPER FLAKES (PUL BIBER)

Also known as Aleppo pepper, this is made from ground dried Turkish peppers – it has a fruity, aromatic flavour and is not particularly hot.

TURKISH PEPPER PASTE (BIBER SALCASI)

This pepper paste is made from dried chillies or sweet peppers and salt, and is easy to find in Turkish food shops.

URID DHAL

Also known as urad dhal or split black gram, this is made from black lentils that have been split and skinned. It is a popular legume in South Asia, where it is used for making dhal, poppadums, soups and dosas.

YUZU JUICE

Yuzu is a Japanese citrus fruit beloved of chefs everywhere for its wonderful aromatic scent and flavour that is part grapefruit, mandarin, lime and lemon. The whole fruit is not easily found, but the juice is available in larger supermarkets and Asian food shops. Although it is not cheap, the good news is that a little goes a long way.

ZA'ATAR

A versatile Middle Eastern spice mix bursting with the earthy flavours of thyme, sumac and toasted sesame seeds – I especially like the one by Zaytoun.

Index

A

aam panna 158
achaar, apple 94
ajwain seeds 289
    ajwain seed mathis with apple achaar 94
almonds
    asparagus with smoked paneer, brown butter,
        almonds and preserved lemon 106
    romesco sauce 98–100
apples
    apple achaar 94
    apple jalebis with fennel ice cream 272
    apple, pear and blackberry breakfast crumble 56
    fennel and apple slaw 36–9
Asian mushroom ragout with sweet potato gnocchi 124–7
asparagus
    asparagus with smoked paneer, brown butter,
        almonds and preserved lemon 106
    charred asparagus with tofu, cashews, chilli oil and
        soy dressing 108
aubergines
    fragrant pulled goat shoulder with burnt aubergine,
        pine nuts and barberries 230–1
    lamb and aubergine fatteh 222–5
    spicy aubergine salad with peanuts, herbs, eggs
        and jaggery fox nuts 141
avocados
    avocado-yuzu puree 188
    guacamole 42

B

bacon, tamarind and maple 36–9
baharat: lamb and baharat sausage rolls 91
bananas
    banana and cardamom lassi 20
    banana cake with miso butterscotch and Ovaltine
        kulfi 246–9
    banana ketchup 74–7
    coconut caramel bananas 18
barberries, fragrant pulled goat shoulder with burnt
    aubergine, pine nuts and 230–1
beetroot
    beetroot and shankleesh croquetas 85
    beetroot and walnut kibbeh with tahini sauce 86
    beetroot chutney 80–3
bhel puri 118
    Jikoni bhel puri 120–1
biryani 234–5
    Mughlai paigham biryani 236–9
biscuits: jam-filled Indian shortbreads 57
blackberries: apple, pear and blackberry breakfast
    crumble 56
bread
    chicken-fat croutons 202
    cornbread with creamed corn, eggs and green chilli
        relish 28–31
    curried cauliflower and cheese toasted sandwiches 51
    parathas 22–7

Turkish spinach, cheese and egg in a hole 55
bread and butter pudding, spinach, pancetta and cheese 50
broccoli
    charred sprouting broccoli with spelt, cashews
        and miso dressing 109
    dashi broccoli with sesame sauce and tobiko 110
broth: clams moilee with lemon vermicelli upma 172–5
brussels sprouts
    charred brussels sprouts and chestnuts with hot
        and sour dressing 148
    panzanella with panettone croutons 150
buttermilk ice cream 260
butternut squash and shankleesh m'hencha 122
butterscotch: banana cake with miso butterscotch
    and Ovaltine kulfi 246–9

C

cabbage
    kimchi 114
    kimchi parathas 25
    kimchi Royals 116
    Mughlai paigham biryani 236–9
cakes
    banana cake with miso butterscotch and Ovaltine
        kulfi 246–9
    Cointreau caramel and blood orange upside down
        cake 275
Campari: Negroni jelly 266
caramel
    coconut caramel bananas 18
    Cointreau caramel and blood orange upside down
        cake 275
    edible Christmas wreath 282–5
    espresso caramel 278–81
    saffron and orange blossom creme caramel with
        cardamom and orange rhubarb 262
    Vietnamese-style caramel pork ribs with pickled
        daikon and carrot salad 228
cardamom
    banana and cardamom lassi 20
    cardamom and orange rhubarb 262
    carrot, cardamom and vanilla kheer creme brulee 261
carpaccio, pineapple 264
carrots
    carrot, cardamom and vanilla kheer creme brulee 261
    pickled daikon and carrot salad 228
cashews
    charred asparagus with tofu, cashews, chilli oil and
        soy dressing 108
    charred sprouting broccoli with spelt, cashews
        and miso dressing 109
cauliflower
    cauliflower popcorn with black vinegar dipping sauce 70
    curried cauliflower and cheese toasted sandwiches 51
cavolo nero, paneer gnudi with saag and 144–7
ceviche: sea bass ceviche with aam panna and
    tomato oil 158
channa dhal 289
    channa dhal with wild garlic puree 130–1
chard, feta, pine nut and preserved lemon fatayer 88

cheelas: oat and chickpea flour cheelas with fried mushrooms and soured cream 45

cheese
asparagus with smoked paneer, brown butter, almonds and preserved lemon 106
beetroot and shankleesh croquetas 85
butternut squash and shankleesh m'hencha 122
chard, feta, pine nut and preserved lemon fatayer 88
curried cauliflower and cheese toasted sandwiches 51
lamb wellington with feta, pine nuts and sumac 220
paneer-stuffed padron peppers 96
pomegranate quail with giant couscous, feta and rose watermelon 196
spinach, pancetta and cheese bread and butter pudding 50
sweet potato latkes with fried manouri cheese and honey 44
Turkish spinach, cheese and egg in a hole 55
cherries: strawberry, raspberry, pomegranate and cherry salad 274
chestnuts: charred brussels sprouts and chestnuts with hot and sour dressing 148
chevdho, baked cornflake 69
chicken 198–9
Indian-style khao suey 207
kikapu chicken with plantain chips 200–1
kuku paka 206
roast chicken salad with chicken-fat croutons and green tahini dressing 202
chickpea (gram) flour 289
Franca's chickpea chips 84
oat and chickpea flour cheelas with fried mushrooms and soured cream 45
chickpeas
Jikoni bhel puri 120–1
lamb and aubergine fatteh 222–5
chillies 290
chilli salt 255
fennel seed and chilli salt 72
green chilli relish 28–31
chips
Franca's chickpea chips 84
plantain chips 200–1
chocolate
coconut, white chocolate and holy basil panna cotta with pineapple carpaccio 264
edible Christmas wreath 282–5
chorizo
grilled concertina squid with Jerusalem artichokes and chorizo crumbs 170
sweetcorn pancakes with guacamole and chorizo crumbs 42
choux pastry: edible Christmas wreath 282–5
Christmas panzanella with panettone croutons 150
Christmas wreath, edible 282–5
chutney
beetroot chutney 80–3
coriander chutney 184–7
green chutney 120–1
mint-coriander chutney 164–7
tamarind chutney 120–1, 128
tomato, tamarind and mint chutney 182

citrus salad 266
clams moilee with lemon vermicelli upma 172–5
clementines: edible Christmas wreath 282–5
clove-smoked venison samosas with beetroot chutney 80–3
cockles with tomatoes, saffron and coriander 171
coconut 290
coconut sambol 227
coconut milk
clams moilee with lemon vermicelli upma 172–5
coconut kadhi with pea and potato pakoras and tomato and mint salsa 136–9
coconut, white chocolate and holy basil panna cotta with pineapple carpaccio 264
duck rendang 212
Indian-style khao suey 207
kuku paka 206
overnight tapioca porridge with passion fruit and coconut caramel bananas 18
pina colada pancakes 32–5
cod
pea and mint stuffed fishcakes 52–4
saffron fish pie 176
salt cod fofos with romesco sauce 98–100
coffee
coffee rasgullas with mascarpone ice cream and espresso caramel 278–81
espresso caramel 278–81
Cointreau caramel and blood orange upside down cake 275
condensed milk
guava kulfi with chilli salt 255
Ovaltine kulfi 246–9
confit salmon with mint-coriander chutney and pomegranate-pistachio crust 164–7
congee: roasted scallops and congee with chilli oil 178
coriander
cockles with tomatoes, saffron and coriander 171
coriander chutney 184–7
lime pickle and coriander yoghurt 123
mint-coriander chutney 164–7
cornbread with creamed corn, eggs and green chilli relish 28–31
cornflakes
baked cornflake chevdho 69
kikapu chicken with plantain chips 200–1
courgette flowers: Keralan crab-stuffed courgette flowers 184–7
courgette tzatziki 226
couscous: pomegranate quail with giant couscous, feta and rose watermelon 196
crab: Keralan crab-stuffed courgette flowers 184–7
cream
coconut, white chocolate and holy basil panna cotta with pineapple carpaccio 264
guava kulfi with chilli salt 255
miso butterscotch 246–9
Turkish delight trifles with pashmak 250
creme brulee, carrot, cardamom and vanilla kheer 261
creme caramel: saffron and orange blossom creme caramel with cardamom and orange rhubarb 262

crisps
    rose and pistachio crisps 268–71
    sweet potato crisps 126–7
croquetas, beetroot and shankleesh 85
croutons
    chicken-fat 202
    panettone croutons 150
crumble
    apple, pear and blackberry breakfast crumble 56
    rhubarb, pomegranate and pink peppercorn crumble
        with buttermilk ice cream 260
curry
    biryani 234–5
    curried cauliflower and cheese toasted sandwiches 51
    curry hollandaise 52–4
    duck rendang 212
    goose leg qorma 214
    Indian-style khao suey 207
    kuku paka 206
    makkai paka 142
    massaman pork and peanut curry with pineapple
        relish 216–19
    Mughlai paigham biryani 236–9
    shalgam gosht 215
custard: Turkish delight trifles with pashmak 250

D

daikon: pickled daikon and carrot salad 228
dashi 289
    dashi broccoli with sesame sauce and tobiko 110
dates
    date and pistachio parathas 26–7
    roast parsnips with dates, tamarind chutney
        and yoghurt 128
dhal: channa dhal with wild garlic puree 130–1
dosas, smoked mackerel and potato 48
doughnuts: mango doughnuts with lime leaf
    sherbet 58–60
dressings
    chilli-ginger dressing 112
    ginger and soy 46
    green tahini dressing 202
    hot and sour dressing 148
    lime pickle and coriander yoghurt 123
    miso dressing 109
    soy dressing 108
dried fruit: jaggery and fennel seed granola 21
drinks: banana and cardamom lassi 20
duck
    duck and pistachio pierogi with hot yoghurt sauce
        and pul biber butter 208–11
    duck rendang 212

E

eggs 40
    buttermilk ice cream 260
    cornbread with creamed corn, eggs and green chilli
        relish 28–31
    edible Christmas wreath 282–5
    fennel ice cream 272
    meringue roulade with poached stonefruit and
        orange blossom cream 256–9
    pina colada pancakes 32–5
    prawn toast Scotch eggs 74–7
    spicy aubergine salad with peanuts, herbs, eggs
        and jaggery fox nuts 141
    Turkish spinach, cheese and egg in a hole 55
espresso caramel 278–81

F

fatayer, chard, feta, pine nut and preserved lemon 88
fatteh, lamb and aubergine 222–5
fennel
    fennel and apple slaw 36–9
    Levantine salmon tartare with pickled fennel
        and labneh 156
fennel seeds
    fennel ice cream 272
    fennel seed and chilli salt 72
    jaggery and fennel seed granola 21
fenugreek 289
    fenugreek waffles 36–9
feta cheese
    chard, feta, pine nut and preserved lemon fatayer 88
    lamb wellington with feta, pine nuts and sumac 220
    pomegranate quail with giant couscous, feta and
        rose watermelon 196
filo pastry: butternut squash and shankleesh m'hencha 122
fish 152–91, 290
    confit salmon with mint-coriander chutney and
        pomegranate-pistachio crust 164–7
    frying 180
    green tea rice bowls with salmon and ginger and soy
        dressing 46
    Levantine salmon tartare with pickled fennel
        and labneh 156
    pan-fried mackerel with pineapple rojak 168
    pea and mint stuffed fishcakes with curry
        hollandaise 52–4
    saffron fish pie 176
    salt cod fofos with romesco sauce 98–100
    sea bass ceviche with aam panna and tomato oil 158
    skate with lime pickle brown butter, tempura samphire
        and nori 190
    smoked mackerel and potato dosas 48
    a sort of Indian fritto misto di mare with tomato,
        tamarind and mint chutney 182
flatbreads
    chicken-fat croutons 202
    date and pistachio parathas 26–7
    kimchi parathas 25
    parathas 22–7
fofos: salt cod fofos with romesco sauce 98–100
fox nuts 289
    jaggery fox nuts 141
fragrant pulled goat shoulder with burnt aubergine,
    pine nuts and barberries 230–1
Franca's chickpea chips 84

freekeh, pistachio and preserved lemon stuffing 240
fritters: salt cod fofos with romesco sauce 98–100
fritto misto di mare, a sort of Indian 182
fruit
    meringue roulade with poached stonefruit and
      orange blossom cream 256–9
    see also dried fruit *and individual types of fruit*

G

ghee 132–3, 290
    ghee-fried wild mushroom and truffle khichdee 135
gin: Negroni jelly 266
ginger 291
gnocchi, sweet potato 124–7
gnudi: paneer gnudi with saag and cavolo nero 144–7
goat: fragrant pulled goat shoulder with burnt aubergine,
    pine nuts and barberries 230–1
goat's cheese: beetroot and shankleesh croquetas 85
goose leg qorma 214
granita, orange 266
granola, jaggery and fennel seed 21
green beans: tofu and green bean larb in lettuce
    cups 113
green chutney 120–1
green tea rice bowls with salmon and ginger and soy
    dressing 46
guacamole 42
guava 252–3
    guava kulfi with chilli salt 255

H

herbs: spicy aubergine salad with peanuts, herbs,
    eggs and jaggery fox nuts 141
hollandaise, curry 52–4
honey
    honeyed quince 268–71
    sweet potato latkes with fried manouri cheese
      and honey 44

I

ice cream
    buttermilk ice cream 260
    fennel ice cream 272
    guava kulfi with chilli salt 255
    mascarpone ice cream 278–81
    Ovaltine kulfi 246–9
    pina colada pancakes 32–5
    tahini ice cream with honeyed quince and
      rose and pistachio crisps 268–71
Indian-style khao suey 207
ingredients 288–91

J

jaggery 290
    jaggery and fennel seed granola 21
    jaggery fox nuts 141
jalebis: apple jalebis with fennel ice cream 272
jam-filled Indian shortbreads 57
jelly: Negroni jelly with orange granita and citrus salad 266
Jerusalem artichokes: grilled concertina squid with
    Jerusalem artichokes and chorizo crumbs 170
Jikoni bhel puri 120–1

K

kale: crispy 'seaweed' 126–7, 188
Keralan crab-stuffed courgette flowers with coriander
    chutney 184–7
ketchup, banana 74–7
khadi: coconut kadhi with pea and potato pakoras
    and tomato and mint salsa 136–9
khao suey, Indian-style 207
kheer: carrot, cardamom and vanilla kheer creme
    brulee 261
khichdee, ghee-fried wild mushroom and truffle 135
kibbeh: beetroot and walnut kibbeh with tahini sauce 86
kikapu chicken with plantain chips 200–1
kimchi 114
    kimchi parathas 25
    kimchi Royals 116
koftas: pea koftas with saffron yoghurt 73
kuku paka 206
kulfi
    guava kulfi with chilli salt 255
    Ovaltine kulfi 246–9

L

labneh, Levantine salmon tartare with pickled fennel
    and 156
lamb
    lamb and aubergine fatteh 222–5
    lamb and baharat sausage rolls 91
    lamb wellington with feta, pine nuts and sumac 220
    Mughlai paigham biryani 236–9
    shalgam gosht 215
    spicy scrag end pie 232
    za'atar lamb cutlets with courgette tzatziki 226
larb: tofu and green bean larb in lettuce cups 113
lassi, banana and cardamom 20
latkes: sweet potato latkes with fried manouri cheese
    and honey 44
lemongrass poussin with green mango and peanut
    salad 204
lemons
    asparagus with smoked paneer, brown butter,
      almonds and preserved lemon 106
    chard, feta, pine nut and preserved lemon fatayer 88
    freekeh, pistachio and preserved lemon stuffing 240
    lemon vermicelli upma 172–5

lettuce
    charred gem lettuce salad with prawns and
        chilli-ginger dressing 112
    tofu and green bean larb in lettuce cups 113
Levantine salmon tartare with pickled fennel
    and labneh 156
lime leaves
    lime leaf and togarashi peanuts 68
    lime leaf sherbet 58–60
lime pickle 290
    lime pickle and coriander yoghurt 123
    skate with lime pickle brown butter, tempura
        samphire and nori 190

M

mackerel
    pan-fried mackerel with pineapple rojak 168
    smoked mackerel and potato dosas 48
makkai paka 142
mangoes
    aam panna 158
    lemongrass poussin with green mango and
        peanut salad 204
    mango doughnuts with lime leaf sherbet 58–60
manouri cheese: sweet potato latkes with fried
    manouri cheese and honey 44
maple syrup: tamarind and maple bacon 36–9
masala, tomato 236–9
mascarpone
    mascarpone ice cream 278–81
    meringue roulade with poached stonefruit and
        orange blossom cream 256–9
massaman pork and peanut curry with pineapple
    relish 216–19
mathis: ajwain seed mathis with apple achaar 94
meringue roulade with poached stonefruit and orange
    blossom cream 256–9
m'hencha, butternut squash and shankleesh 122
mint
    mint-coriander chutney 164–7
    pea and mint stuffed fishcakes with curry
        hollandaise 52–4
    tomato, tamarind and mint chutney 182
miso 290
    banana cake with miso butterscotch and Ovaltine
        kulfi 246–9
moilee: clams moilee with lemon vermicelli upma 172–5
Mughlai paigham biryani 236–9
mushrooms
    Asian mushroom ragout with sweet potato
        gnocchi 124–7
    ghee-fried wild mushroom and truffle khichdee 135
    oat and chickpea flour cheelas with fried mushrooms
        and soured cream 45
mussel, sweetcorn and rice soup 159
mutton: Mughlai paigham biryani 236–9

N

Negroni jelly with orange granita and citrus salad 266
noodles
    Indian-style khao suey 207
    lemon vermicelli upma 172–5
nori: tempura samphire 190
nuts
    baked cornflake chevdho 69
    jaggery and fennel seed granola 21

O

oats
    apple, pear and blackberry breakfast crumble 56
    jaggery and fennel seed granola 21
    oat and chickpea flour cheelas with fried mushrooms
        and soured cream 45
oil, tomato 158
orange blossom water
    orange blossom and saffron shrikhand 26–7
    orange blossom cream 256–9
    saffron and orange blossom creme caramel with
        cardamom and orange rhubarb 262
oranges
    cardamom and orange rhubarb 262
    Cointreau caramel and blood orange upside down
        cake 275
    Negroni jelly with orange granita and citrus salad 266
Ovaltine kulfi 246–9
overnight tapioca porridge with passion fruit and coconut
    caramel bananas 18
oysters 160
    oyster pani puris 163

P

paanch phoran 290
padron peppers, paneer-stuffed 96
pakoras, pea and potato 136–9
pancakes
    pina colada pancakes 32–5
    smoked mackerel and potato dosas 48
    sweetcorn pancakes with guacamole and chorizo
        crumbs 42
pancetta: spinach, pancetta and cheese bread and
    butter pudding 50
paneer
    asparagus with smoked paneer, brown butter,
        almonds and preserved lemon 106
    paneer gnudi with saag and cavolo nero 144–7
    paneer-stuffed padron peppers 96
panettone croutons 150
pani puris, oyster 163
panna cotta: coconut, white chocolate and holy basil
    panna cotta with pineapple carpaccio 264
panzanella with panettone croutons 150
parathas 22
    date and pistachio parathas 26–7

kimchi parathas 25
parsnips
    panzanella with panettone croutons 150
    roast parsnips with dates, tamarind chutney and
        yoghurt 128
pashmak, Turkish delight trifles with 250
passion fruit: overnight tapioca porridge with passion fruit
    and coconut caramel bananas 18
peanut butter: makkai paka 142
peanuts
    lemongrass poussin with green mango and peanut
        salad 204
    lime leaf and togarashi peanuts 68
    massaman pork and peanut curry with pineapple
        relish 216–19
    spicy aubergine salad with peanuts, herbs, eggs and
        jaggery fox nuts 141
pears: apple, pear and blackberry breakfast crumble 56
peas
    pea and mint stuffed fishcakes with curry
        hollandaise 52–4
    pea and potato pakoras 136–9
    pea koftas with saffron yoghurt 73
    spicy scrag end pie 232
peppers
    paneer-stuffed padron peppers 96
    romesco sauce 98–100
pickles 92–3
    pickled daikon and carrot salad 228
    pickled fennel 156
pierogi: duck and pistachio pierogi with hot yoghurt
    sauce and pul biber butter 208–11
pies
    saffron fish pie 176
    spicy scrag end pie 232
pina colada pancakes 32–5
pine nuts
    chard, feta, pine nut and preserved lemon fatayer 88
    fragrant pulled goat shoulder with burnt aubergine,
        pine nuts and barberries 230–1
    lamb wellington with feta, pine nuts and sumac 220
pineapple
    pina colada pancakes 32–5
    pineapple carpaccio 264
    pineapple relish 216–19
    pineapple rojak 168
pistachios
    confit salmon with pomegranate-pistachio crust 164–7
    date and pistachio parathas 26–7
    duck and pistachio pierogi with hot yoghurt sauce
        and pul biber butter 208–11
    freekeh, pistachio and preserved lemon stuffing 240
    rose and pistachio crisps 268–71
plantain chips 200–1
pomegranate 291
    confit salmon with pomegranate-pistachio crust 164–7
    pomegranate quail with giant couscous, feta and
        rose watermelon 196
    rhubarb, pomegranate and pink peppercorn crumble
        with buttermilk ice cream 260
    strawberry, raspberry, pomegranate and cherry
        salad 274

Turkish delight trifles with pashmak 250
Pondicherry prawn puffs 66
popcorn: cauliflower popcorn with black vinegar
    dipping sauce 70
pork
    massaman pork and peanut curry with pineapple
        relish 216–19
    pork scratchings with fennel seed and chilli salt 72
    tamarind and maple bacon 36–9
    tandoori pork chops with coconut sambol 227
    Vietnamese-style caramel pork ribs with pickled
        daikon and carrot salad 228
porridge: overnight tapioca porridge with passion fruit
    and coconut caramel bananas 18
potatoes
    beetroot and walnut kibbeh with tahini sauce 86
    kimchi Royals 116
    pea and mint stuffed fishcakes 52–4
    pea and potato pakoras 136–9
    saffron fish pie 176
    smoked mackerel and potato dosas 48
    spicy scrag end pie 232
poussin: lemongrass poussin with green mango
    and peanut salad 204
prawns
    charred gem lettuce salad with prawns and
        chilli-ginger dressing 112
    Pondicherry prawn puffs 66
    prawn toast Scotch eggs with banana ketchup 74–7
    saffron fish pie 176
    a sort of Indian fritto misto di mare with tomato,
        tamarind and mint chutney 182
puff pastry
    lamb and baharat sausage rolls 91
    lamb wellington with feta, pine nuts and sumac 220
    Pondicherry prawn puffs 66
pul biber butter 208–11
pumpkin: panzanella with panettone croutons 150
puris
    bhel puri 118
    Jikoni bhel puri 120–1
    oyster pani puris 163

Q

qorma, goose leg 214
quail: pomegranate quail with giant couscous,
    feta and rose watermelon 196
quail's eggs: prawn toast Scotch eggs with banana
    ketchup 74–7
quince, honeyed 268–71

R

radishes: kimchi 114
ragout: Asian mushroom ragout with sweet potato
    gnocchi 124–7
rasgullas 277
    coffee rasgullas with mascarpone ice cream and
        espresso caramel 278–81

raspberries
strawberry, raspberry, pomegranate and cherry salad 274
Turkish delight trifles with pashmak 250
relishes
green chilli relish 28–31
pineapple relish 216–19
rendang, duck 212
rhubarb
cardamom and orange rhubarb 262
rhubarb, pomegranate and pink peppercorn crumble with buttermilk ice cream 260
rice
carrot, cardamom and vanilla kheer creme brulee 261
ghee-fried wild mushroom and truffle khichdee 135
green tea rice bowls with salmon and ginger and soy dressing 46
Mughlai paigham biryani 236–9
mussel, sweetcorn and rice soup 159
roasted scallops and congee with chilli oil 178
smoked mackerel and potato dosas 48
rojak, pineapple 168
romesco sauce, salt cod fofos with 98–100
rose and pistachio crisps 268–71
roulade: meringue roulade with poached stonefruit and orange blossom cream 256–9
rum: pina colada pancakes 32–5

S

saag 144–7
saffron
cockles with tomatoes, saffron and coriander 171
orange blossom and saffron shrikhand 26–7
saffron and orange blossom creme caramel with cardamom and orange rhubarb 262
saffron fish pie 176
saffron-roasted turkey with freekeh, pistachio and preserved lemon stuffing 240
saffron yoghurt 73
salads
charred gem lettuce salad with prawns and chilli-ginger dressing 112
citrus salad 266
fennel and apple slaw 36–9
lemongrass poussin with green mango and peanut salad 204
panzanella with panettone croutons 150
pickled daikon and carrot salad 228
pineapple rojak 168
roast chicken salad with chicken-fat croutons and green tahini dressing 202
spicy aubergine salad with peanuts, herbs, eggs and jaggery fox nuts 141
strawberry, raspberry pomegranate and cherry salad 274
tofu and green bean larb in lettuce cups 113
salmon
confit salmon with mint-coriander chutney and pomegranate-pistachio crust 164–7
green tea rice bowls with salmon and ginger and soy dressing 46
Levantine salmon tartare with pickled fennel and labneh 156
pea and mint stuffed fishcakes 52–4
salsas
tomato and mint salsa 136–9
tomato salsa 222–5
salt 289, 290
chilli salt 255
fennel seed and chilli salt 72
salt cod fofos with romesco sauce 98–100
sambol, coconut 227
samosas 78–9
clove-smoked venison samosas with beetroot chutney 80–3
samphire, tempura 190
sandwiches, curried cauliflower and cheese toasted 51
sausage rolls, lamb and baharat 91
scallops
pan-fried scallops with avocado-yuzu puree and crispy 'seaweed' 188
roasted scallops and congee with chilli oil 178
Scotch eggs, prawn toast 74–7
sea bass ceviche with aam panna and tomato oil 158
seaweed
crispy 'seaweed' 126–7, 188
dashi broccoli with sesame sauce and tobiko 110
sesame seeds: dashi broccoli with sesame sauce and tobiko 110
shalgam gosht 215
shankleesh
beetroot and shankleesh croquetas 85
butternut squash and shankleesh m'hencha 122
sherbet, lime leaf 58–60
shortbreads, jam-filled Indian 57
shrikhand
orange blossom and saffron shrikhand 26–7
sumac and strawberry shrikhand 274
skate with lime pickle brown butter, tempura samphire and nori 190
slaw, fennel and apple 36–9
smoked mackerel and potato dosas 48
snake beans: pineapple rojak 168
a sort of Indian fritto misto di mare with tomato, tamarind and mint chutney 182
soups
coconut kadhi 136–9
mussel, sweetcorn and rice soup 159
soured cream, oat and chickpea flour cheelas with fried mushrooms and 45
spelt
charred sprouting broccoli with spelt, cashews and miso dressing 109
sweetcorn pancakes 42
spicy aubergine salad with peanuts, herbs, eggs and jaggery fox nuts 141
spicy scrag end pie 232
spinach
saag 144–7
saffron fish pie 176
spinach, pancetta and cheese bread and butter pudding 50
Turkish spinach, cheese and egg in a hole 55

squid
    grilled concertina squid with Jerusalem artichokes and chorizo crumbs 170
    a sort of Indian fritto misto di mare with tomato, tamarind and mint chutney 182
strawberries
    strawberry, raspberry, pomegranate and cherry salad 274
    sumac and strawberry shrikhand 274
    Turkish delight trifles with pashmak 250
stuffing, freekeh, pistachio and preserved lemon 240
sumac 291
    lamb wellington with feta, pine nuts and sumac 220
    sumac and strawberry shrikhand 274
sweet and sour tamarind tomatoes 143
sweet potatoes
    Jikoni bhel puri 120–1
    roast sweet potato with lime pickle and coriander yoghurt 123
    sweet potato crisps 126–7
    sweet potato gnocchi 124–7
    sweet potato latkes with fried manouri cheese and honey 44
sweetcorn
    cornbread with creamed corn, eggs and green chilli relish 28–31
    makkai paka 142
    mussel, sweetcorn and rice soup 159
    sweetcorn pancakes with guacamole and chorizo crumbs 42

T

tahini
    green tahini dressing 202
    tahini ice cream with honeyed quince and rose and pistachio crisps 268–71
    tahini sauce 86
tamarind 291
    sweet and sour tamarind tomatoes 143
    tamarind and maple bacon 36–9
    tamarind chutney 120–1, 128
    tomato, tamarind and mint chutney 182
tandoori pork chops with coconut sambol 227
tapioca: overnight tapioca porridge with passion fruit and coconut caramel bananas 18
tartare: Levantine salmon tartare with pickled fennel and labneh 156
tempura samphire 190
toasted sandwiches, curried cauliflower and cheese 51
tobiko, dashi broccoli with sesame sauce and 110
tofu
    charred asparagus with tofu, cashews, chilli oil and soy dressing 108
    tofu and green bean larb in lettuce cups 113
tomatoes
    cockles with tomatoes, saffron and coriander 171
    guacamole 42
    Jikoni bhel puri 120–1
    sweet and sour tamarind tomatoes 143
    tomato and mint salsa 136–9
    tomato masala 236–9

tomato oil 158
tomato salsa 222–5
    tomato, tamarind and mint chutney 182
trifles: Turkish delight trifles with pashmak 250
truffle: ghee-fried wild mushroom and truffle khichdee 135
turkey: saffron-roasted turkey with freekeh, pistachio and preserved lemon stuffing 240
Turkish delight trifles with pashmak 250
Turkish peppers 291
Turkish spinach, cheese and egg in a hole 55
turnips: shalgam gosht 215
tzatziki, courgette 226

U

upma, lemon vermicelli 172–5
urid dhal 291

V

vanilla: carrot, cardamom and vanilla kheer creme brulee 261
venison: clove-smoked venison samosas with beetroot chutney 80–3
vermouth: Negroni jelly 266
Vietnamese-style caramel pork ribs with pickled daikon and carrot salad 228

W

waffles, fenugreek 36–9
walnuts: beetroot and walnut kibbeh 86
watermelon, pomegranate quail with giant couscous, feta and rose 196
whitebait: a sort of Indian fritto misto di mare 182
wild garlic puree 130–1

Y

yoghurt
    banana and cardamom lassi 20
    courgette tzatziki 226
    hot yoghurt sauce 208–11
    Jikoni bhel puri 120–1
    labneh 156
    lamb and aubergine fatteh 222–5
    lime pickle and coriander yoghurt 123
    orange blossom and saffron shrikhand 26–7
    roast parsnips with dates, tamarind chutney and yoghurt 128
    saffron yoghurt 73
    sumac and strawberry shrikhand 274
yuzu 291
    avocado-yuzu puree 188

Z

za'atar 291
    za'atar lamb cutlets with courgette tzatziki 226

With Thanks

Writing a book, opening and running a restaurant, and getting married – all in under three years – is not a solo project (nor for the faint-hearted). None of these things would have been achieved without the love and unending support of many people. You all have a part in this book.

Nadeem, I really was through with love before you persuaded me otherwise. You are the most loving, kind-hearted and supportive husband and best friend, and you have made it your mission to help me achieve my dreams. I don't think I will ever know anyone with a kinder heart or a more illuminated soul than yours. Thank you for inspiring me to be a little better always.

To my parents-in-law, Moaz and Shany Nanjuwany, I am so grateful that Nadeem and I have you in our lives. Thank you for being the greatest role models both personally and professionally, for your open hearts, endless love, support and advice, your belief in our dreams and for embracing me with such warmth and love when I needed it the most. Thank you for making me part of your family.

To my parents, grandparents and wider family, for all the experiences, memories and stories that bind us together. Mum – thanks for showing me that cooking for others is an act of love.

Avneet Rehal – ravishingly beautiful inside and out – we have howled with laughter and tears together and I couldn't have wished for a brighter light to see me through the good times and the bad. Soul sisters forever.

Gulzar Kanji, thank you for your wisdom. For your listening ear. For your grace. For your compassion. I am in awe of you.

Sandeep, Ollie and Devinder Aunty – I love you so much. The power of your love has got me through so many challenges. Thank you for the endless warm hugs and open-hearts and -doors policy.

Rahil Ahmad, for your love, support, generosity and championing of me, Nadeem and Jikoni. For your beautiful photos of us, our guests and our food. There is always a thimble of champagne at the bar for you.

For the entire team at Jikoni – I am so proud to work with some of the most brilliant people in the industry. Thank you for your care and conscientious efforts, day in and day out, to make our guests feel loved, welcomed and pampered; for sharing our values, and for choosing to be kindred spirits on this journey with me and Nadeem.

Dominique, Marcus and the wonderful people at Fraser – the dream team. Thank you for your friendship and professional support, and for endless cheerleading, enthusiasm and kindness.

Zoe Ross – thank you for your support with this book, and for your enthusiasm and guidance even through the anxious, wobbly moments.

Richard Atkinson and Natalie Bellos, thank you for believing in this book and being part of it. I am so delighted we got to work together, albeit briefly. Xa Shaw Stewart, thank you for your kindness, patience, sensitivity and wisdom – for eking out all the extra stories, even when I thought there were no more to be written. Lisa Pendreigh, thank you for believing in me, Jikoni and the banana cake right from the very beginning. Thank you, Alison Cowan, for your meticulous eye and wisdom. Thank you all for supporting my animal vision, even though it sounded mad and impossible, and for allowing me to be involved in every aspect of this book.

Kristin Perers, I loved every moment of working with you. From the first moment I met you, I knew you were formidable. Thank you for bringing such love, grace, wisdom, light and talent to every photograph.

Tabitha Hawkins, one of the best humans – your energy is astounding and I couldn't have hoped for a better friend and prop stylist to work on this book. They say God is in the details and you certainly brought something other-worldly to the shoot every day. Thank you for your fragile magic.

Joss Herd, I can't thank you enough. You inspired me every time I worked with you – you are a 100/10. Thank you for showing me and my recipes such love. Aside from your culinary wizardry, you give the best hugs and let out the most infectious giggles.

Lizzie Kamenetzky – what a joy to be brought together with this project. Thank you for bringing such beauty, enthusiasm and love to the shoots, and I will never forget those mango doughnuts!

Hattie Arnold, you're an ocean of calm and wearer of excellent dresses – I wish I could have you in my kitchen every day. You have the best energy, and your work ethic is the 100 emoji.

Sandra Zellmer, thank you – I know how hard you worked on this book. Thank you for your enthusiasm and for bringing such a beautiful and considered design to life.

Adam Grout, you have a genius for imagination in its purest form. Thank you for bringing your astounding creativity to so many of my projects over the last few years. With your eloquent design work, you always manage to express what is in my heart.

Sham Sandhu, you have been like a brother to me over the years – thank you for believing in Jikoni and me. Clive, so much gratitude to you for taking time out to bring your handsome pup Lord Pedro Carlos to our set – watching you wrestle that pork chop from his jaws will be an enduring memory.

Thank you to Roushan and Rahil V, for believing in our work and vision, and for all your enthusiasm and support.

Pip McCormac, thank you for showing Jikoni such unfiltered love and support from the very beginning – it has meant so much to me, and I love working with you. Thank you for bringing Jennifer to the set. She was an absolute pro. Your stories about her indifference and tyranny always make me laugh and smile – she loves you really!

To our suppliers at Jikoni – Serge, Stan and Simon – thank you for showing such generosity and support always.

Thank you Jerry, from Our Amazing Animal World, for the beautiful Belinda, Olive and Felipe – I will never forget your gentle spirit and your calm, happy animals.

Thank you Charlie McCorry and the amazing team at Ruuby, for always playing a supporting role in getting me looking my best.

Finally, a heartfelt thank you to all our guests and supporters at Jikoni and my dear readers. Thank you for giving me the privilege to share food, recipes and stories, because without you eating, reading or listening – what is the point? I am full of immense gratitude.

BLOOMSBURY PUBLISHING
Bloomsbury Publishing Plc
50 Bedford Square, London, WC1B 3DP, UK

BLOOMSBURY, BLOOMSBURY PUBLISHING
and the Diana logo are trademarks of Bloomsbury Publishing Plc

First published in Great Britain 2020

A catalogue record for this book is available from the British Library

Library of Congress Cataloguing-in-Publication data has been applied for

ISBN: HB: 978-1-5266-0144-5; eBook: 978-1-5266-2292-1

10 9 8 7 6 5 4 3 2 1

Project editor: Alison Cowan
Designer (interior pages): Sandra Zellmer
Designer and illustrator (cover): Adam Grout
Photographer: Kristin Perers
Food stylists: Joss Herd and Lizzie Kamenetzky
Prop stylist: Tabitha Hawkins
Indexer: Vanessa Bird

Printed and bound in China by C&C Offset Printing Co., Ltd.

Bloomsbury Publishing Plc makes every effort to ensure that the
papers used in the manufacture of our books are natural, recyclable
products made from wood grown in well-managed forests. Our
manufacturing processes conform to the environmental regulations
of the country of origin. To find out more about our authors and books
visit www.bloomsbury.com and sign up for our newsletters